# Political Activism across the Life Course

How do people of different ages experience and engage with politics in their everyday lives, and how do these experiences and engagements change over their life course and across different generations? Age, life course and generation have become increasingly important experiences for understanding political participation and political outcomes, and current policies of austerity across the world are affecting people of all ages. This book contributes towards an interdisciplinary understanding of the temporalities of everyday political encounters.

At a time when social science is struggling to understand the rapid and unexpected changes to contemporary political landscapes, the contributors to this book present examples of activism and politics across everyday experiences of homes, communities, online platforms, local environment, playgrounds and educational spaces. The research takes ethnographic, biographical and action research approaches, and the studies described feature interlocutors as young as four and as old as ninety-two who reside in Europe, North and South America and South Asia. This is an eclectic text that brings together a number of themes and ideas not typically associated with political activism, and is intended for students and academic researchers across the humanities, social and political sciences interested in the temporalities of everyday political participation.

This book was originally published as a special issue of *Contemporary Social Science*.

**Sevasti-Melissa Nolas** is a Senior Lecturer in Sociology at Goldsmiths College, University of London, UK. Her research focuses on the relationship between childhood and public life, everyday childhoods, temporalities of everyday politics and publics creating methodologies.

**Christos Varvantakis** is an Anthropologist, working as a researcher at Goldsmiths College, University of London, UK. His research focuses on the intersections of childhood and public life, politics and urban environments, as well as on visual and multimodal research methodologies.

**Vinnarasan Aruldoss** is a Research Fellow at Goldsmiths College, University of London, UK. His main research interests are childhood theories, post-colonial childhood, early years provision, children's politics and social policy.

# Contemporary Issues in Social Science

*Contemporary Social Science*, the journal of the **Academy of Social Sciences**, is an inter-disciplinary, cross-national journal which provides a forum for disseminating and enhancing theoretical, empirical and/or pragmatic research across the social sciences and related disciplines. Reflecting the objectives of the Academy of Social Sciences, it emphasises the publication of work that engages with issues of major public interest and concern across the world, and highlights the implications of that work for policy and professional practice.

The *Contemporary Issues in Social Science* book series contains the journal's most cutting-edge special issues. Leading scholars compile thematic collections of articles that are linked to the broad intellectual concerns of *Contemporary Social Science,* and as such these special issues are an important contribution to the work of the journal. The series editor works closely with the guest editor(s) of each special issue to ensure they meet the journal's high standards. The main aim of publishing these special issues as a series of books is to allow a wider audience of both scholars and students from across multiple disciplines to engage with the work of *Contemporary Social Science* and the Academy of Social Sciences.

*Series editor: David Canter, University of Huddersfield, UK*

For a full list of titles in this series, please visit www.routledge.com/Contemporary-Issues-in-Social-Science/book-series/SOCIALSCI .

# Political Activism across the Life Course

*Edited by*
**Sevasti-Melissa Nolas, Christos Varvantakis
and Vinnarasan Aruldoss**

LONDON AND NEW YORK

First published 2018
by Routledge
2 Park Square, Milton Park, Abingdon, Oxon, OX14 4RN, UK

and by Routledge
711 Third Avenue, New York, NY 10017, USA

*Routledge is an imprint of the Taylor & Francis Group, an informa business*

Introduction & Chapter 5 © 2018 Sevasti-Melissa Nolas, Christos Varvantakis
and Vinnarasan Aruldoss
Chapter 1–4 & 6–11 © 2018 Academy of Social Sciences

*British Library Cataloguing in Publication Data*
A catalogue record for this book is available from the British Library

ISBN 13: 978-0-8153-8533-2

Typeset in Myriad Pro
by RefineCatch Limited, Bungay, Suffolk

**Publisher's Note**
The publisher accepts responsibility for any inconsistencies that may have
arisen during the conversion of this book from journal articles to book chapters,
namely the possible inclusion of journal terminology.

**Disclaimer**
Every effort has been made to contact copyright holders for their permission to
reprint material in this book. The publishers would be grateful to hear from any
copyright holder who is not here acknowledged and will undertake to rectify
any errors or omissions in future editions of this book.

# Contents

# CONTENTS

# Citation Information

The chapters in this book were originally published in *Contemporary Social Science*, volume 12, issue 1–2 (March–June 2017). When citing this material, please use the original page numbering for each article, as follows:

**Introduction**

*Political activism across the life course*
Sevasti-Melissa Nolas, Christos Varvantakis and Vinnarasan Aruldoss
*Contemporary Social Science*, volume 12, issue 1–2 (March–June 2017) pp. 1–12

**Chapter 1**

*Embodying 'the Next Generation': children's everyday environmental activism in India and England*
Catherine Walker
*Contemporary Social Science*, volume 12, issue 1–2 (March–June 2017) pp. 13–26

**Chapter 2**

*Teenage girls' narratives of becoming activists*
Jessica K. Taft
*Contemporary Social Science*, volume 12, issue 1–2 (March–June 2017) pp. 27–39

**Chapter 3**

*Narrative resources and political violence: the life stories of former clandestine militants in Portugal*
Raquel da Silva
*Contemporary Social Science*, volume 12, issue 1–2 (March–June 2017) pp. 40–51

**Chapter 4**

*Politicisation in later life: experience and motivations of older people participating in a protest for the first time*
Jonathan R. Guillemot and Debora J. Price
*Contemporary Social Science*, volume 12, issue 1–2 (March–June 2017) pp. 52–67

**Chapter 5**

*Talking politics in everyday family lives*
Sevasti-Melissa Nolas, Christos Varvantakis and Vinnarasan Aruldoss
*Contemporary Social Science*, volume 12, issue 1–2 (March–June 2017) pp. 68–83

For any permission-related enquiries please visit:
http://www.tandfonline.com/page/help/permissions

# Notes on Contributors

**Molly Andrews** is Professor of Political Psychology, and co-director of the Centre for Narrative Research at the University of East London, UK. Her research interests include political narratives, the psychological basis of political commitment, political identity and patriotism.

**Vinnarasan Aruldoss** is a Research Fellow at Goldsmiths College, University of London, UK. His main research interests are childhood theories, post-colonial childhood, early years provision, children's politics and social policy.

**Veronica Barassi** is a Lecturer in the Department of Media and Communications at Goldsmiths, University of London, UK. She is currently the chair of the E-Seminars of the Media Anthropology Network of the European Association of Social Anthropology. Her research work focuses on digital citizenship and participation. She is the author of *Activism on the Web: Everyday Struggles Against Digital Capitalism* (Routledge, 2015), and has written extensively about social movements and social media.

**Raquel da Silva** is a British Academy Research Fellow in the International Development Department at the University of Birmingham, UK. Her current research explores the interplay between narratives of intervention and statebuilding and the life stories of former foreign fighters in Syria and Iraq.

**Thalia Dragonas** is Professor of Social Psychology, Dean of the School of Educational Sciences at the National and Kapodistrian University of Athens, Greece. She has written extensively on psychosocial identities, intercultural education and ethnocentrism in the educational system.

**Jonathan R. Guillemot** is a Researcher and Lecturer at Universidad San Francisco de Quito, Ecuador, at the College of Health and Medicine. He is currently writing his PhD at the department of Global Health & Social Medicine and Institute of Gerontology at King's College London, UK. His current research interest focuses on the sociology of ageing and medical sociology.

**Andrea Jones** is a Project Manager in the fields of health and housing. She was recently awarded her PhD at the University of Sussex, UK.

**Sheila Marie Katz** is Assistant Professor of Sociology at the University of Houston, USA, and an affiliated faculty with UH's Women's, Gender, and Sexuality Studies Program. Her qualitative sociological research focuses on gender and poverty, specifically low-income women's experiences in domestic violence, grassroots activism and higher education.

She serves on the boards of the National Center for Student Parent Programs and the journal, *Social Problems*.

**Sevasti-Melissa Nolas** is a Senior Lecturer in Sociology at Goldsmiths College, University of London, UK. Her research focuses on the relationship between childhood and public life, everyday childhoods, temporalities of everyday politics and publics creating methodologies.

**Debora J. Price** is a Professor of Social Gerontology at the University of Manchester, UK, where she directs MICRA. Her research centres on social policy for an ageing population, with particular focus on well-being in later life. She is currently the president of the British Society of Gerontology.

**Rachel Rosen** is Senior Lecturer in the sociology of childhood at University College London, UK. Her research focuses on the politics of children and childhood.

**Jessica K. Taft** is an Associate Professor of Latin American and Latino Studies at the University of California at Santa Cruz, USA. She is the author of *Rebel Girls: Youth Activism and Social Change across the Americas* (2011) as well as several articles on youth politics and civic engagement.

**Christos Varvantakis** is an Anthropologist, working as a researcher at Goldsmiths College, University of London, UK. His research focuses on the intersections of childhood and public life, politics and urban environments, as well as on visual and multimodal research methodologies.

**Anni Vassiliou** is a Social Psychologist by training, and a youth and community worker by experience. Having been involved in numerous diverse projects in the fields of education, preventative social health and adult education since 1980, she practices, teaches and supervises socio-cultural youth-work in Greece.

**Catherine Walker** is a Postdoctoral Research Associate in Human Geography at the University of Leicester, UK. Her research interests lie in children's and youth geographies, sustainability education and intergenerational approaches to theorising agency.

# Foreword

## Political activism is not just for the young

*David Canter*

The usual image of political activism is of young people, often students, waving banners or even throwing cobbles at serried ranks of law enforcement. But as these eleven papers, brought together in this volume by Sevasti-Melissa Nolas, Christos Varvantakis and Vinnarasan Aruldoss, show there is a case to be made that political activism extends right across the life course.

Indeed, where one finds themselves in their life may shape what social issues they engage with. As Catherine Walker argues from discussions with children between the ages of 11 and 14, their position as 'the next generation' gives them a perspective on what needs to be done now to protect their futures. This can enable them to be catalysts for environmental actions, not just symbolic representations for other people's action.

This awareness of the possibility for political engagement is shown to have roots in those families in which talking politics is an everyday family activity. Although, as Melissa Nolas and her colleagues uncovered from in-depth study of three families, the recognition that political issues can be talked about is crucial, rather than any specific political orientation.

The power of the family even continues into the online sphere. Veronica Barassi examined the digital identities of activists. Somewhat surprisingly, these activists often went to some trouble to integrate their childhood and families into their web profiles. They emphasise the importance of family life in shaping their political development.

Teenage girls provide another illustration of how age, and in their case gender, influences their narratives of engagement with political campaigns. Jessica Taft interviewed activist girls in North and South America. She discovered that these teenagers found significance in joining political groups. It helped them to differentiate themselves from their peers, who did not really care about what was going on around them. It allowed them to feel they were developing as citizens and adults.

Other contributions to the collection explore the process of committing to political action. Raquel da Silva, using detailed discussions with two Portuguese, former clandestine militants, explores the ways in which past actions are used to shape current identities. Her interviewees, as we all do, re-interpreted their past to give meaning to their current circumstances. Their feeling of having contributed to a moment in history becomes a dominant part of their identity.

Participation in protest is not limited to intellectuals or those with time on their hands, as may sometimes be believed. Sheila Katz from the University of Houston, discusses how women's participation in grassroots activism allowed them to feel less ashamed about being on welfare. They felt empowered through being made aware of the ways in which their own debilitating circumstances related to broader social inequalities. Challenging the processes that produced those inequalities was itself effective in giving them feelings of self-worth.

Examples of activism unfolding across the life course challenge the notion that taking up a cause requires the energy and stamina of youth. Jonathan Guillemot and Debora Price indicate that the physical frailty of older people can be used as a political tool to shame decision makers. As in all other contexts, support from those around them and the facilitation of group membership can lead those who feel threatened to take up a cause, even when constrained by a wheelchair.

Activism can take many forms. Rachel Rosen makes the case for aspects of children's play to be considered a form of political engagement. Thalia Dragonas and her colleague Anni Vassilou describe how youth workshops that bring together Muslim and Christian young people in a wide range of creative and artistic activities contribute to reducing the historic conflict inherent in Thrace where they live.

Andrea Jones identifies an even more implicit example of activism in the decision made by some older people to live in co-operative, non-conventional housing. Although the residents of these places do not see themselves as political activists, it is clear that they are making a stand against what is on offer in housing in order to make their own lives more liveable and also to contribute to a better society as they see it.

Finally, Molly Andrews summarises the overall sweep of the studies in this volume, revisiting her own seminal work on political commitment. Activism exists right across the life course, across genders and classes. It emerges as an aspect of identity from within the family and develops, in different ways for different people, into a set of commitments that are shaped by and shape the account that people give of themselves, their personal narratives.

# Political activism across the life course

Sevasti-Melissa Nolas, Christos Varvantakis and Vinnarasan Aruldoss

**ABSTRACT**
The study of political activism has neglected people's personal and social relationships to time. Age, life course and generation have become increasing important experiences for understanding political participation and political outcomes (e.g. Brexit), and current policies of austerity across the world are affecting people of all ages. At a time when social science is struggling to understand the rapid and unexpected changes to the current political landscape, the essay argues that the study of political activism can be enriched by engaging with the temporal dimensions of people's everyday social experiences because it enables the discovery of political activism in mundane activities as well as in banal spaces. The authors suggest that a values-based approach that focuses on people's relationships of concern would be a suitable way to surface contemporary political sites and experiences of activism across the life course and for different generations.

## Introduction

People's personal and social relationships to time has been a neglected topic of inquiry in the study of political activism. Research at the intersections of political activism, age, life course and generations can be found in diverse disciplinary endeavours but these projects seldom cross paths and have not coalesced into an area of study (Braungart & Braungart, 1986). Yet, such temporal relationships are becoming increasingly important. Age legitimates institutional political participation (e.g. voting) and generational belonging shapes life chances and political activism (Alwin, Cohen, & Newcomb, 1991; Elder, Modell, & Parke, 1993; Hughes, 2015; Moran-Ellis, Bandt, & Sünker, 2014; Pilcher & Wagg, 1996; Wagg & Pilcher, 2014; Weisner & Bernheimer, 1998), as well as shaping election outcomes (Grasso, Farrall, Gray, Hay, & Jennings, 2017). At a time when popular imagination and the research literature continue to be preoccupied with youth as a site of revolt, this essay engages with the experiences of those people not considered to be 'young'. Does an interest in public life, issues of common concern and collective action only emerge during 'youth' and dissipate after 'young adulthood'? Where do 'younger children' and 'older adults' fit within discourses and practices of social and political change?

How does a life course approach to political activism expand the ways in which political activism might be defined? How might political activism across the life course be studied? We argue that bringing questions of people's personal and social relationships to time into conversation with political activism challenges commonly held beliefs and practices about political participation.

These questions also have a contemporary resonance. The consequences of neoliberal socioeconomic policies are affecting people of different age groups across all aspects of their everyday lives, from housing and employment to health and social care. Following almost a decade of austerity policies since the financial crisis of 2008, the electorate in a number of countries is responding in ways that shift the political landscape in unanticipated directions. Age and generational belonging have played a key role in those shifts (e.g. Brexit). At the same time, these social changes are happening to a backdrop of demographic shifts, 'youth bulges' in the Global South and greying populations in the North, which have consequences for individuals, public sector organisation and nation states (e.g. child care; pensions). As such, the conditions that gave rise to the iconic, and formative for many, social movements of the last century (Seidman, 2004), have shifted and so too must the ways we think about the profile of who gets involved in political activism as well as what is valued as political activism.

The contributions to the special issue accompanying this essay emerged from an open call for papers and a workshop, *Activism on the edge of age*, organised by the guest editors and held at the Friends Meeting House in Brighton on 2 and 3 June 2016. At the workshop participants explored the meanings of activism for younger children and older adults, those on either side of 'youth'. We called this being at 'the edges of age'. The themed issue brings together scholars from across the social sciences whose research has been carried out in diverse geographical locations; their contributions to the special issue are all concerned with the ways that age, life course and generations intersects with activism and everyday life.

## Notes on 'political activism'

Pippa Norris (2009) defines 'political activism' as 'the ways that citizens participate, the processes that lead them to do so, and the consequences of these acts'. The study of political participation draws on Almond and Verba's (1963) seminal work, *The civic culture*. In disciplinary terms, research on political activism sits at the intersections of political science and psychology. Reading the introduction of Almond and Verba's (1963) classic text it is hard not to be struck by the authors' anxieties, 'that the continental European nations will discover a stable form of democracy in the West' (p. 1), at the same time as finding these anxieties to resonate over 50 years later. Preoccupations with 'the social psychology of participation' (Allport, 1945) and 'the political culture of democracy' (Almond & Verba, 1963, p. 1), emerged in direct response to the rise of Fascism and Communism in the interwar period and the atrocities and aftermath of the Second World War. Pre-occupations with political participation intensified with the subsequent threat of nuclear war and civic disorder that haunted international relations between Eastern and Western blocs following the War and until the early 1990s. From the outset then, the study of political participation has focused on understanding democratic stability and the ways in which psychology (broadly defined) might rule citizens 'through their freedoms, their choices, and their solidarities' (Rose, 1998, p. 117). In this respect, the 'what' of political participation has been most notably defined in relation to acts that promote stability such as voting, an activity likely to involve the largest number of citizens (Norris, 2009). Campaigning, community organising and protest politics (demonstrations, petitions, strikes) are also identified in the literature as political acts, though ones involving a much smaller number of people.

These political activities have not remained static over time. A number of social changes have occurred over the last century transforming the nature of political participation (Norris, 2009). In Western Democracies voter turnout has declined as has political party membership. How much people participate in public life is contested. On the civic side of public life, there is evidence from the US context that participation in community life has declined over the years (Putnam, 2000). However, the cross-cultural evidence of dwindling participation in traditional associations is more difficult to interpret and there is no easily discernible pattern of increase or decrease in community association in other countries (Norris, 2009). On the political side of public life, it is clearer that 'cause-oriented activism' has risen considerably in various locations around the world as well as transnationally with new social movements becoming an important avenue for political mobilisation (Norris, 2009; Tilly & Tarrow, 2015). These changing civic and political trends have led scholars to re-think the meaning and practices of political participation. Indeed, we would argue that Norris's curation of a number of political acts under the banner of 'political activism' signals in itself, a notable semantic shift in terminology. It is an invitation to engage with the conceptual and empirical ambiguity that the term 'activism' offers (Yang, 2016).

In the last year, the need to re-think how citizens participate in society is also echoed in the soul searching that has started to emerge across the social sciences (Davies, in press; Nielsen, 2016) following the surprise outcomes of the UK General Election 2015, the 2016 UK Referendum of European Membership, and the 2016 US Presidential Elections. Calls are being made for researchers, policy-makers, politicians and the media to engage with other forms of knowledge when it comes to people's politics. For example, Leo Coleman (2016) has suggests that psychoanalysis and ethnography might speak to gaps in current under-standing of political participation because they are knowledge traditions which deal with the relationship between our inner and outer worlds as well as being traditions that pay close attention to the details of everyday life.

The call to engage with people's everyday experiences of the social world, if heeded, would result in redefining the categories of politics and activism in unexpected ways. As recent research on new publics (Mahony, Newman, & Barnett, 2010) and new social movement (Bayat, 2010) formation shows, what matters to people, and the dynamics and processes of people coming together over what matters, is largely emergent and unpredictable. It is therefore important that research on political activism (broadly defined) starts to pay closer attention to people's engagement with public life in the round, which Barnett (2014) describes as 'a family of practices of sharing with others'. Barnett argues that any analysis of entanglements with public life must pay close attention to ordinary contexts of everyday life and to seriously consider what matters to people, engaging with what he calls people's 'vocabularies of worth'.

In this respect, values-based definitions of political activism are beginning to emerge (Dave, 2012; Fassin, 2015; Flyvbjerg, 2001; Lambert, 2010). Values-based approaches seek to understand political activism as an assemblage of meanings and practices that express relationships of concern to the world (Sayer, 2011). Sayer (2011, p. 1) puts it well when he writes about people's relationship to the world as being about the things that matter most to them:

> the most important questions people tend to face in their everyday lives are normative ones of what is good and bad about what is happening, including how others are treating them, and of how to act, and what to do for the best.

In such approaches, researchers have foregrounded the importance of affect and ethics and have formulated an understanding of activism as the subjective experiences of challenging social norms. For example, while the older people whom Jones interviewed in her study on housing (2017) did not self-define as 'activists', many of their housing decisions were underpinned by ethical and affective considerations and their housing choices clearly challenged prevailing normative housing pathways. Conversely, Walker (2017) shows how children's everyday environmental activism at home and at school can be viewed both as experience but also as a social norm, a behaviour that is expected of children and against which they may push back. Activism here can be understood as critique, invention and creative practice which challenges social norms (Dave, 2012). Thinking about political activism in terms of resistance and challenge to social norms allows a broadening of the definition of political participation as a response to that which stifles and suppresses identities and practices which do not conform.

## Thinking about personal and social relationships to time: age, the life course and generations

The focus on understanding political activism almost exclusively in terms of voting, coupled with entrenched stereotypes of age and political activity (Andrews, 2017), has resulted in little, if any, serious exploration of the intersections of age, life course, generation and activism. Commonly held beliefs of activism remain closely intertwined with youth. The countercultural revolution of the 1960s in North America and Western Europe, the events of May 1968 in Europe, and student-led responses to repressive political regimes internationally, have contributed to such social imaginaries (Dubinsky, Krull, & Lord, 2009; Hughes, 2015; Seidman, 2004), which continue to be reproduced in youth research, policy and practice (presented co-editors included). Yet, genealogies of care and concern are manifest and can be mobilised in everyday life across all ages, and so the question remains: how do those who are not 'young people' or 'young adults' fit into the imaginary normative distribution of political participation, which sees the onset of political identity in the teenage years and its trailing off at the end of young adulthood?

A useful way to start to answer this question is by looking at a key term for thinking about political participation: 'the citizen' (Dalton, 2009; Norris, 2009). There is a long debate in the social sciences about the many exclusions embedded in this term including exclusions on the grounds of age (see below), gender (Lister, 2003; McAfee, 2000; Roseneil, 2013), racial, ethnic (Hall, 1993) and sexual (Plummer, 2003) identities. Such exclusions are closely linked with disciplinary power dynamics and the central role that psychology and psychoanalysis have played in the modern invention of the self (Rose, 1998; Steedman, 1998). Endeavours to understand the processes of political participation have been underscored by behavioural and functionalist models of personhood (knowledge, attitudes, behaviours) (cf. Moran-Ellis et al., 2014) that are characteristically a-historical and a-cultural and which interiorise the self.

Such models of personhood have long been critiqued in social psychology, a key intellectual home of 'the science of democracy' (Rose, 1998), as well as elsewhere. In line with theorising in cultural studies, feminism, social constructionism and post-structuralism alike (Fine & Sirin, 2007; Flax, 1990; Gergen, 2011; Griffiths, 1993), socio-behavioural conceptualisations have given way to an understanding of person-hood as configurations of thinking–acting–feeling beings in relationships with others and with their environments. Carolyn Pedwell, drawing on the work of Jane Bennett, calls this 'the mind-body-environment assemblage' (quoted in Pedwell, 2017, p. 95). Values-based approaches to political activism resonate with these relational approaches to understanding people by providing a more inclusive concept of citizen-ship as an affective and ethical relationship between a fluid self and a networked society. Yet, much of this scholarship has remained silent on the relationship between activism and age.

Our thinking in relation to activism and age emerged initially in response limitations in the literature about what political activism meant for younger children; those children in early and middle childhood who are rarely, if ever, thought of in political terms. Cockburn (2013) has argued, children, together with older people, have from ancient times been excluded from definitions of the 'citizen' on account of their competence. This is curious because children's involvement in educational (Ndlovu, 2006) and labour move-ment activism internationally (Liebel, Overwien, & Recknagel, 2001) has been well docu-ment if not always well known. Instead, what this points towards is the historical and cultural specificities of how childhood is constructed at any given time and place, and how these 'constructions' permeate public understandings of children.

Over the last 25 years, representations of children as a-political have been challenged. In particular, the issue of children's competences to participate in matters that concern them has been widely questioned by the children's rights movement and partially over-turned by international conventions (cf. Nolas, 2015 for a review). Nevertheless, the issue of age, as Lister (2007) argues, remains an important consideration in relation to childhood because the arguments for political participation are far more compelling the older a child is; an observation that is supported by empirical evidence (Peterson-Badali, Ruck, & Ridley, 2003). Furthermore, when children are thought of as citizens it is usually as 'citizens-in-waiting', 'learner citizens' or 'apprentice citizens' (Lister, 2007) and not citi-zens in the here-and-now.

To address these conceptual shortcomings, researchers have drawn on feminist theo-rising, in particular ethics of care philosophies developed by Joan Tronto and Carol Gilli-gan, to re-think children's citizenship (Cockburn, 2013). An ethics of care approach challenges the strict and impermeable boundaries between the public and the private found in traditional moral theories. It also challenges the separation of morality from poli-tics. Finally, instead of a top-down, technical and expert view of personhood it advocates for an understanding of people in terms of what matters to them (Cockburn, 2013). Relat-edly, the concepts of 'lived citizenship' (James, 2011; Lister, 2007) and 'living rights' (Hanson & Nieuwenhuys, 2012) have also come to the fore as a way of understanding chil-dren's civil and political experiences in everyday life.

A similar situation can be discerned for older people who, like children, experience dependency and exclusion from the labour market (Craig, 2004). The pathologisation of older people as ill and incapacitated is also well-established (Bytheway, 2005). Higgs (1995) has argued that the erosion of the welfare state and the marketization of public services require a rethinking of social models of citizenship. He concludes that under neo-liberalism older people are more likely to become alienated than they are to be empowered. The media regularly reproduce such representations of older age. Yet, such conclusions do not necessarily hold up in practice. Andrews's (1991) and Jones's (2017) studies referenced earlier precisely challenge ideas of alienation. Equally, Guillemot and Price (2017) document the case of later life politicization in a group of elderly women who had no previous 'habit of responding' to issues of common concern (Andrews, 2017) other than by voting. This group found themselves as first-time protesters to the closure of a charity-run day centre which they all cared deeply about as a space of communion and commensality.

While values-based approaches to political activism have yet to engage with age, these approaches are highly amendable to exploring political activism in relation to age and generation and across the life course. These temporal lived experiences of growing up, getting by and getting on, and of encountering public life in time and over time, open new vistas for thinking about political activism.

Furthermore, looking at 'the edges of age', childhood and older age, together and in relation to activism, enables a reframing of political socialisation as a lifelong process with inter-generational connections. As Guillemot and Price (2017) note, much of the political socialisation literature has confined itself to the study of youth and the influences of home, school and media on their political attitude formation (see also Barassi, 2017; Nolas, Varvantakis, & Aruldoss, 2017b). Important though these influences are known to be (Pancer, 2015), a focus on people's various relationships to time (age, life course, and generation), its experience and passage provides insights into the vicissitudes of life and political activism alike. These are insights that can account for both continuity and change in political orientations (Linden & Klandermans, 2007), the pathways in and out of activism or voluntary action (Fisher, 2012) and/or what Jones (2017) calls 'intermittent activism': the ways in which lives criss-cross 'resonant sites of activism' (Rosen, 2017) (see also Taft, 2017 and Da Silva, 2017).

## Resonant sites of activism

While noted to be ambiguous (Yang, 2016), the term activism has been used to refer to high-cost, high-risk protests and revolutionary movements, such as participation in the clandestine militant movements in Portugal (Da Silva, 2017), as well as the everyday practices of environmental protection (Walker, 2017). In relation to such definitions, voting booths, streets, empty buildings and public squares are all familiar sites of political activism. A focus on age, life course and generation, however, expands and introduces new resonant sites of activism. Engaging with people's relationships to and experiences of time forces us to look for and locate activism in diverse sites challenging and expanding commonly held beliefs about political participation. Communities, schools and colleges (Dragonas & Vassiliou, 2017; Katz, 2017), home and family life (Jones, 2017; Walker, 2017), and the internet (Barassi, 2017) all emerge as resonant sites of activism. For example, Rosen (2017) draws our attention to the playground and children's imaginative play as a site in which gender norms and social inequalities of childhood might be challenged. While Nolas et al. (2017b) demonstrate how the everyday spaces of the home can be transformed into temporary *agoras* for political oration.

These resonant sites suggest that a temporal engagement with political activism moving forward will also require an engagement with the impossible geometries of the public–private–personal–political. Feminists have long argued that the personal is political. More recently, political economist Will Davies (in press) has suggested that as: '[public life] becomes corrupted, [sociology] must delve further into the private realm in search of some future public'. Meanwhile, research on political talk supports the idea that conversations of a political and public nature require the most intimate and trusting of private spaces and personal relationships in order to be aired (Nolas et al., 2017b). The public and the private, the personal and the political are not just analytical counterparts to be explored and experimented with. As digital technologies accelerate and make visible experiences of 'context collapse' (Marwick & boyd, 2011) it will become necessary to relinquish the idea that political activism occupies only one 'proper' place (de Certeau, 1984). Instead, it might be more productive to think about political activism as mobile and fluid practices that cut across variously connected 'mind-body-environment assemblage' that are at once public and private, personal and political.

## Encountering activism over time

How might political activism across the life course be studied? Much of the research on activism is limited in its geographical (mostly western) and methodological (survey methods) breadth (Norris, 2009; Sapiro, 2004; Schmitt-Beck & Lup, 2013). Action-oriented and comparative design approaches are starting to emerge in the literature, and will be necessary going forward in order to move beyond the over-represented, in the political participation literature, U S and the tendency for single-country study designs (Norris, 2009). For example, reflections on an action research educational intervention for language learning and youth inclusion over a 20-year period (1997-to date) in the multi-cultural borderland of North-Eastern Greece (Dragonas and Vassiliou, 2017) reveals the ways in which intergroup relationships are historically sedimented and explores how they can be locally reconfigured through dialogue and joint activities. Research on political activism also has started to take a comparative approach by, for example, contrasting experiences across European and South Asian societies (Barassi, 2017; Nolas et al., 2017b; Walker, 2017). Such cross-national conversations contextualise political experiences allowing for commonalities and differences across cultures to emerge that challenge universalising notions of both politics and participation (Nolas, Varvantakis, & Aruldoss, 2017a; 2017b).

Barassi (2017) argues that much of the literature on political activism has to-date neglected the biographical aspects of how activism comes about. Research and everyday understandings of political activism rely heavily on the tropes of programmatic and spectacular moments (Dave, 2012) tending to ignore, for instance, the narrative imagination, the lived experience and the storied life (Andrews, 2014) which we find to be of great significance for a nuanced understanding of political activism. By contrast life history and biographical methods produce rich narrative analyses of the range of stories that activists tell about themselves and their activism. Indeed, as Da Silva (2017), and others (Taft, 2017) have argued narrative itself becomes a resource for making sense and reflecting on one's activism. Meanwhile, ethnographic approaches and the practice of spending time in the field enable researchers to capture children and adults' fleeting and ephemeral encounters with public life such as in the case of political talk in the home (Nolas et al., 2017b).

These methodological approaches give rise to questions around the relationships between commitment and intermission and the ways in which everyday life and familial obligations might intervene to disrupt old, as well as generate new trajectories of activism. For example, Andrews (2017), reflecting on her seminal life history research on the political commitment of a group of older, white British socialist (1991) suggests that maintaining political commitment depends on cultivating a 'habit of responding'. Pedwell (2017) has recently argued that habits are not just mindless repetition that sustains the status quo. They are also the sustained action required once consciousness has been raised and altered as thinking–acting–feeling bodies interact with their environments. In both read-ings, habits require time to form and to be recognised as such. This processual view of acti-vism helps us to understand how activism comes about and unfolds over time.

Importantly, such research approaches that engage with people's relationship to time (temporality) allow us to move beyond a (largely imaginary and largely empty) singular moment of *enrolment*, in which one's activism 'switches on'. Instead, we can begin to see the political/activist identity as something that is nuanced through time, that is both cultural and social, that has a history and a future, and which is also fluid and flexible in response to changes and interpretations over time. Additionally, an in-depth ethno-graphic orientation allows for a more nuanced understanding of aspects of the political in everyday life (families, talk, storytelling, discussion, online narratives, etc) and takes us beyond the spectacular moments of social action. Thus, such methodological (and epis-temological) views, we would argue, assist to substantiate a more *political* political science (Schram, Flyvbjerg, & Landman, 2013).

## Conclusion

In the study of political activism people's personal and social relationships to time have received scarce attention. Stereotypes of age and generational belonging have been instrumental in maintaining a research agenda that largely ignores the experiences of the very young or the very old and diversity of experience within generations. Yet recent political developments, and life course research, suggest that relationship to time is an important social category and lived experience which shapes political outcomes as much as political participation.

The concepts of age, life course and generation bring in aspects of time to the study of political activism. In this essay, we have called for a more open and inclusive approach to political activism that accounts for the hitherto overlooked experiences at the edge of age. We have reviewed a number of research examples which challenged the notion that only young people or young adults are politically active in an institutional sense. The literature reviewed for this essay provides research examples of encounters with public life and pol-itical participation from as young as four (Rosen, 2017) to as old as 92 (Guillemot & Price, 2017). Thinking about personal and social relationships to time not only broadens our notions of who might be a citizen, it also forces us to look at citizenship relationally in the context of family life and friendships groups. People of all ages are interdependent on each other, yet these inter-dependencies are most visible on the edges of age. Thinking about activism through the prism of age forces us to engage with the times and places in which those inter-dependencies unfold as people make sense of their living and dining arrangements, as they play and talk, go to school and go online.

Our understanding of political activism has been influenced by values-based literatures. Values-based approaches seek to understand political activism as a configuration of meanings and practices that express relationships of concern to the world (Sayer, 2011). Accordingly, we highlighted the ways in which the understanding of political activism could be enriched through granular, qualitative research approaches, such as life history, ethnographic and action research methods all of which engage to a greater or lesser extent with time. Stories that surface 'habits of responding' (Andrews, 2017) help to challenge the commonly held belief that activism is always something spectacular and remarkable and the exclusive purview of youth. Instead, by engaging with the pasts, presents and imagined futures of activism, we discover that political activism can be found in mundane activities as well as in banal spaces. Such methodological diversity in the scientific enquiry of political activism contributes a more nuanced understanding of individual biographies and cultural and historical contexts in which political activism takes place.

The special issue that follows this essay brings together a number of themes and ideas that have not typically been associated with political activism. It is our hope that the collection of papers make a modest, initial contribution towards an interdisciplinary social science that engages with the cares and concerns of people across the life course, who live in and through different circumstances, generations and geographical locations.

## Acknowledgement

We would like to thank David Canter and Charles Watters for feedback on an earlier draft of this essay.

## Disclosure statement

No potential conflict of interest was reported by the author.

## Funding

The research and the *Activism on the edge of age* workshop was funded by the FP7 European Research Council Starting Grant [ERC-StG-335514] to Sevasti-Melissa Nolas.

# References

Allport, G. (1945). The psychology of participation. *Psychological Review, 52*(3), 117–132.

Almond, G. A., & Verba, S. (1963). *The civic culture: Political attitudes and democracy in five nations.* London: Sage.

Alwin, D. F., Cohen, R. L., & Newcomb, T. M. (1991). *Political attitudes over the life span: The Bennington women after fifty years.* Madison: The University of Wisconsin Press.

Andrews, M. (1991). *Lifetimes of commitment: Aging, politics, psychology.* Cambridge: Cambridge University Press.

Andrews, M. (2014). *Narrative imagination and everyday life.* Oxford: Oxford University Press.

Andrews, M. (2017). Enduring ideals: Revisiting *Lifetimes of Commitment* twenty-five years later. *Contemporary Social Science, 12*(1–2). doi:10.1080/21582041.2017.1325923

Barassi, V. (2017). Digital citizens? Data traces and family life. *Contemporary Social Science, 12*(1–2). doi:10.1080/21582041.2017.1338353

Barnett, C. (2014). Theorising emergent public spheres: Negotiating democracy, development, and dissent. *Acta Academica, 46*, 1–21.

Bayat, A. (2010). *Life as politics: How ordinary people change the Middle East.* Stanford, CA: Stanford University Press.

Braungart, R. G., & Braungart, M. M. (1986). Life-course and generational politics. *Annual Review of Sociology, 12*, 205–231.

Bytheway, B. (2005). Ageism and age categorization. *Journal of Social Issues, 61*(2), 361–374.

Cockburn, T. (2013). *Rethinking children's citizenship.* Basingstoke: Palgrave Macmillan.

Coleman, L. (2016, November 18). Why to read Winnicott after the US election, and how. *Somatosphere.* Retrieved April 28, 2017, from http://somatosphere.net/2016/11/why-to-read-winnicott-after-the-us-election-and-how.html

Craig, G. (2004). Citizenship, exclusion and older people. *Journal of Social Policy, 33*(1), 95–114.

Da Silva, R. (2017). Narrative resources and political violence: The life stories of former clandestine militants in Portugal. *Contemporary Social Science, 12*(1–2). doi:10.1080/21582041.2017.1335878

Dalton, R. J. (2009). *The good citizen: How a younger generation is reshaping American politics.* Washington: CQ Press.

Dave, N. (2012). *Queer activism in India: A story in the anthropology of ethics.* Durham, NC: Duke University Press.

Davies, W. (in press). *Review essay: Strangers in their own land: Anger and mourning on the American Right, Arlie Russell Hochschild.* New York: New Press, 2016. *International Journal of Politics, Culture and Society.* Retrieved from http://www.springer.com/social+sciences/journal/10767

de Certeau, M. (1984). *The practice of everyday life.* Chicago: University of Chicago Press.

Dragonas, T., & Vassiliou, A. (2017). Educational activism across the divide: Empowering youths and their communities. *Contemporary Social Science, 12*(1–2). doi:10.1080/21582041.2017.1327668

Dubinsky, K., Krull, C., & Lord, S. (2009). *New world coming: The sixties and the shaping of global consciousness.* Toronto: Between the Lines.

Elder, G. H., Modell, J., & Parke, R. D. (1993). *Children in time and place: Developmental and historical insights.* Cambridge: Cambridge University Press.

Fassin, D. (2015). Troubled waters: At the confluence of ethics and politics. In M. Lambek, V. Das, D. Fassin, & W. Keane (Eds.), *Four lectures on ethics: Anthropological perspectives* (pp. 175–210). Chicago, IL: The University of Chicago Press.

Fine, M., & Sirin, S. R. (2007). Theorizing hyphenated selves: Researching youth development in and across contentious political contexts. *Social and Personality Psychology Compass*, *1*(1), 16–38.

Fisher, D. R. (2012). Youth political participation: Bridging activism and electoral politics. *Annual Review of Sociology*, *38*, 119–137.

Flax, J. (1990). *Thinking fragments: Psychoanalysis, feminism and postmodernism in the contemporary west*. Berkeley, CA: University of California Press.

Flyvbjerg, B. (2001). *Making social science matter: Why social inquiry fails and how it can succeed again*. Cambridge, UK: Cambridge University Press.

Gergen, K. (2011). *Relational being: Beyond self and community*. Oxford: Oxford University Press.

Grasso, M. T., Farrall, S., Gray, E., Hay, C., & Jennings, W. (2017, January 26). Thatcher's children, Blair's babies, political socialization and trickle-down value change: An age, period and cohort analysis. *British Journal of Political Science*. Advanced online publication. doi:10.1017/S0007123416000375

Griffiths, C. (1993). *Representations of youth*. Cambridge: Polity Press.

Guillemot, J., & Price, D. (2017). Politicisation in later life: Experience and motivations of older people participating in a protest for the first time. *Contemporary Social Science*, *12*(1–2). doi:10.1080/21582041.2017.1326620

Hall, S. (1993). Culture, community, nation. *Cultural Studies*, *7*(3), 349–363.

Hanson, K., & Nieuwenhuys, O. (2012). Living rights, social justice, translations. In Karl Hanson & Olga Nieuwenhuys (Eds.), *Reconceptualizing children's rights in international development: Living rights, social justice, translations* (pp. 3–26). Cambridge: Cambridge University Press.

Higgs, P. (1995). Citizenship and old age: The end of the road? *Ageing and Society*, *15*, 535–550.

Hughes, C. (2015). *Young lives on the left: Sixties activism and the liberation of the self*. Manchester: Manchester University Press.

James, A. (2011). To be(come) or not to be(come): Understanding children's citizenship. *The Annals of the American Academy of Political and Social Science*, *633*, 167–179.

Jones, A. (2017). Housing choices in later life as unclaimed forms of housing activism. *Contemporary Social Science*, *12*(1–2). doi:10.1080/21582041.2017.1334127

Katz, S. (2017). Welfare mothers' grassroots activism for economic justice. *Contemporary Social Science*, *12*(1–2). doi:10.1080/21582041.2017.1335879

Lambert, M. (2010). *Ordinary ethics: Anthropology, language and action*. New York, NY: Fordham University Press.

Liebel, M., Overwien, B., & Recknagel, A. (2001). *Working children's protagonism: Social movements and empowerment in Latin America, Africa and India*. Frankfurt, Germany: IKO-Verlag für Interkulturelle Kommunikation.

Linden, A., & Klandermans, K. (2007). Revolutionaries, wanderers, converts, and compliants: Life histories of extreme right activists. *Journal of Contemporary Ethnography*, *36*(2), 184–201.

Lister, R. (2003). *Citizenship: Feminist perspectives* (2nd revised ed.). London: Palgrave Macmillan.

Lister, R. (2007). Why citizenship: Where, when and how children? *Theoretical Inquiries in Law*, *8*(2), 693–717.

Mahony, N., Newman, J., & Barnett, C. (2010). *Rethinking the public: Innovations in research, theory and politics*. Bristol: The Policy Press.

Marwick, A. E., & boyd, d. (2011). I tweet honestly, I tweet passionately: Twitter users, context collapse, and the imagined audience. *New Media & Society*, *13*(1), 114–133.

McAfee, N. (2000). *Habermas, Kristeva and citizenship*. Ithaca, NY: Cornell University Press.

Moran-Ellis, J., Bandt, A., & Sünker, H. (2014). Children's well-being and politics. In A. Ben-Arieh, F. Casas, I. Frønes, & J.E. Korbin (Eds.), *Handbook of child well-being: Theories, methods and policies in global perspective* (pp. 415–435). New York: Springer.

Ndlovu, S. M. (2006). The Soweto uprising. In B. Theron (Ed.), *The road to democracy in South Africa volume 2 [1970–1980]* (pp. 317–350). Unisa: Unisa Press, University of South Africa.

Nielsen, R. K. (2016). *A desk is a dangerous place from which to view the world: Social science and the 2016 elections*. Retrieved June 5, 2017, from https://rasmuskleisnielsen.net/2016/11/09/a-desk-is-a-dangerous-place-from-which-to-view-the-world-social-science-and-the-2016-elections/

Nolas, S.-M. (2015). Children's participation, childhood publics and social change: A review. *Children & Society*, *29*(1), 157–167.

Nolas, S.-M., Varvantakis, C., & Aruldoss, V. (2017a, May 2). Children of the financial crisis. *Discover Society*, Issue 44. Retrieved May 20, 2017, from http://discoversociety.org/2017/05/02/children-of-the-financial-crisis/

Nolas, S.-M., Varvantakis, C., & Aruldoss, V. (2017b). Talking politics in everyday family lives. *Contemporary Social Science*, *12*(1–2). doi:10.1080/21582041.2017.1330965

Norris, P. (2009). Political activism: New challenges, new opportunities. In Carles Boix & Susan C. Stokes (Eds.), *The oxford handbook for comparative politics* (pp. 628–649). Oxford: Oxford University Press.

Pancer, S. M. (2015). *The psychology of citizenship and civic engagement*. Oxford: Oxford University Press.

Pedwell, C. (2017). Transforming habit: Revolution, routine and social change. *Cultural Studies*, *31*(1), 93–120.

Peterson-Badali, M., Ruck, M. D., & Ridley, E. (2003). College students' attitudes toward children's nurturance and self-determination rights. *Journal of Applied Social Psychology*, *33*, 730–755.

Pilcher, J., & Wagg, S. (1996). *Thatcher's Children?: Politics, childhood and society in the 1990s and 1990s*. London: Falmer Press.

Plummer, K. (2003). *Intimate citizenship: Personal decisions and public dialogues*. Seattle: University of Washington Press.

Putnam, R. (2000). *Bowling alone: The collapse and revival of American community*. New York, NY: Simon & Schuster Paperbacks.

Rose, N. (1998). *Inventing our sevles: Psychology, power, and person hood*. Cambridge: Cambridge University Press.

Rosen, R. (2017). Play as activism? Early childhood and (inter)generational politics. *Contemporary Social Science*, *12*(1–2). doi:10.1080/21582041.2017.1324174

Roseneil, S. (Ed.). (2013). *Beyond citizenship? Feminism and the transformation of belonging*. London: Palgrave MacMillan.

Sapiro, V. (2004). Not your parents' socialisation: Introduction for a new generation. *Annual Review of Political Science*, *7*(1), 1–23.

Sayer, A. (2011). *Why things matter to people: Social science, values and ethical life*. Cambridge: Cambridge University Press.

Schmitt-Beck, R., & Lup, O. (2013). Seeking the soul of democracy: A review of recent research into citizens' political talk culture. *Swiss Political Science Review*, *19*(4), 513–538.

Schram, S. F., Flyvbjerg, B., & Landman, T. (2013). *Political* political science: A phronetic approach. *New Political Science*, *35*(3), 359–372.

Seidman, M. M. (2004). *The imaginary revolution: Parisian students and workers in 1968*. Oxford: Berghahn Books.

Steedman, C. (1998). *Strange dislocations: Childhood and the idea of human interiority*. Cambridge, MA: Harvard University Press.

Taft, J. (2017). Teenage girls' narratives of becoming activists. *Contemporary Social Science*, *12*(1–2). doi:10.1080/21582041.2017.1324173

Tilly, C., & Tarrow, S. (2015). *Contentious politics* (2nd ed.). Oxford: Oxford University Press.

Wagg, S., & Pilcher, J. (2014). *Thatcher's grandchildren: Politics and childhood in the twenty first century*. New York: Springer.

Walker, C. (2017). Embodying 'the next generation': Children's everyday environmental activism in India and England. *Contemporary Social Science*, *12*(1–2). doi:10.1080/21582041.2017.1325922

Weisner, T., & Bernheimer, L. P. (1998). Children of the 1960s at midlife: Generational identity and the family adaptive project. In Richard A. Shweder (Ed.), *Welcome to middle age! (and other cultural fictions)* (pp. 211–257). Chicago, IL: The University of Chicago Press.

Yang, G. (2016). Activism. In B. Peters (Ed.), *Digital keywords: A vocabulary of information society and culture* (pp. 1–17). Princeton, NJ: Princeton University Press.

# Embodying 'the Next Generation': children's everyday environmental activism in India and England

Catherine Walker ⓘ

**ABSTRACT**

The symbolic evocation of 'the next generation' might be considered as valuable in buttressing calls for concerted public and political action on climate change, whilst assigning to children a unique identity and role in engendering sustainable transitions. Yet does an identity that is in essence equated with futurity stifle possibilities for children's own actions in the present, and conflict with policy expectations that children can be 'agents of (pro-environmental) change'? Drawing on multi-method doctoral research carried out with children (aged 11–14) and their families in varying socio-economic contexts in India and England, this paper considers the use and utility of generational identities in prompting environmental concern and explores how generationally framed imaginaries of childhood feature in children's and family narratives of everyday environmental activism. Building on theoretical arguments of generational interdependence and ethics of care, the paper argues for greater recognition of children's actual and potential contributions to engendering sustainable futures, whilst drawing attention to the ways in which children's agency to act on environmental knowledge is supported by – and interdependent with – that of adult actors, not least parents.

## Introduction

In recent years, everyday household practices have become a new arena for the performance of morality, as policies lead individuals to consider these practices in relation to concerns about the planet and its present and future residents (Agrawal, 2005; Boddy et al., 2016; Hobson, 2013; Miller, 2012). Across global settings, environmental policies are increasingly premised on the idea of individuals taking on the role of the 'environmental subject [...] for whom the environment constitutes a critical domain of thought and action' (Agrawal, 2005, p. 16), although it is notable that understandings of 'environmentally friendly' behaviours are contextually situated rather than universally understood (Boddy et al., 2016; Guha, 2006; Shiva, 1993). The role of the 'environmental subject' materialises as everyday practices become associated with contextually situated understandings of environmental 'friendliness' or harm, and as understandings resonate with individuals' concerns about valued aspects of their environments (Agrawal, 2005; Beck, 2010).

Taking on of the role of the 'environmental subject' in and through one's everyday practices constitutes what I refer to in this paper as 'everyday environmental activism'. Such activism might be defined as individual and collective efforts to change, adapt or disrupt one's own and others' everyday practices in response to concerns about the negative impact of these practices on the environment as it is known, valued and imagined. Efforts could encompass activities commonly associated with an 'activist' lifestyle, for example, attending climate demonstrations or joining an environmental campaigning group; however, the activism defined here is a phenomenological – or lived – form of activism motivated by relationships of concern and materialised through emotions and practices in private as well as public spaces.

This definition of activism is encompassing of human–environmental interdependence, understanding that neither are human beings impervious to the unpredictable effects of nature, nor is the non-human world a passive force supporting human activity (Manuel-Navarrete & Buzinde, 2010; Szerszynski & Urry, 2010). Such activism is grounded theoretically in an ethic of care, premised on understandings of interdependence between humans (and non-humans) across times and spaces (Tronto, 1993). It is also influenced by Horton and Kraftl's consideration of 'implicit' or 'modest activisms', emerging from individuals' emotional encounters with the world around them (2009, p. 14), and by Nolas, Varvantakis, and Aruldoss' experiential exploration of children's awareness of, access to, orientation towards and action on 'issues of common concern', as a way of extending literatures of childhood, activism and prefiguration (2016, p. 252).

Symbolic evocations of 'the next generation' underpin moral arguments for 'sustainable transitions' and many policy instruments hinge on the planetary legacy for 'future generations' (Renton & Butcher, 2010; United Nations Children's Fund, 2008; United Nations Children's Fund UK, 2013). As the present-day embodiment of this symbolic identity, children and young people[1] are often evoked to animate abstract environmental concerns as policy-makers speak of their offspring as a motivator for action.[2] However, children's inclusion in environmental policies is not only symbolic. The United Nations' Education for Sustainable Development initiative, rolled out globally through the Decade of Education for Sustainable Development (2005–2014), has sought to 'integrate the principles, values and practices of sustainable development into all aspects of education and learning' (United Nations Educational Scientific and Cultural Organisation [UNESCO], n.d.). Through this initiative, children are centrally implicated in policy endeavours to materialise environmental knowledge and cultivate environmental subjectivities as 'agents of change', envisaged to influence the practices of those around them through their environmental knowledge and 'pester power' (Ballantyne, Connell, & Fien, 1998; Satchwell, 2013; Uzzell et al., 1994; Walker, 2017).

Children's imagined role as 'agents of change' assumes a straightforward crossover between childhood's symbolic power to influence high-level change and children's embodied and emotive 'pester power' in everyday life. However, this assumption is frequently underexplored in relation to children's lived experiences in societies that sociologists of childhood have argued are 'generationally ordered', making children 'the less powerful part in an adult world' (Qvortrup, 2005, p. 20; for discussion, see Alanen, 2009; Mayall, 2002; Punch, 2007). It is therefore pertinent to consider the extent to which the imagined and assigned identities associated with childhood – those mobilised in making the moral case for 'pro-environmental' action and in allocating a role for children in such action – translate to lived experiences of everyday environmental activism in childhood and if children have anything more than a symbolic role to play in engendering sustainable planetary futures.

## Aims and contribution of this paper

The above discussion introduces the potential difficulties presented for children in reconciling their assigned, imagined and lived identities as 'the next generation'. The remainder of the paper aims to tease out the complexities and contradictions inherent in children's societal positioning as 'the next generation' and consider the value of this identity for supporting children's (and other generations') everyday environmental activism. The paper considers the following questions:

- How do children make sense of their assigned identity as 'the next generation'?
- Does an identity that is in essence equated with futurity stifle possibilities for children's own actions in the present, and conflict with policy expectations that children can be 'agents of (pro-environmental) change'?
- What contradictions might be raised as children seek to engender and encourage sustainable transitions in contexts where their social influence is frequently lessened by their generational positioning?

The paper draws on the work of sociologists of childhood, who have developed 'generation' as a 'conceptual starting point and an analytical tool for framing the study of childhood' (Alanen, 2009, p. 163). The paper considers the use and utilities of generational identities – in particular the trope of 'the next generation' – in prompting environmental concern and explores how generationally framed imaginaries of childhood feature in children's and family narratives of everyday environmental activism.

## Assigned, imagined and lived identities: the trope of 'the next generation'

Across global contexts, the legally and socially constituted period of childhood is commonly viewed as a transition from dependence and lesser political and moral agency to increased participation, independence and responsibility (Nolas, 2015; Oswell, 2013; Panelli, Punch, & Robson, 2007). The symbolic power of generation to imagine and assign political and social identities for children might be considered amongst what James, using a metaphor of fabric, presents as 'the commonalities of childhood – social stratification, culture, gender [and] generational relations' (2010, p. 493). James presents these as 'common threads that permeate the fabric of the social category of childhood, and which are used to define childhood structurally, as a separate generational space'. These are woven through with the 'weft' of lived childhoods across times and spaces, creating the 'detailed patterns [of] childhood' (2010, pp. 493–494).

The vulnerability of children's bodies to climate-related events, the frequent entwinement in the public imagination of childhood and nature and today's children's historical positioning growing up in an age of environmental concern mean that the trope of 'the next generation' is powerfully mobilised in contemporary environmental policies (Renton & Butcher, 2010). Indeed, it is the cross-temporality of childhood that affords its central policy positioning, as policy-makers recognise that 'if practices consistent with sustainable development are to be carried forward through time, then children must be the bridge conveying their value and ways' (Heft & Chawla, 2006, p. 199). Despite this apparent logic, the imagined, assigned and lived identities that cohere in the narrative trope of 'the next generation' present a number of contradictions that children are tasked with negotiating in their everyday lives.

A commonly assigned identity for children in environmental policy is as 'agents of change', acting on the knowledge they receive through environmental education and influencing the practices of their family members through their 'pester power' (Satchwell, 2013). This assigned role maps directly onto what is termed in this paper as children's imagined identity as 'the next generation' – as those who inspire and lead action on issues of common concern, either indirectly through their symbolic positioning in the social imagination or directly by using 'pester power' to influence change. This identity is neatly summed up by Kraftl, who identifies a persistent imaginary of childhood as 'a universalising affective condition [...] characterised by very simplistic, and often problematic, notions of hope, logic and futurity' (2008, p. 82). As Kraftl continues, the persistent attribution of childhood with 'spectacular', future-oriented forms of hope can mean that children's more 'modest' articulations of hope are overlooked, potentially stifling children's agency to achieve their modest hopes in their present-day lives (2008, p. 85; see also Horton & Kraftl, 2009). Kraftl's argument that children become a 'repository for hope in the diverse political agendas of human rights and wellbeing' (2008, p. 83) has resonance with the arguments of other scholars who have identified state agendas (for example, the shaping and governance of 'good citizens') in children's assigned political and social participation (Aitken, Lund, & Kjørholt, 2007; Nolas, 2015).

In an age in which individuals' everyday practices are increasingly scrutinised in relation to 'good' and 'bad' paradigms of environmental behaviour, the making of children as 'environmental subjects' might be seen as one manifestation of what Agrawal (2005) has termed 'environmentality'. In a study of citizen participation in environmental regulation practices in North India, Agrawal develops 'environmentality' as an 'analytical optic' adapted from Foucault's notion of 'governmentality', and defines this as 'the knowledges, politics, institutions and subjectivities that come to be linked together with the emergence of the environment as a domain that requires regulation and protection' (2005, p. 226). Children's assigned environmental subjectivities can be understood as part of this 'analytical optic'. However, children's agency – including their agency to act on environmental knowledge – is indelibly shaped by societal notions of childhood as a time of futurity, learning and 'becoming' (Aitken et al., 2007; Kraftl, 2008; Lee, 2013). Whilst these notions are to some extent axiomatic – children will, in the main, have longer futures than most adults – a danger is that these notions position children as 'a defective form of adult, social [and political] only in their future potential but not in their present being' (James, Jenks, & Prout, 1998, p. 6). This understanding is most clearly materialised through age-defined political suffrage; however, sociologists of childhood have identified this in the everyday difficulties encountered by children as they negotiate decisions in adult-dominated worlds (Alanen, 2009; Mayall, 2002; Punch, 2007; Qvortrup, 2005). Thus, in their lived identity as 'the next generation', children must reconcile being 'environmental subjects' with a generational positioning that means they are frequently disadvantaged in their everyday interactions and negotiations.

## Methodology

Building on the above framework of assigned, imagined and lived identities, this paper explores the everyday contradictions of embodying 'the next generation' through children's narratives of everyday life and environmental concern in a range of settings.

The narratives presented and analysed in this paper are drawn from multi-method doctoral research with eighteen 11- to 14-year-old children[3] and their families in a variety of socio-economic contexts in India and England, as part of the cross-national study *Family Lives and the Environment* (FLE).[4] The doctoral research was concerned with children's everyday experiences, understandings and practices of environment and aimed to critically consider theories of children's agency to act on expressed environmental concerns by analysing children's and family narratives of environment and everyday life (Walker, 2016). A second aim of the research, entwined within the first, was to explore the local particularities of how 'global' environmental concerns are experienced, understood and narrated by children in different contexts. This aim underpinned the construction of a multiply-varied research sample across two countries and was informed by political ecological literature on the cultural specificity of environmental concern (see, for example, discussions by Guha, 2006; Peet, Robbins, & Watts, 2011; Shiva, 1993) and calls for more critical and globally informed childhood scholarship (Balagopalan, 2011; Nieuwenhuys, 2013; Punch & Tisdall, 2012). For Balagopalan, attending to the 'multiple modernities' of childhood may be one way of challenging the 'discourse of 'lack' associated with childhood in the majority world (2011, p. 291). By incorporating intersecting structural varieties into its sample, the research design allowed for attention to how children's varying exposures to globally situated environmental hazards are woven into other forms of structural disadvantage, incorporating socio-economic positioning, rural–urban location and gender.

The PhD research and FLE shared a research design and sample. Participants lived in London and Hyderabad, South India (cities of around 8 million people) and two predominantly rural areas in Southern England and Andhra Pradesh. Researchers contacted families through fee-paying and non-fee-paying schools in an aim to recruit a socio-economically varied sample, and worked with an equal number of boys and girls. In total, 24

**Table 1.** Research sample.

| Type and location of school | Participant pseudonym (gender, age at time of research) |
| --- | --- |
| Fee-paying international school, Hyderabad | Amrutha (F, 12), Aamir (M, 12) |
| Fee-paying private school, Hyderabad | Gomathi (F, 12), Rahul (M, 12) |
| Non-fee-paying government school, Hyderabad | Mamatha (F, 12), Anand (M, 14) |
| Fee-paying international school, regional city in Andhra Pradesh | Reethika (F, 12), Nageshwar (M, 12) |
| Fee-paying private school, rural Andhra Pradesh | Chitra (F, 12), Hemant (M, 12) |
| Non-fee-paying government school, rural Andhra Pradesh | Dharani (F, 12), Chandrasekhar (M, 12) |
| Fee-paying independent school, rural England | Rosie (F, 12) |
| Non-fee-paying state school, rural England | Helena (F, 12), Callum (M, 11) |
| Fee-paying independent school, London | Humphrey (M, 12) |
| Non-fee-paying state schools, London | Tamsin (F, 12), Solomon (M, 11) |

children and families participated in *FLE*. Eighteen of these children were included in the research sample for the doctoral study. The sample is detailed in Table 1.

Data were generated through a multi-method research design, incorporating individual interviews with caregivers and children, group interviews with families at home and children in school and a range of multi-sensory activities with children and other family members. These activities included mobile interviews, cognitive mapping, responses to hypothetical vignettes and a photo elicitation activity carried out over approximately one week that culminated in a family discussion of photos taken by different family members. In both countries, the research was carried out in small teams (see Acknowledgements for details of researchers). Many of the research activities in India were carried out in translation, with research team member Madhavi Latha interviewing children and families in Telugu and translating responses into English. Using a research design that included group interviews and activities with family members and school peers allowed for consideration of how children's narratives of environmental concern and everyday activism develop in dialogue with other key actors in their lives.

Children's narratives are analysed in this paper using a case-based narrative approach, which attends to how participants construct identities through stories, and considers the ways in which participants exercise 'agentic choice' in how they present themselves across research activities (Phoenix, 2013; Riessman, 2011). Whilst attentive to participants' agency in constructing stories and identities, this analytic approach is cognisant of how narratives are shaped by the social, political and interpersonal contexts in which they are told, as 'events perceived as important are selected, organised, connected, and evaluated as meaningful for a particular audience' (Riessman, 2008, p. 3).

Although children's narratives were generated across a range of spaces (as detailed above), this paper focuses on children's narratives of attempts to act on environmental knowledge in their homes, often in collaboration with other family members. There are a number of reasons for this focus. Firstly, the home is often cited by scholars as the place where children have the most opportunities – comparative to schools and other public spaces – for reflexive action and negotiation with those around them (Mayall, 2002; Punch, 2007; Valentine, 2004). Secondly, focusing on the home encompasses attention to intergenerational negotiations and, therefore, possibilities for intergenerational action on environmental concerns. Finally, attention to domestic forms of activism might contribute to a broadening of what is considered *as* activism, as explored by a number of scholars (Brown & Pickerill, 2009; Horton & Kraftl, 2009; Nolas et al., 2016). I return to these considerations in the closing discussion.

## Children's narratives of everyday environmental activism

Research activities described in the above section were designed to provide children with multiple opportunities to interpret 'big' environmental messages in relation to any concerns about their immediate environments, and to recollect – by telling stories, either individually or jointly with family members or peers – changes they had made to everyday practices in response to their concerns.

Some children's stories presented changes as relatively straightforward to enact. Dharani, living in rural India, recounted the following story in response to a prompt in her school group activity for participants to share examples of environmental messages that had led them to act differently at home:

Dharani:    We are cutting trees, we should not do this. The trees are dying because we are felling them. Devoid of trees we will not get any fresh air, and naturally no rains. And so, first of all we should not cut trees but save them and protect them.
Madhavi:    How did your family members respond to that? What did your mother tell you?
Dharani:    She said 'we too shall grow trees'. And from that time onwards we started growing plants at home.
Madhavi:    What plants?
Dharani:    She started growing flowering plants and also our own kitchen garden. And because of that, the environmental pollution also came down and we have fresh air all around us now. (Dharani, 12, school group activity, rural India)

Prompted by the researchers' questions, in Labovian terms,[5] Dharani's story of how her family began planting at home moves directly from the abstract – 'we are cutting trees, we should not do this' – to an evaluation of the problem – 'devoid of trees we will not get any fresh air', a proposed solution – 'we should not cut trees but save and protect them' – and a resolution, 'from that time onwards we started growing plants at home … we have fresh air all around us now'. There is no complicating action in terms of resistance from family members around the value of planting or the practicalities of this activity. It may be notable that Dharani presents her mother as the active agent in the story, whose decision brings about the positive resolution. However, this decision results from Dharani's expressed concerns about air pollution and her identification of a (partial) solution by drawing on her scientific knowledge. Dharani's story, which initially appears to read as a template for the assigned role of children as 'agents of change' in their families, shows the importance of family support in enabling children's concerns to be translated into action.

Other children's narratives of household changes to everyday practices gave insights into the ongoing negotiations that environmental messages prompted in homes. Rosie, living in rural England, gave various examples of attempts to enact her environmental knowledge at home. This included a time when she had tried to remind herself and other family members to turn off lights by sticking 'post-it' notes next to light-switches. In another story, the role was reversed as Rosie presented her reaction to her father reminding family members of the need to turn off lights:

Rosie:    Certainly lights get left on when no one's using them. And my dad goes round counting how many lights are on in the house. He goes round every morning and goes, 'One, two, three, four, five, six.' I just go, 'Oh, shut up! I'm just trying to get some sleep!' (Rosie, 12, individual interview, rural England)

The shifting roles taken by different family members in engaging with and reminding one another of environmental messages were also seen in this family as Rosie's parents alternated in how they presented different generations in their family as more or less aware of environmental problems. At times, they drew on their historical positioning of having seen greater environmental changes over their lifetime to support their environmental concerns, whilst at other times they presented Rosie and her brother as 'more aware' of these changes, as those growing up in an era when environmental concerns are more commonly vocalised in everyday life.

Some research activities led to *in-situ* negotiations of environmental knowledge, which demonstrated the emotional and imaginative work undertaken by children in their attempts to influence family practices, particularly where the relevance of their messages was contested. A family discussion in Hyderabad, Amrutha's mother's recollection of how Amrutha and her sister often asked her to turn off air-conditioning to 'save polar bears', led to one such negotiation:

| Aruna [*mother*]: | In what ways you save polar bears by doing that? |
|---|---|
| Alekhya [*sister*]: | By not by not turning on the AC [air conditioning]! |
| Amrutha: | By not turning on the AC because it kills a lot of polar bears in the Arctic. |
| Aruna: | Do we see polar bears around us? |
| Amrutha: | Not around us but in the Arctic we can see. |
| Aruna: | How do they affect, ah? How do you save them by turning it off? |
| Amrutha: | We won't get to see, but if you use all the AC then you won't get more AC in the future. It's like that. (Amrutha, 12, and family, group discussion, Hyderabad) |

The causality between 'AC' and polar bears constructed by Amrutha in this extract demonstrates the power of symbolic images to promote 'pro-environmental' messages. Aruna's scepticism, however, leads Amrutha to call upon another environmental narrative – future resource scarcity – to support her case for the family reducing their use of 'AC'. Following further discussion, Amrutha's parents conceded that Amrutha's concerns were scientifically grounded and used the opportunity to demonstrate their own environmental knowledge:

| Vijay [*father*]: | [AC's] use a lot of CFC gases, Amrutha. So those gases kind of impact the ozone layer which in turn is fastening [sic] the melting cycles of the arctic. So no snow, no ice, polar bears are, um (.) going to extinction. |
|---|---|
| Aruna: | Yeah, that is correct. (Family group discussion, Hyderabad) |

This exchange indicates Amrutha's capacities to influence family understandings of a formerly taken-for-granted practice, later exemplified as Aruna described how she sometimes reminded Amrutha of her own message: 'Whenever she turns on the AC when she wants to sleep, I tell her "polar bears are crying, why are you switching on the AC?"'. However, this *in situ* negotiation of everyday practices also shows the difficulties for children (and indeed, all family members) of acting on as-yet temporally and spatially distant concerns. Although Amrutha's parents' ultimately endorsed this particular message, this and other examples illuminate how children's attempts to influence family practices involve negotiations between 'new' knowledge and parents' existing knowledge, which may be supported by parents' claims to authoritative knowledge based on comparatively greater life experience.

Understandings of age-related 'maturity' were vocalised by a number of children and parents in the research, in what might be seen as a refutation of the narrative of 'the next generation' acting as 'agents of change' in lieu of a narrative of parental responsibility to teach children to use resources sustainably. Aamir, living in Hyderabad, spoke in self-deprecating terms of his own attempts at reducing his use of 'gadgets' in response to his knowledge of their environmental impact. In contrast, he presented his parents as 'obviously' better at acting on this knowledge:

| | |
|---|---|
| Aamir: | I actually tried to change some things in my house but then I am lazy enough to just leave it and, like, never mind anything (Aamir laughs). |
| | [Discussion ensues about the nature of attempted changes] |
| Catherine: | And when you were trying to make those changes, did you tell your family that that's what you were doing? |
| Aamir: | Yeah. Actually <u>they</u> tried their best and even I did the same, but I ended up doing it for short time whereas they did it for, uh, a longer time. |
| Catherine: | Oh really? Could you tell me who in your family was good at remembering to not use AC so much? |
| Aamir: | Uh, my mother, obviously (…) mother and my father. (Aamir, 12, school group discussion, Hyderabad; emphasis in the original) |

Aamir's assessment that his parents were 'obviously' better than he was at remembering to use less 'AC' cohered with a family narrative of responsible resource use as something learned over time and with the help of older family members, vocalised by various members of Aamir's family in research activities. This could be seen in the family discussion of a hypothetical vignette presented by the research team, premised on a child suggesting that the family use less water in response to teaching at school about the threat of regional drought:

| | |
|---|---|
| Aafiya [*cousin*]: | Maybe his mother, she changes her mind and uses less water everywhere, every day. |
| Aamir: | Depends on the mother. |
| Zoya [*mother*]: | If she were a mother like me she would have definitely changed. |
| Natasha: | OK. And why do you think she would change the way she uses her water? |
| Zoya: | Because she is old enough to understand the situation. The child has understood, he has come home fully prepared that this is how he is going to save water, so now it is the mother who <u>has to</u> understand, so being a very mature person in the family she understands and then she cuts down the use of water. (Aamir, 12, and family, group discussion, Hyderabad; emphasis in the original) |

Zoya's intervention amidst the boys' responses suggests parental responsiveness to the hypothetical child's concerns, whilst reinforcing a position of parental authority and responsibility for managing household resources. This understanding of parental authority, vocalised by both parents and children in the research, presents a disjunction from simplistic notions of children acting as 'agents of change' and leading family members to 'pro-environmental' practices by their examples.

This observation is not intended to minimise the important role that children have in influencing family attempts to make connections between 'big' environmental concerns and everyday domestic practices, and to adapt these practices accordingly. Indeed, case examples seen above present insights into children's capacities to interpret complex environmental messages, to make moral decisions based on their interpretations and – in Amrutha's case in particular – to use their generational positioning as those who will live with the consequences of present-day practices to influence the way in which previously taken-for-granted practices are understood. It is important to note, however, that children's attempts to influence practices and the 'new' knowledge used in such attempts must be negotiated alongside parents' own (claims to) authoritative knowledge generated though their greater life experience. Thus, family attempts to adapt practices in

21

'pro-environmental' ways might be better conceived of as collaborative actions, involving intergenerational negotiations of knowledge and symbolic authority. Within such negotiations, children's symbolic connection to the future is a powerful motivator for action. However, translating future-oriented concerns into action is mediated through prevailing understandings of children's and parents' roles in the home and family members' existing knowledge.

## Closing discussion: what place for children in everyday environmental activism?

By critically considering the ways in which the trope of 'the next generation' is used in environmental policies, and in societal framings more broadly, this paper has attended to the assigned, imagined and lived identities that cohere in this generational identity, and has considered the extent to which this identity is useful in prompting children's (and other generations') everyday environmental activism. This was defined as individual and collective efforts to change, adapt or disrupt one's own and others' everyday practices in response to concerns about the negative impact of these practices on the environment as it is known, valued and imagined.

Case examples presented above offer insights into ways in which children in different contexts are responding to their assigned role as 'agents of (pro-environmental) change'. Children's narratives of attempts to adapt their everyday practices and to influence how such practices are understood and engaged in by other family members show their capacities to interpret complex messages and to act reflexively, thus demonstrating what Mayall (2002) terms children's 'moral agency'. Moreover, children's attempts to act on spatially and temporally distant environmental concerns, using their imagination to construct causalities between distant times and spaces, illuminate their capacities to engage in meaningful action motivated by an 'ethic of care' (Tronto, 1993), albeit action of a more modest order than that commonly understood to constitute 'activism'. Such insights support arguments for renewed consideration of what is considered to constitute activism, including where this takes place and who is involved (Brown & Pickerill, 2009; Horton & Kraftl, 2009; Nolas et al., 2016). In particular, children's narratives in this paper suggest that ideas that children do not engage in 'activism' have less to do with children's (frequently underexplored) capacities for political action and more to do with the reductive ways in which 'activism' is often understood as 'spectacular' public action, engaged in by those of voting age and above.

Children's and family narratives of everyday environmental activism display the symbolic ways that the identity of 'the next generation' can prompt present-day action, as children embody the need for action to assure the future security of the planet. In this regard, the close associations between childhood and futurity do not necessarily mean that children's possibilities for action in the present are stifled. Rather, children's imagined identity as 'repositories of hope' for the future (Kraftl, 2008) can be useful in supporting environmental activism. However, children's role should not only be viewed as symbolic. The important role that children have in negotiating environmental knowledge and adaptations to everyday practices highlights the need for a revaluation of the diminished political and social role with which children are imbued in many contexts (James et al., 1998; Mayall, 2002; Qvortrup, 2005).

The examples presented above caution against making too straightforward a connection between childhood's symbolic power and children's 'pester power' to influence change. In particular, children's narratives show that their possibilities for action – in the home at least – depend to large extent on their proposed actions being taken seriously by other family members. In this way, the potential stifling of children's possibilities to engage in every-day environmental activism remains a risk where attention is not paid to the ways in which children's agency and propensity to act is supported by – and interdependent with – that of their parents. Thus, rather than a policy focus on building children's agency to act as 'agents of change', a more helpful and ultimately more sustainable approach might be to focus on the ways in which family members work together to enact changes in their everyday lives, amidst ongoing conflicts and negotiations. This fits with the arguments of scholars who have argued for greater attention to familial interdependence and to human interdependence in general (Oswell, 2013; Punch, 2007; Richards, Clark, & Boggis, 2015; Tronto, 1993).

An important area of consideration not explored in depth in this paper is the way in which children's and family agency to act on environmental concerns might be stifled by the structural inadequacies of their environments, particularly for families living in materially poor circumstances. In the research informing this paper, children in low-income settings often expressed concerns and frustrations over environmental problems that they sensed in their everyday lives but felt unable as individuals to do anything to change (e.g. exposed waste, traffic pollution or stagnant water). In contrast to the largely future-oriented concerns seen in this paper, these concerns were part of children's present-day environmental experiences, adding weight to the moral imperative for structural interventions to support children and families in responding to these present-day concerns.

In conclusion, responses to complex environmental and political challenges require interdependent action. Children's identity as 'the next generation' – as those with lives envisaged to cross temporalities and trajectories of planetary degradation – can and should support their contributions to engendering sustainable futures. Indeed, the examples presented above show children's potential to act and influence in ways that are more than symbolic. However, ongoing political work is needed to 'upgrade childhood as social status' (Mayall, 2002, p. 12) so that children's everyday environmental activism, carried out in partnership with other generations, is taken seriously.

## Notes

1. Henceforth in this paper, I use the term 'children' to refer to those under the age of 18. This is in keeping with scholars of childhood, whose work has been influential to this paper and who have explored and theorised the ways in which children are generationally positioned vis-à-vis adults. In using the terms 'children' and 'childhood' in this paper, I refer to the generational positioning of 'children' as a societal group distinguished from 'adults', whilst acknowledging that many legally and societally constituted 'children' identify as 'young people'.
2. As exemplified in an interview with Christiana Figueres, UN Chief Negotiator on Climate Change, published shortly before the 2015 Paris Summit (see Harvey, 2015).
3. The intention of the research team was to work with a smaller age range (11–12) by presenting the research to children from the same school year (year seven) when visiting schools. However, some schools in India had a high rate of older children in attendance in year seven. In one case, this resulted in us working with a 14-year-old boy who was in the same school year as the other children in the sample.

4. FLE was a constituent project of the ESRC National Centre for Research Methods node NOVELLA (Narratives of Varied Everyday Lives and Linked Approaches), which used and developed narrative approaches to analyse everyday family life (see Phoenix, 2011 and www.novella.ac.uk for details).
5. Labov's (1972) systematic approach to the interpretation of narratives categorises talk into abstract, orientation, complicating action, evaluation, and result. Occasionally speakers use a coda to 'sign off' the narrative and signify that its telling is complete.

## Acknowledgements

Many thanks to the *Connectors* research team (and editors of this special issue) for the opportunity to present an earlier version of this paper at a highly stimulating workshop, and for their and other workshop participants' feedback on this paper.

The PhD research underpinning this paper was supervised by Professors Ann Phoenix and Janet Boddy, who were respectively principal investigators for the NOVELLA research node and the Family Lives and the Environment study in which the PhD was embedded. The PhD research owes much of its design and intellectual framing to how Ann and Janet designed and led these studies.

Data presented in this chapter were generated by the following researchers in England and India: Helen Austerberry, Janet Boddy, Hanan Hauari, Madhavi Latha, Natasha Shukla and Catherine Walker.

Finally and most importantly, thanks are due to the participants who so generously gave their time, energy and imagination to the research.

## Disclosure statement

No potential conflict of interest was reported by the authors.

## Funding

This PhD work and the study in which it was embedded were funded as part of the ESRC National Centre for Research Methods Phase III Node, Narratives of Varied Everyday Lives and Linked Approaches (NOVELLA) [Grant Number RES-576-25-0053].

## ORCID

*Catherine Walker* ⓘ http://orcid.org/0000-0003-3390-9272

## References

Agrawal, A. (2005). *Environmentality: Technologies of government and the making of subjects*. Durham, NC: Duke University Press.

Aitken, S. C., Lund, R., & Kjørholt, A. T. (2007). Why children? Why now? *Children's Geographies, 5*(1–2), 3–14. doi:10.1080/14733280601108114

Alanen, L. (2009). Generational order. In J. Qvortrup, W. A. Corsaro, & M.-S. Honig (Eds.), *The Palgrave handbook of childhood studies* (pp. 159–174). Basingstoke: Palgrave Macmillan.

Balagopalan, S. (2011). Introduction: Children's lives and the Indian context. *Childhood*, *18*(3), 291–297. doi:10.1177/0907568211413369

Ballantyne, R., Connell, S., & Fien, J. (1998). Students as catalysts of environmental change: A framework for researching intergenerational influence through environmental education. *Environmental Education Research*, *4*(3), 285–298. doi:10.1080/1350462980040304

Beck, U. (2010). Climate for change, or how to create a green modernity? *Theory, Culture & Society*, *27*(2–3), 254–266. doi:10.1177/0263276409358729

Boddy, J., Phoenix, A., Walker, C., Vennam, U., Austerberry, H., & Latha, M. (2016). Telling 'moral tales'? Family narratives of responsible privilege and environmental concern in India and the UK. *Families, Relationships and Societies*, *5*(3), 357–374. doi:10.1332/204674316X14758399286843

Brown, G., & Pickerill, J. (2009). Space for emotion in the spaces of activism. *Emotion, Space and Society*, *2*, 24–35. doi:10.1016/j.emospa.2009.03.004

Guha, R. (2006). *How much should a person consume: Environmentalism in India and the United States*. Berkeley: University of California Press.

Harvey, F. (2015, November 27). Christiana Figueres, the woman tasked with saving the world from global warming. *The Guardian*. Retrieved from http://www.guardian.co.uk

Heft, H., & Chawla, L. (2006). Children as agents in sustainable development: The ecology of competence. In C. Spencer, & M. Blades (Eds.), *Children and their environments: Learning, using and designing spaces* (pp. 199–216). Cambridge: Cambridge University Press.

Hobson, K. (2013). On the making of the environmental citizen. *Environmental Politics*, *22*(1), 56–72. doi:10.1080/09644016.2013.755388

Horton, J., & Kraftl, P. (2009). Small acts, kind words and 'not too much fuss': implicit activisms. *Emotion, Space and Society*, *2*, 14–23. doi:10.1016/j.emospa.2009.05.003

James, A., Jenks, C., & Prout, A. (1998). *Theorising childhood*. London: Polity.

James, A. L. (2010). Competition or integration? The next step in childhood studies? *Childhood*, *17*(4), 485–499. doi:10.1177/0907568209350783

Kraftl, P. (2008). Young people, hope, and childhood-hope. *Space and Culture*, *11*(2), 81–92. doi:10.1177/1206331208315930

Labov, W. (1972). *Language in the inner city: Studies in the black English vernacular*. Oxford: Basil Blackwell.

Lee, N. (2013). *Childhood and biopolitics: Climate change, life processes and human futures*. Basingstoke: Palgrave Macmillan.

Manuel-Navarrete, D., & Buzinde, C. N. (2010). Socio-ecological agency: From 'human exceptionalism' to coping with 'exceptional' global environmental change. In M. Redclift & G. Woodgate (Eds.), *The international handbook of environmental sociology* (2nd ed., pp. 136–149). Cheltenham: Edward Elgar.

Mayall, B. (2002). *Towards a sociology for childhood*. Maidenhead: Open University Press.

Miller, D. (2012). *Consumption and its consequences*. Cambridge: Polity Press.

Nieuwenhuys, O. (2013). Theorizing childhood(s): Why we need postcolonial perspectives. *Childhood*, *20*(1), 3–8. doi:10.1177/0907568212465534

Nolas, S.-M. (2015). Children's participation, childhood publics and social change: A review. *Children & Society*, *29*, 157–167. doi:10.1111/chso.12108

Nolas, S.-M., Varvantakis, C., & Aruldoss, V. (2016). (Im)possible conversations? Activism, childhood and everyday life. *Journal of Social and Political Psychology*, *4*(1), 252–265. doi:10.5964/jspp.v4i1.536

Oswell, D. (2013). *The agency of children: From family to global human rights*. Cambridge: Cambridge University Press.

Panelli, R., Punch, S., & Robson, E. (2007). From difference to dialogue: Conceptualising global perspectives on rural childhood and youth. In R. Panelli, S. Punch, & E. Robson (Eds.), *Global perspectives on rural childhood and youth* (pp. 1–13). Abingdon: Routledge.

Peet, R., Robbins, P., & Watts, M. (2011). Global nature. In R. Peet, P. Robbins, & M. Watts (Eds.), *Global political ecology* (pp. 1–47). Abingdon: Routledge.

Phoenix, A. (2011). Narrative analysis in research on families' habitual practices. *Methods news: Winter 2011*. Southampton: National Centre for Research Methods.

Phoenix, A. (2013). Analysing narrative contexts. In M. Andrews, C. Squire & M. Tamboukou (Eds.), *Doing narrative research* (2nd ed., pp. 72–87). London: Sage.

Punch, S. (2007). Generational power relations in rural Bolivia. In R. Panelli, S. Punch, & E. Robson (Eds.), *Global perspectives on rural childhood and youth* (pp. 151–164). Abingdon: Routledge.

Punch, S., & Tisdall, E. K. M. (2012). Exploring children and young people's relationships across majority and minority worlds. *Children's Geographies, 10*(3), 241–248. doi:10.1080/14733285. 2012.693375

Qvortrup, J. (2005). *Studies in modern childhood: Society, agency, culture.* Basingstoke: Palgrave Macmillan.

Renton, Z., & Butcher, J. (2010). Securing a sustainable future for children and young people. *Children & Society, 24*(2), 160–166. doi:10.1111/j.1099-0860.2009.00280.x

Richards, S., Clark, J., & Boggis, A. (2015). *Ethical research with children: Untold narratives and taboos.* Basingstoke: Palgrave Macmillan.

Riessman, C. K. (2008). *Narrative methods for the human sciences.* Thousand Oaks, CA: Sage.

Riessman, C. K. (2011). What's different about narrative inquiry? Cases, categories and contexts. In D. Silverman (Ed.), *Qualitative research: Issues of theory, method and practice* (pp. 310–324). London: Sage.

Satchwell, C. (2013). 'Carbon literacy practices': textual footprints between school and home in children's construction of knowledge about climate change. *Local Environment, 18*(3), 289–304. doi:10. 1080/13549839.2012.688735

Shiva, V. (1993). The greening of the global reach. In W. Sachs (Ed.), *Global ecology: A new arena of political conflict* (pp. 149–156). London: Zed Books.

Szerszynski, B., & Urry, J. (2010). Changing climates: Introduction. *Theory, Culture & Society, 27*(2–3), 1–8. doi:10.1177/0263276409362091

Tronto, J. (1993). *Moral boundaries: A political argument for an ethic of care.* Abingdon: Routledge.

United Nations Children's Fund. (2008). *Our climate, our children, our responsibility: The implications of climate change for the world's children.* London: UNICEF.

United Nations Children's Fund UK. (2013). *Climate change: Children's challenge.* London: UNICEF.

United Nations Educational Scientific and Cultural Organisation (UNESCO). (n.d.). Education for sustainable development: Three terms and one goal. Retrieved February 23, 2015, from http://www. unesco.org/new/en/education/themes/leading-the-international-agenda/education-for-sustainable-development/three-terms-one-goal/

Uzzell, D., Davallon, J., Jensen, B. B., Gottesdiener, H., Fontes, P., Kofoed, J., & Vognsen, C. (1994). *Children as catalysts of environmental change.* (Report to DGXII/D-5 Research on Economic and Social Aspects of the Environment (SEER)). Brussels: SEER.

Valentine, G. (2004). *Public space and the culture of childhood.* London: Ashgate.

Walker, C. (2016). *Environment and children's everyday lives in India and England: Experiences, understandings and practices* (Unpublished doctoral dissertation). UCL Institute of Education, London.

Walker, C. (2017). Tomorrow's leaders and today's agents of change? Children, sustainability education and environmental governance. *Children & Society, 31*(1), 72–83. doi:10.1111/chso.12192

# Teenage girls' narratives of becoming activists

Jessica K. Taft

**ABSTRACT**

Stories about individuals' entry into activism are an important part of collective identity formation within social movements. This article, based on in-depth interviews and participant observation with teenage girl activists in five cities in North and South America, looks at narratives of the process of becoming an activist in order to understand how these narratives function for teenagers. Drawing on the conventions of coming of age narratives as well as developmental ideas of adolescence as a time of self-discovery, teenage girl activists produce narratives of the activist self that are influenced by these age-based discourses. The article identifies features of these narratives, including concerns with the subject's outsider status, transformative peer relationships, growing social awareness, and a self-in-process. It argues that girl activists' emphasis on themselves as 'becoming' rather than 'being' activists enables valuable political flexibility and openness but also contributes to their own invisibility and dismissal.

In March of 2003, hundreds of thousands of high school students all over the world took to the streets to protest the impending US-led war in Iraq. Emily, from the San Francisco Bay Area, was 13 at the time. When I interviewed her several years later, a senior in high school, she told me that the main thing she remembers about 8th grade was all the anti-war protests. She went to every possible rally, student walkout, and march. But these anti-war protests were not the end of her teenage activism; over the next five years she coordinated an organisation for women's rights at her high school, worked to oppose California ballot measures that would restrict the reproductive rights of teenage girls, and continued to go to protests and rallies on a variety of national issues. Similarly, Celia, an Italian exchange student who I met while she was living in Venezuela described the lead-up to war as the spark that led her and many of her peers to become activists. She was 14 at the time.

> I began to educate myself more about this issue because I wanted to oppose what was being done. And many other youth were also doing this, like me, so a lot of spontaneous protests were born almost without organization at the beginning. And afterward we began to discuss and decide how to organize ourselves in order to continue with other activities and other projects.

Like Emily, Celia didn't stop there. In fact, she was so interested in social movements that she convinced her parents to let her spend a year living in Venezuela where she'd be able to see the unfolding political changes.

What leads girls like Emily and Celia to become involved in social movements? How do they understand this involvement? And how do they narrate their developing identities as teenage activists? This article analyses girls' stories about their entry into activism, examining how they talk about the process of 'becoming an activist'. In particular, I show how girl activists' constructions of their activist identities replicate many of the narrative conventions of coming of age tales as well as popular discourses of adolescence as a time of self-development. After describing some of the narrative themes found in these activist coming of age tales, I argue that girl activists' emphasis on themselves as still 'becoming' rather than 'being' activists enables a valuable political flexibility, openness, and the mobilisation of their peers but also has the unintended consequence of contributing to their own invisibility and to the widespread dismissal of young people's politics as merely practice for the future.

## Mobilisation and narrative

Sociologists who study social movements have spent decades considering the forces that lead people to social movement participation (Corning & Myers, 2002). They have variously emphasised rational and calculated self-interest (McCarthy & Zald, 1977), social-psychological factors such as efficacy and strong identification with the group whose grievances the movement addresses (Klandermans, 1984; Snow & Oliver, 1993), participation in social networks from which individuals are recruited (Diani, 2004; McAdam & Paulsen, 1993), the processes of frame alignment (Snow, Rochford, Worden, & Benford, 1986), and family background, class, education, and other elements of political socialisation that support activist engagement (Sherkat & Blocker, 1994). Rather than taking up a position in these long-standing debates over the factors that are most predictive of participation, this paper instead follows a growing number of studies that examine how activists themselves talk about their routes into activism (Lyson, 2014; McGuire, Stewart, & Curtin, 2010; Ruiz-Junco, 2011; Valocchi, 2013). By looking to activists' identity narratives, these newer studies focus not why some individuals participate while others do not, but instead seek to understand the processes by which individuals come to see themselves as activists and how these processes are shaped by larger social structures, dynamics, and discourses.

Polletta (2006) has shown that storytelling plays a vital role in contemporary social movements. Stories, she argues, are politically potent but present their own significant limitations. One genre of social movement story is the 'becoming activist' tale, or the narrative of one's entry into activism. Distinct from the mobilisation tales that describe the emergence of a movement, 'becoming activist' stories are personal, highlighting activist biographies. However, they are not merely individual. Activist entry stories can serve to define the meaning of activist (Bobel, 2007), to construct the collective identity of an organisation or broader movement, specifying who 'belongs' or 'fits' and who does not (Lyson, 2014; Lyytikäinen, 2013), and to lay out a trajectory for how others may come to be mobilised (Oyakawa, 2015). Further, activist stories of the self are socially patterned and embedded in larger cultural vocabularies, interpretive frameworks, and discursive contexts (Valocchi, 2013).

In their study of the life histories of extreme-right activists Linden and Klandermans (2007) outline three types of activist entry narratives: continuity, conversion, and compliance. Each type of narrative is linked to a distinct activist biography and trajectory. But activist entry stories are far from universal; recent scholarship highlights how class, race, and gender all influence the ways that individuals narrate their activist biographies (Lyson, 2014; Lyytikäinen, 2013; Valocchi, 2013). For example, Valocchi's (2013) important contribution highlights three very different activist entry narratives for activists from distinct class backgrounds: activism as career, activism as calling, and activism as a way of life. This article contributes to this growing literature by exploring how dynamics of age and discourses of adolescence can structure and infuse activists' narratives. In doing so, it adds another type of activist biographical story to those already catalogued by other scholars: the activist coming of age tale. In identifying and describing the features of girls' activist coming of age tales, I am not suggesting that these features are entirely absent from adults' narratives. Instead, I catalogue the elements of these narratives in order to explore their relationships with two prominent discourses of adolescence: the coming of age story and developmental discourses of adolescence as a time of 'becoming'.

Rishoi (2003) traces the literary history of the coming of age genre to its roots in the *bildungsroman*, or novel of development. She argues that while male coming of age stories have been defined largely by a rugged individualism and search for self, women's coming of age tales instead, given the norms of gender socialisation, propose a socially connected model for growing up. In both cases, however, the coming of age narrative

> privileges the autonomous individual who feels at odds with society ... the subjects of coming of age narratives, like those of the earlier genres, construct themselves as outsiders, but unlike them they choose to remain marginalized at the end of their texts. (p. 63)

Rishoi also suggests that coming of age narratives tend to highlight a widening scope of consciousness and a growing sense of awareness. Given that the formulas of the coming of age tale are pervasive in contemporary discussions of adolescence (Lesko, 2001), it is not surprising to find these narrative conventions also appearing in girl activists' identity talk.

Critical scholars of childhood, adolescence, and youth have all identified how developmentalist discourses that position young people as 'becoming' rather than 'being' have served to define young people as incapable, partial, and deficient in contrast to an imagined vision of the capable, complete, and rational adult (James, Jenks, & Prout, 1998; Wyn & White, 1997). The developmental narratives deployed by popular psychology, educational institutions, and media/culture industries continually invoke ideas that youth are lacking in various ways: lacking in reason, lacking in empathy, lacking in moral clarity, and lacking in understanding of social rules and norms (Lesko, 2001). Scholars have argued that these discourses marginalise and disempower young people and dismiss their experiences in the present by focusing primarily on their status as future-adults (Gordon, 2010). However, narratives of youth as a time of becoming continue to be powerful and pervasive, and thus are often taken up by young people themselves (Budgeon, 2003) despite the fact that they can have negative consequences for young people's power and authority and are rooted in ageist and adult-centric modes of thinking (Gordon, 2010).

In contrast to the important critiques of narratives of young people as 'becoming' found in the scholarship on childhood and youth, post-structuralism, performance studies, and contemporary feminist theories have generally embraced the idea that subjects and identities are always in-process or always becoming, doing, or performing, rather than ontological beings (Butler, 1990; Rattansi & Phoenix, 2005). From this vantage, scholars of youth and childhood might consider embracing the idea of youth as becoming, and argue instead that all people, including adults, are becoming, rather than seeking to include youth in the domain of 'being' or consider thinking about all people as both being and becoming (Uprichard, 2008). This debate is far beyond the scope of this particular article, but in the analysis that follows, I indicate some of the ways that girls themselves use the vocabulary of becoming when they are narrating their activist identities and, in the conclusion, suggest some of the complex and mixed implications of their use of this discourse.

## Methods

This analysis of girls' narratives of becoming activists is part of a larger study that explores the political identities and practices of teenage girl activists in five cities in North and South America – Vancouver, San Francisco, Mexico City, Caracas, and Argentina (Taft, 2011). I conducted, recorded, and transcribed in-depth semi-structured interviews with 75 girls, approximately 15 per city, attended and took extensive field notes on dozens of political events involving these teenage girls, and collected printed materials from the organisations in which these girl activists participated. Conducted in 2005–2006, the research focused on high-school aged girls who were actively involved in progressive or Leftist social movements. They organised around a wide range of social problems, including labour issues and youth labour rights, educational reform, environmental racism, economic justice, corporate power, human rights, gender equality, anti-racism, media democracy, indigenous rights, and political repression. In addition to being part of issue-specific groups and campaigns, some were also involved in socialist, communist, anarchist, Zapatista-informed, feminist, and other ideologically defined progressive parties, collectives, and youth organisations. Their ages ranged from 13 to 19, but the majority were 16 or 17 at the time they were interviewed. 17% identified as either poor or working class, 21% as lower middle class, 49% as middle class, and 13% as upper middle class. Ten said that they were lesbian, bisexual, or questioning. Given the complexities of racial and ethnic identities in these five very different locations it is difficult to quantify and summarise the racial breakdown of this group. But, as a very simplified descriptor, 21% of the girls identified as part of a non-dominant racial group in their country.

Interview transcripts, printed materials, and field notes were all imported into Atlas.ti, a qualitative coding and data analysis programme, and were coded by the author using an inductive process. In the case of this article, that meant first identifying the narrative patterns in girls' activist entry tales and then considering the various cultural tropes, narrative conventions, and discourses with which they were engaging – coming of age tales and vocabularies of becoming. Interviews and transcripts were in both English and Spanish, and I worked with and coded the interviews and quotes in the original language, only translating a quote near the end of the writing process. In this paper, for reasons of space, I focus primarily on themes and patterns that emerged across the five locations rather than on differences between or within national and local contexts. My analysis primarily focuses on discourses of age, rather than those of gender due to both space limitations and the paucity of comparable examples of teenage boys' activist narratives.

## Becoming activist: narrative themes

Coming of age narratives often highlight an individual's outsider status, exploring their feelings of non-belonging (Rishoi, 2003). Amongst girl activists, this outsider status is articulated as a sense of their difference from other teens, a feeling that they are unlike many of their peers (Taft, 2011). As I discuss in my larger work based on this research, many girl activists distinguished themselves from the other girls in their schools, saying that they just are not like the self-absorbed, silly, and foolish girls in their school who, in their view, only care about boys, shopping and the latest movies (Taft, 2011). Becoming an activist is a way of finding others who are 'like you', of finding a place to 'be oneself' in a world where you were not yet sure you fit. Finding activism, for them, is partly about finding somewhere to belong.

Ixtab, a lower middle-class Mexicana with a nose ring and a casual, easy-going attitude, grew up in a household where her family discussed politics and was supportive of social movements, but her parents were not themselves activists. She was politically aware from a young age, but did not know anyone her own age who was also interested in social movements:

> For my whole life, from the time I was little, my parents made me see how things are. So, from the time I was little I knew who Che Guevara was, who others were. When the EZLN emerged I was only six years old, but I knew that they came out of earlier struggles, about the national liberation struggles and all of this. I was always interested [in social movements]. I remember in primary school I fought with the teachers about the strike at UNAM. They were against it, and said that it was just a bunch of rebels at UNAM who were just making the University look bad. And I fought with them and told them that they should realize that the students were fighting this struggle because right now it might just be one peso, but tomorrow it could be two, then three and then when our children want to go to the university it will just be a private school.

In addition to fighting with teachers, Ixtab said she would get frustrated that 'in my school, nobody cared about these issues'. Her friends, she said, 'didn't think like me'. She began to read more, but still didn't have a place where she could talk with people who shared her ideas and interests. Until

> one day one of the activists from the newspaper collective came to sell at my school, and he sold me the first issue. He invited me to a forum; it was one year ago on October 2nd … It was really interesting, I met a lot of other people, and I began to go to more and more meetings. And, then, now, here we are, one year later.

Ixtab's story of becoming an activist is primarily the story of her shift from being a lone political thinker to a member of a group. It is a move from a lonely outsider position, to a significantly more supported one.

As with Ixtab's finding her activist self through finding a community, many girls described their entry into activism as being facilitated by personal relationships, both friendly and romantic, with other youth who were already involved. Friends and peers are key characters in girls' stories of their entry into activism. Niamh, a white teen from California described how her friend 'just dragged me to a meeting one day and she was like, come to this, and I was like, mmmm [unsure noise]. But we ended up going and I was like, I never knew all this action was happening'. This meeting was not, however, just a fluke. Niamh's story of becoming an activist is much longer. As a sixth grader,

> I covered my backpack with like, 'save the world' and 'hug a tree' and I like tried to be a veg-etarian … I always was like interested in like environmental stuff and I was like, oh, environ-mental day, I'll have to go to that, or like, have to make sure to recycle and all that stuff.

Then, as she got into high school, she started to become more interested in 'social justice stuff'. She continued,

> this is kinda weird to say to some people, but like the Catholic church, I've been involved in my youth group for a really long time and that is the only like movement where I've actually gone out and like worked with the homeless and like done like that kind of thing.

This service work was good, but she said, she

> wished that I could do more, like create an organization that could give them jobs so it wouldn't be like here's a package of food every once in a while. So doing things like that started getting me into social activism.

Volunteering was better than just writing slogans on her backpack, but it still wasn't quite what she wanted to do in terms of changing the world. When her friend took her to a social movement meeting, Niamh was excited about the prospect of other approaches to social change. Her friend was a key character in the tale, but the story is also about Niamh's own personal search for the right kind of social action for her. Now, Niamh is not just a volunteer, but an activist who is part of several groups that work on issues of fair trade, corporate power, and immigrant rights. In her narrative, becoming an activist was presented as the last step in a longer process of figuring out how she wanted to engage with the world and create the kinds of changes she imagined.

In contrast to the transformative and supportive role of peers, parents have a very different place in coming of age tales. Instead of being the source of self-discovery, parents represent a more passive childhood that must be left behind through the process of individuation and growing up. Coming of age, as a narrative trope, is partly about distinguishing oneself from one's parents and background. The same is true in girls' stories of their activist selves, but this takes two different forms, depending on the level of political affinity between the girl and her family. Park (1993) argues that there are two competing approaches to understanding the motivations of youth activists as they relate to their parents: generational conflict and lineage socialisation, or 'are they rebelling against the historical legacy of the older generation or simply "living out" their parents' values in practice' (p. 172). While neither of these images is entirely fair to youth in that both assume youth activist motivations to be very different from the political motivations of adults *and* both treat youthful politics as primarily irrational or automatic, youth activists' narratives about their relationships to activism do make reference to the political views and practices of their parents.

Nearly thirty percent of the girl activists I interviewed said they held very different political views from their parents, but only a handful experienced major conflict with their parents over politics. And, while disagreement with their parents was part of the context of their activism, the girls themselves never described it as a reason for their involvement. Obviously, few people would expect youth to acknowledge the possibility that their political engagement is just a form of rebellion against parents. But, if the few girls who were experiencing conflict with their parents over their activism were, in fact, engaged in activism for the sake of rebellion, we could expect them to emphasise this conflict, the pleasure of upsetting their parents, or other elements of this relationship far more than they did. Instead, they tended to shrug off these conflicts, saying that the disagreements were just 'kinda annoying', but 'not really a big deal'. And, like other girl activists, they were passionate about their beliefs, articulate about social problems, and appeared to have become engaged in activism for political, and not just personal, reasons. The idea of rebelling against one's parents was simply not part of young women's narratives about their own routes into activism.

Representing the other side of this debate are those girls who come from long family traditions of Left activism and for whom activism has always been a part of daily life. Approximately a quarter of the girls I interviewed had a parent who was still, or had once been, engaged in social movements and activism. Ramona, a bisexual middle-class Mexicana with light skin, medium-brown dreadlocks and funky, brightly coloured clothing is one example of a girl from an activist family. Her parents 'were involved in lots of things and I always went with them when they went to meetings. From the time I was little, I went with them'. As she got older, she went from being taken to activist events with parents to doing activism alongside her parents. In middle school, she and several of her friends kept getting in trouble because they were resisting the administration's dress code which required skirts below their knees and shoes without heels. 'It was a scandal. And my parents, when they came, they came to give out fliers! So, that was my first political work.' While this story may not at first appear to be one of differentiation, Ramona and other girls like her went to great lengths to describe how their activism differed from that of their parents. A senior in high school when I met her, Ramona was quick to point out that her activism now was her own and not the activism of her parents. She was one of the founding members of a new Zapatista-inspired *cubiculo* in her school, and, she says that this mode of activism, this perspective on politics, is a little bit different than what her parents might want her to be doing. For girls like Ramona, being an activist is more than just being a mirror image of their parents. Their relationships to their activism changed over time and they made political decisions that built upon what they had learned from their families, but also moved in some different directions.

Moving in new political directions sometimes meant using different political tactics than their parents. Clare, a San Francisco Bay Area teen who was concerned with redefining activism so that it goes beyond marches, articulated this definitional expansion as partly about developing political practices that differ from those of her parents and their generation. Her dad grew up in Colombia and her mom in the US, and they were both involved in the student and youth movements of the 60s. Clare thinks about

> The way that they were active, and I think 'that's like, kind of simple, because it's like what's been done.' So that is kinda why I feel like I do about the marches. And I should give them some credit for how they've taught me … I might like shake them off, like 'your beliefs are really oversimplified, you are just living in the sixties where everything was great, we have to look at the real world and we have to take a fresh approach.' But the fact is that they're my parents and they probably know so much more than I do … I guess I'm different from them.

For Clare, being an activist has meant engaging in different types of political action than her parents. Even though she may have begun her activism alongside her family, going to her first march with her mom, she has been working to become her own kind of activist along the way. Countering claims that young activists are simply following in their parents' footsteps, the narratives of girls like Ramona and Clare highlight their changing relationships to activism and the choices they have made as they develop their own distinctive activist identities, again drawing on some of the narrative conventions of a coming of age tale.

In addition to repeating the character types found in coming of age stories (outsider heroes, supportive peers, and confused or restrictive parents), girls' narratives of becoming activists also draw on some of the themes of this genre. In particular, Rishoi (2003) finds that the genre often highlights an individual's widening perspectives on the world around them. These growing insights, or the shift from innocence to knowledge, were an important part of many girls' tales. Sometimes told in terms of an 'aha moment,' and other times described as a steady process of learning more about 'how messed up the world is', the development of a broader social consciousness was a key part of girls' stories of their entry to activism. Haile, a Chinese-Canadian 17-year-old, described her own process of realisation and self-education:

> In middle school I was very into appearance and very ignorant, I think. And it was just kind of an awakening. I've since noticed lots of injustices, but [gender inequality] was the first thing I noticed in my day-to-day life. And once I got into that and did the research I was so, um, feverish with the research. And, once I got that, I broadened and started doing everything - not everything, but a broader variety.

Haile went on to say that, for her, this awareness,

> started personal and then I saw that it was the same kind of thing everywhere … It made me feel better that it wasn' just my family, that it's a problem far and wide. Yeah, and I was inspired because when people get together they can change things. Even on a political level it can affect on the personal level too … So that was kind of my gateway to 'oh, yeah, there's something that's wrong and I can do something about it.' So it was just a change in my head.

Haile's own experiences with gender inequality in her family led her to seek out more information, more social analysis. And, through her reading, she came to see how this issue was a social problem and changeable. She then took this perspective with her into her high school years, becoming involved in her global issues club, a feminist newspaper, and an Asian community newspaper. Haile's story, in emphasising her newfound ideas and insights, emphasises a process of becoming aware – a common feature of coming of age narratives.

A final narrative theme in many girls' stories about their entry into activism is the claim that they are *still* in the process of becoming activists. According to these girls, they had not yet arrived at an activist identity, but were still on a journey toward this identity. Girls' firm claim that they are 'not yet' activists and are still in the process of becoming activists, is perhaps the most distinctive feature of their narratives. Unlike the adult-narrated stories of entry into social movements catalogued in the academic literature (Linden & Klandermans, 2007; Lyson, 2014; Valocchi, 2013), when teenagers tell these stories, they are stories that are very much in-process. Bobel (2007) 'challenges the assumption that social movement participants necessarily and automatically identify as activists' (p. 148). She finds that some people distinguish between 'doing activism' and 'being an activist'. But, while Bobel's young adult interviewees claim to 'do activism' rather than 'be activists', my own research suggests a third possible position in relationship to an activist identity: that of 'becoming activist'. Similar to Bobel's participants who held activists to a very high standard that they felt they did not meet, many of the girls I interviewed also describe activists as people who are truly extraordinary. As Violet said, 'there is a lot of honour that goes with the word "activism" and people who put the energy in … It comes with a lot of honour, a lot of, I don't know – "wow, an activist"'. Activists, in this view, are accomplished, committed, passionate, knowledgeable, and effective organisers. Although many girls described activist identity as quite special, and as something they are not yet worthy of claiming, they didn't see it as out of reach. As Diana put it,

> activist is such a like, up-there word. Like it sounds like anyone who is activist, who in my mind I admire, and who I think has done like amazing things for other people, and I think I'm maybe on my way to being an activist, but it is something that I would like to be and that I hope to be. And I'll have to put a lot of work into it.

These girls narrate themselves as being on the continuing route to becoming an activist.

Rosa, a Mexicana active in both a school *cubiculo* and a youth collective that organises in her neighbourhood, was one of the approximately 20 girls, located in all five cities, who explicitly stated that they did not feel like they deserved to identify themselves as activists (yet). She said that she couldn't really claim the mantle of activist because she is 'still lacking a lot, so much'. Even though she spoke eloquently and clearly on her reasons for being 'opposed to capitalism, globalization, neoliberalism', and her thoughts on Marxism and anarchism, Rosa told me, 'I'm not well informed politically. Yes, I've read a lot of things, but I'm still missing a lot more.' Although Rosa was, in part, dismissing what she knows, framing her story as a tale of 'becoming activist' also let her articulate what she has learned and read while maintaining a socially acceptable level of both feminine and youthful humility. Similarly, Gloria indicated that she wasn't working hard enough or putting enough time in to really be an activist:

> I think of activists as participating actively in politics, in the community, in leadership, and I don't participate *really* actively because I am in school. But the time that I have left after my studies, I dedicate to this. In reality, I put more time into this than into my studies. I study in the morning and the rest of the afternoon I dedicate to the movement … But this isn't totally active because I know a lot of people who spend the whole day on this.

Despite spending several hours every day on political activities and the student movement, Gloria felt she just wasn't active enough to claim the mantle of activist. Narratives of *becoming* activists give girls the space to talk about what they know and about what they have accomplished, but also allow them to simultaneously highlight their on-going growth and development. However, it is my argument that given the power and prevalence of widespread ideas about adolescence as a period of growth, self-discovery and self-change, their emphasis on becoming is not only a way to manage their relationship to what Bobel calls 'the perfect standard' for activist identity, but is also an age-inflected narrative practice. The focus on becoming activist rather than being activist suggests that girl activists continue to see themselves, as young people, as unfinished subjects-in-process.

## The teenage activist self-in-formation

Girls' narratives of themselves as becoming activists invoke and repeat several key elements of contemporary coming of age tales: the search for belonging and figuring out where one fits in the world, a growing and expanding awareness, transformative peer relationships, and differentiation from parents. In addition to repeating tropes of this powerful cultural resource, their varied narratives also indicate that there is no singular route into activism. Although there are some patterns and common features in these narratives, their diversity suggests that the process of becoming an activist is not entirely predictable. For some girls, it was seen as a logical and obvious development of who they already were and what they already believed. They had just been waiting for the right opportunity or group to present itself. For others, it was something they came upon through new friends, sought out after a particular experience, or began to engage in due to what they saw as a new social problem.

Girls' stories of their entry to activism detail processes of both continuity and change. However, unlike the adult model described by Linden and Klandermans (2007), compliance, or the idea of entering activism due to circumstances beyond one's control, is largely absent from their narratives. Their narratives of becoming activist are also not stories of a major break from their past nor are they tales of simply continuing to act as they always have (Linden & Klandermans, 2007), but instead are accounts of changing selves that are growing up, becoming aware, and discovering new possibilities for who they want to be and what they want to do in their lives. And, more importantly, unlike adults, their stories tend to emphasise the *on-going* process of becoming an activist, rather than offering a completed tale that ends with the individual now 'being' an activist (Oyakawa, 2015; Valocchi, 2013). Drawing on both coming of age conventions and developmental discourses on adolescence as a time of exploration and formation of self (Lesko, 1996; Wyn & White, 1997), girls produce an age-inflected set of activist identity narratives.

To conclude, I want to consider some of the implications of girls' construction of an activist self that is in-process, rather than an activist self that is fixed or already achieved. The open-ended quality of their coming of age narratives highlights the fact that they think that they have a great deal still to learn, that they themselves are still growing and changing. It suggests an openness to new ideas, new suggestions, and to discussion, rather than a dogmatic or already determined position on any given issue. Their stories of selves-in-process encourage girl activists to be particularly flexible, creative, and willing to engage with a variety of different ideas in their activism. As I've written elsewhere (Taft, 2011), they tend not to think they have found 'the answer' to a given political problem, but instead strive to create opportunities for young people to discuss political issues, learn from one another, and develop political responses together.

Girls' tales of becoming activists are also strategically and practically useful for encouraging the political participation of their peers. Their emphasis on the process of becoming an activist serves to create a welcoming atmosphere within their political organisations: if you do not have to already *be* an activist to participate, anyone can begin engaging in activism. Girl activists present themselves as teens who have started moving in a direction that any other teen can also take, and they invite other teens to join them. Their narratives of becoming activists are not tales of heroism, of overcoming barriers, or celebrations of their incredible feats, but are instead stories of on-going growth and learning, something that is open to all youth. Girls' activist coming of age narratives highlight the process by which they, ordinary girls, become activists. Anyone, they say, can become an activist.

Framing themselves as becoming activists also gives girls a chance to acknowledge some of the things that they have done and achieved, while still maintaining humility. This is a distinctly gendered process; 'good girls' are modest and humble, while those who speak too forcefully about their accomplishments are often considered arrogant (Bent & Switzer, 2016; Brown, 2016). Such gendered expectations push girls to dismiss and downplay their accomplishments out of fear of appearing too bold, too proud, and too self-assured. The gendered quality of girls' narratives here is confirmed by findings that white male youth activists more often construct themselves as radical teen superheroes (Gordon, 2010). Like many other high-achieving girls and young women, girl activists do not want to appear to be too proud of themselves and their accomplishments. However, girl activists' humility also unfortunately contributes to their continued invisibility within social movements. If they do not loudly proclaim their activist abilities, it is not likely that adults will realise their valuable contributions and impressive political organising skills.

Finally, in drawing on the traditions of coming of age narratives and developmental discourses on adolescence, girls also unwittingly replicate ideas about young people as subordinate, incomplete, or deficient. Coming of age narratives inevitably position childhood as 'lacking,' and the child as innocent, incapable, unable, and not a full subject. Even the adolescent, as the one who is still 'in-process,' is assumed to be less than what he or she will be as an adult. In contrast to the previous points, coming of age narratives are not necessarily a celebration of the perpetually learning, perpetually changing self, but also suggest that this period of growth and change will end and that the adolescent will, eventually, arrive at a better and more enlightened adult state. In this way, by emphasising their 'becoming' rather than their 'being' activists, these girls also unwittingly contribute to the long-standing idea that the experiences of childhood and youth are primarily relevant for how they impact the supposedly more 'real' world of adulthood and adult politics (Gordon, 2010; James et al., 1998).

Looking at activists' stories of their entry into social movements and activism sheds light on the collective identities being created within a given social movement terrain. My research with teenage girls suggests that these stories may be shaped by age categories and are not universal. Drawing on a particular set of cultural discourses about adolescence as a time of self-creation and self-discovery, teenage girl activists produce narratives of the activist self that are distinct from those produced by adults. In addition to illuminating some of the dynamics and implications of these narratives for the identities and practices of teenage girl activists, this research also suggests the need for further scholarship on the diversity of narratives of mobilisation and social movement participation. Much as age is relevant to these stories and to versions of the activist self that they produce, we should consider how differences of race, nation, ability, religion, or the specific movement context intersect to shape activists' narratives of entry, and how these differences change a movements' collective identity processes, mobilisation strategies, and political practices.

## Disclosure statement

No potential conflict of interest was reported by the authors.

## Funding

This work was supported by a National Science Foundation [Graduate Research Fellowship], Division of Social and Economic Sciences.

## References

Bent, E., & Switzer, H. (2016). Oppositional girlhoods and the challenge of relational politics. *Gender Issues*, *33*(2), 122–147.

Bobel, C. (2007). I'm not an activist, though I've done a lot of it: Doing activism, being activist, and the perfect standard in a contemporary movement. *Social Movement Studies*, *6*(2), 147–159.

Brown, L. M. (2016). *Powered by girl: A field guide for supporting youth activists*. Boston, MA: Beacon Press.

Budgeon, S. (2003). *Choosing a self: Young women and the individualization of identity*. Westport, CT: Praeger.

Butler, J. (1990). *Gender trouble: Feminism and the subversion of identity*. New York, NY: Routledge.

Corning, A. F., & Myers, D. J. (2002). Individual orientation toward engagement in social action. *Political Psychology*, *23*(4), 703–729.

Diani, M. (2004). Networks and participation. In D. A. Snow, S. A. Soule, & H. Kriesi (Eds.), (pp. 339–359). Malden, MA: Blackwell.

Gordon, H. (2010). *We fight to win: Inequality and the politics of youth activism*. New Brunswick, NJ: Rutgers University Press.

James, A., Jenks, C., & Prout, A. (1998). *Theorizing childhood*. Cambridge: Polity Press.

Klandermans, B. (1984). Mobilization and participation: Social-psychological expansions of resource mobilization theory. *American Sociological Review*, *49*(5), 583–600.

Lesko, N. (1996). Denaturalizing adolescence: The politics of contemporary representations. *Youth and Society*, *28*(2), 139–161.

Lesko, N. (2001). *Act your age!: A cultural construction of adolescence*. New York, NY: Routledge.

Linden, A., & Klandermans, B. (2007). Revolutionaries, wanderers, converts, and complaints: Life histories of extreme right activists. *Journal of Contemporary Ethnography*, *36*(2), 184–201.

Lyson, H. C. (2014). Social structural location and vocabularies of participation: Fostering a collective identity in urban agriculture activism. *Rural Sociology*, *79*(3), 310–335.

Lyytikäinen, L. (2013). Gendered and classed activist identity in the Russian oppositional youth movement. *The Sociological Review*, *61*(3), 499–524.

McAdam, D., & Paulsen, R. (1993). Specifying the relationship between social ties and activism. *American Journal of Sociology*, *99*, 640–647.

McCarthy, J. D., & Zald, M. N. (1977). Resource mobilization and social movements: A partial theory. *The American Journal of Sociology*, *82*(6), 1212–1241.

McGuire, K., Stewart, A. J., & Curtin, N. (2010). Becoming feminist activists: Comparing narratives. *Feminist Studies*, *36*(1), 99–125.

Oyakawa, M. (2015). 'Turning private pain into public action': The cultivation of identity narratives by a faith-based community organization. *Qualitative Sociology*, *38*(4), 395–415.

Park, B.-C. (1993). An aspect of political socialization of student movement participants in Korea. *Youth & Society*, *25*(2), 171–201.

Polletta, F. (2006). *It was like a fever: Storytelling in protest and politics*. Chicago, IL: University of Chicago Press.

Rattansi, A., & Phoenix, A. (2005). Rethinking youth identities: Modernist and postmodernist frameworks. *Identity: An International Journal of Theory and Research*, *5*(2), 97–123.

Rishoi, C. (2003). *From girl to woman: American women's coming-of-age narratives*. Albany, NY: State University of New York Press.

Ruiz-Junco, N. (2011). 'Losing neutrality in your everyday life' framing experience and activist identity construction in the Spanish environmental movement. *Journal of Contemporary Ethnography*, *40*(6), 713–733.

Sherkat, D. E., & Blocker, J. (1994). The political development of sixties' activists: Identifying the influence of class, gender, and socialization on protest participation. *Social Forces*, *72*(3), 821–842.

Snow, D. A., & Oliver, P. E. (1993). Social movements and collective behavior: Social-psychological dimensions and considerations. In K. S. Cook, G. A. Fine, & J. S. House (Eds.). Boston, MA: Allyn & Bacon.

Snow, D. A., Rochford, E. B., Worden, S. K., & Benford, R. D. (1986). Frame alignment processes, micromobilization, and movement participation. *American Sociological Review*, *51*(4), 464–481.

Taft, J. (2011). *Rebel girls: Youth activism and social change across the Americas*. New York, NY: New York University Press.

Uprichard, E. (2008). Children as 'beings and becomings': Children, childhood and temporality. *Children & Society*, *22*, 303–313.

Valocchi, S. (2013). Activism as a career, calling, and way of life. *Journal of Contemporary Ethnography*, *42*(2), 169–200.

Wyn, J., & White, R. (1997). *Rethinking youth*. Thousand Oaks, CA: Sage.

# Narrative resources and political violence: the life stories of former clandestine militants in Portugal

Raquel da Silva

**ABSTRACT**

This study analyses the experiences, both violent and non-violent, of two former clandestine militants who were part of distinct politically violent organisations in the past in Portugal. It explores the narrative resources at the origin of personal political awareness and their influence on political activism, taking into (particular) account the impact of the early family narrative environment and of the moment in history in which individuals were living. It also demonstrates the ways in which past experiences are reconstructed by self-constructions and representations in the present. Activism at the edge of age is, thus, shaped by the meanings of past memories, which are used dialogically to preserve a valued identity.

Individuals respond to the conditions and stimuli of their environment in ways which are consistent with their life stories, that is, with the perceptions they hold about themselves, others and their political, social, cultural, economic and historical milieu (McAdams, 2008). Such perceptions are generated by the narrative resources available to individuals, which derive from their personal cultural repertoire composed by the 'early narrative environment of the family', by the stories individuals access while growing up (Wang & Brockmeier, 2002, p. 54) and by the social interactions that occur across their life course (Elder, 1994).

Personal stories of involvement in politically motivated violence are the focus of the present article. This social phenomenon has been explored very little in the Portuguese context, but it can still be retrieved from one of the few places where it lives: the memory of the individuals who took part in armed organisations. Therefore, I suggest that the stories people tell about their lives are connected with and shed light on the social, cultural, political, historical and human contexts which frame these same stories and these same lives, enriching the study of political violence. Yet, it is important to note that personal stories are socially constructed and cannot be taken as *the* representation of *the* reality, but as *a* representation of *a* reality (see Esin, Fathi, & Squire, 2013). Stories are the vehicles through which individuals represent their experiences, based on the narratives available at their temporal and spatial locations; narratives which constitute the cultural and social resources which enable individuals to put their stories together (Spector-Mersel, 2010), giving meaning to themselves and to the world (Bruner, 1986;

Polkinghorne, 1988), and shaping their personal identities (McAdams, 1993). Thus, story and narrative are different. As Smith (2016) argues, 'people tell stories, not narratives', but their stories draw on their narrative resources or, in other words, on their cultural knowledge, on their relationship with the receiver, and on the shared and divergent understandings of which stories are appropriate in different contexts (Gubrium & Holstein, 1997).

## Storytelling, history and autobiographical memory

According to Cohler (1982), and corroborated by several other studies (see for example, Habermas & Paha, 2001; Habermas & de Silveira, 2008), the acquisition of a coherent life story narrative is possible for the first time at the life stage of adolescence. In developmental terms, it is only at this point in life that individuals are able to give both internal and external context to their life stories and to 'integrate memories and self-concept into a coherent overall account' (Habermas & Hatiboğlu, 2014, p. 38). Adolescence enables individuals to conceive and talk about themselves and others biographically, recognising the temporal linearity of their stories, how stories connect and offer explanations for different life events, and what social, cultural and historical contexts surround and influence their lives (Habermas & Hatiboğlu, 2014). At this stage, individuals start building their narrative identity, which, according to McAdams (2008, p. 243), corresponds to 'an individual's internalized, evolving, and integrative story of the self'. In this sense, as Somers argues (1994, p. 606),

> it is through narrativity that we come to know, understand, and make sense of the social world, and it is through narratives and narrativity that we constitute our social identities [...] all of us come to be who we are (however ephemeral, multiple, and changing) by being located or locating ourselves (usually unconsciously) in social narratives rarely of our own making.

In this sense, stories do not only work 'for people', but they also work 'on people', leading their construction and understanding of reality, and their course of action (Frank, 2010, p. 3). In this context, Jackson argues that:

> Our lives are storied. Were it not for stories, our lives would be unimaginable. Stories make it possible for us to overcome our separateness, to find common ground and common cause. To relate a story is to retrace one's steps, going over the ground of one's life again, reworking reality to render it more bearable. A story enables us to fuse the world within and the world without. In this way we gain some purchase over events that confounded us, humbled us, and left us helpless. In telling a story we renew our faith that the world is within our grasp. (Jackson, 2002, p. 245)

Personal stories are also closely linked to history, portraying historical shifts in a culture, establishing collective memories and bridging cultural history and personal biography (Plummer, 2002). As defended by Andrews (2002, p. 84), 'stories are products of their times'. Thus, the historical contexts of people's stories are therefore key to their understanding. Plummer adds:

> Narrative processes refer to a wide array of social actions that make stories and narratives work. Structures of narration speak to the historical and cultural structural contexts in which these processes are embedded. With these concepts in mind, storytelling becomes a

creative political and symbolic strategy to bridge the macro and micro, the process and the structures: it becomes a key human active way of transforming how we grasp, connect to and change the world. (Plummer, 2017, p. 3)

This author suggests that there is a new area of storytelling and politics emerging which focuses on the organisation of stories under different political systems. This is particularly relevant to the present article, because the stories of my interviewees encompass different political systems in Portugal and showcase a 'before' – life under an authoritairan regime – and an 'after' – life after the Revolution and within a democratic system. Such a transition creates opportunities for new stories to emerge and to tell stories differently, in a more open and democratic way.

Finally, through stories, individuals also attach meanings to episodes stored in their auto-biographical memory, which in itself is 'an active construction embedded in a social weave of dialogues that are negotiated not only between an individual and his or her immediate social environment [...] but also, equally importantly, between the individual and the larger cultural milieu' (Wang & Brockmeier, 2002, p. 47). In this sense, according to Bruner (2003, p. 213), the self relies on selective remembering to 'adjust the past to the demands of the present and the anticipated future'. This is corroborated by Mishler (2004), who considers that the same identity-defining episode may be told very differently in different circumstances, creating multiple life narrative storylines and constructing different identities.

## Storytelling and political violence

The fact that stories are rooted in the place and time in which they exist and in the social relationships in which they are created, repeated and transformed (Frank, 2010) influences the establishment of 'cognitive and affective processes' that may gradually lead to violence and that are strengthened by violence itself (Della Porta, 2013, p. 19). Resorting to political violence is therefore not automatic, but a process: 'actions of some kind associated with other actions and reactions, often expressed in some sort of reciprocal relationship' (Taylor & Horgan, 2012, p. 130). In addition, such actions are often not violent, because various 'underground organisations evolve within and then break away from larger, nonviolent social movement organisations' (Della Porta, 2013, p. 159), and these in turn are permeated by stories and storytelling. Consequently, the aspects driving individuals to political violence involve a relational, but also a cultural component, which highlights the symbolic nature of the phenomenon and its roots in images, stories, experiences and conditions available to individuals at a given time (see, e.g. Arena & Arrigo, 2005; Cordes, 2001; Tololyan, 2001). Thus, stories are shared collectively and individuals grow with such stories and use stories to justify their actions, because stories 'make the unseen not only visible but compelling' (Frank, 2010, p. 41). Selbin adds the following:

It is the articulation of compelling stories [...] that allows people to deploy them in ways which resonate with others and empower them to seek to change the material and ideological conditions of their everyday lives. (Selbin, 2010, p. 6)

This author defends the line of reasoning that research should go beyond the usual material and structural factors and focus on the thoughts and feelings of political activists, recognising the role played by stories and narratives 'of past injustices and struggles as they fight for the future' (Selbin, 2010, p. 9).

In this vein, this article investigates the narrative resources available to two different individuals who engaged in politically violent activism at a younger age and in different periods of time in Portugal. It also looks closely at how the telling of the past is reconstructed in the present and for the present.

## Method

### *Participants*

The data for this study were drawn from my doctoral research on the narratives of political violence in Portugal (see Da Silva, 2016). Former clandestine militants in Portugal were interviewed in-depth, allowing the collection of 28 life stories. These compose a very rich description of the experiences of social actors who, at a certain point in time, took the leap into political violence, but who are much more than former clandestine militants. In the present article, I am only focusing on the stories of two individuals, Rita and Jaime, because despite having been both born during *Estado Novo*'s dictatorial regime,[1] in 1949 and 1958 respectively, their age difference and contextual influences have had a distinct impact on their political activism.

### *Data collection*

Interviews involve a close personal interaction, as well as the production of potentially powerful knowledge, which makes ethics extremely significant during the research process, particularly when it involves sensitive topics (see Renzetti & Lee, 1993). While as a researcher I am aware that interviews assign the interviewer both the role of participant and observer, not all interviewees share such awareness of this duplicity of roles. This is especially so in a setting where the researcher presents him- or herself as very interested in the subject, friendly and trustworthy (which is supported by information sheets and consent forms, holding the impressive university logos). In this context, the responsibility regarding the data collected lies with the researcher, who must reflect the potential 'societal uses of the knowledge produced by academic social science interviews' (Kvale, 2006, p. 497) and, particularly, its impact on the research participants and the ways they can be ethically protected. Therefore, my ethical concerns were not limited to certain stages of the research (e.g. data collection), but were rather present throughout the entire process, from the moment individuals were contacted to take part on the study, to the analysis and representation of their accounts. In this vein, all interviewees received the verbatim transcript of their interviews in order to have the opportunity to correct any inaccuracies, to make sure that their views were correctly represented and to exclude any sections that would make them feel uncomfortable if publicly revealed. At this stage, informed consent was again requested from the interviewees, as suggested by Josselson (2007), in order to make clear that I was going to use their statements to shed light on the subject under analysis and not on their personal lives. In addition, I clarified that their stories would be treated as possible versions of the social world, as expressed by Dingwall (1980), so that they would not feel betrayed or expect me to affirm or endorse their version of events. Lastly, all transcripts were anonymised and the quotations to be included in the final outputs carefully chosen, in order to protect the interviewees' identities and, at the same time, to produce a coherent and thick account of their experiences (Jackson, 2009; Stark & Hedgecoe, 2004).

## Data analysis

Narrative inquiry focuses on the storied nature of human conduct (Sarbin, 1986), considering that 'social reality is primarily a narrative reality' (Spector-Mersel, 2010, p. 211). According to Andrews (2007), the way individuals present themselves through the stories they tell encompasses their past, their present and their imagined future, as well as the audience they are talking to and the narratives they have constructed over the years. This author goes even further and adds that personal narratives do not only talk about the individual, 'but provide a small window into the engines of history and historical change, as we both shape and are shaped by the events of our day' (Andrews, 2007, p. 51).

In order to read narrative texts, Josselson (2004) considers that a hermeneutics of faith or a hermeneutics of suspicion can be put into place. The former reads narrative texts as representations of lived experiences and aims to explore and represent their meanings at a different level of discourse or abstraction, while the latter reads narrative texts as disguised and explores their hidden meanings. In this study, I employ a hermeneutics of faith to understand Rita's and Jaime's meanings as best as I can, and I take interpretive authority (Chase, 1996) for my understanding of their words, which are reproduced for the credibility of my interpretations of their meanings (Polkinghorne, 2007).

## Rita

Rita grew up in a small village in the Alentejo, which is a large region situated in the south of Portugal, between the Lisbon area and the Algarve, geographically marked by its extensive, open, rolling plains. In the Alentejo the population had always relied mainly on agriculture, livestock and forestry, whose production during *Estado Novo*, according to Rita, was in the hands of a few landowners, who would contract workers from the region at a very low wage and in very precarious conditions.

This context of extreme poverty and injustice strengthened the political opposition in the region and attracted the attention of the clandestine Portuguese Communist Party (PCP), which had a strong presence in the area. As Rita affirmed: 'that area provided many members for the party [PCP], which was only natural, because it was the only force that brought some hope to people. People had nothing to lose, really'. Consequently, coming from the Alentejo meant coming from an area marked by resistance to the regime, from a place where daily hardships made people aware of the need to fight the system, fight for justice. In this sense, these people were more likely to join the ranks of the PCP, which was the only active opposition party in the country during the *Estado Novo*, despite it being banned by the regime and forced to stay underground. In the 1950s, Rita's parents opted to go underground in order to work for the PCP, leaving her with her grandparents until she finished primary school. At age 10, Rita joined them, mainly motivated by the 'normal' desire to live with her parents – 'I could not live with my grandparents forever. I wanted to join my parents' – but also by the conviction that it was 'the natural thing to do', because she was brought up to see the misery and repression in which people lived. She described how aware she was of the limitations of life underground: 'we could not go to the movies, we could not play, we could not have close friendships, we could not have a boyfriend. Everything was very limited, so people would not suspect us'. As a consequence, in her adolescence she questioned her choice: 'when we enter adolescence, we understand everything better. At that point we can ask ourselves: do I want to stay here or not?'. Ultimately, she decided that 'continuity is usually the normal way'. Thus, over time Rita's decision became more politically rather than relationally grounded, leading her not only to remain underground for eight years, but also to join a training course in the Soviet Union when she turned 18. Rita spent 18 months in the Soviet Union, where she met her husband with whom she resumed the underground life upon their return to Portugal in order to found the armed organisation Armed Revolutionary Action (ARA). This was again something that Rita considered 'normal' and in her opinion 'well done', as 'everything' was 'working to overthrow the regime'.

Regarding her role within the ARA, Rita considered that it was never operational in terms of the direct commission of actions, because her place was mostly in the background, supporting her husband. Such a role followed the rules of the PCP (the political party behind ARA), which presupposed that women should act as housewives, lending an air of normality to different situations. These rules were justified among ARA members by the position of women in Portuguese society at the time. Rita was the first to recognise that at the time it was very difficult for a woman to move around as freely as a man: 'Men could move around better. We have to situate things. At that time, in the 1960s and 1970s, women did not have, as they do now, freedom to do whatever they wished'. However, Rita was involved in the planning of different actions, going out with her husband and children, for instance to observe possible targets while having a picnic. Her role did not lack challenges and difficulties either, particularly concerning the relationships with the neighbours and raising two children in a context where both parents were living under a false identity. In relation to the first aspect, Rita had to make sure that the neighbours would not connect the armed actions happening around them with her family, particularly her husband, whose picture often appeared in the media. Nonetheless, for Rita, the second aspect was worse for two reasons: health issues and the compulsory separation from children who reached school age (a normal practice of PCP's clandestine militants). The first situation was especially relevant to Rita, because her youngest child had asthma and she said that once she thought that the little girl would die at home. She also always had the separation from her children at the back of her mind and considered it 'a terrible thing':

> When the children reached school age they had to go somewhere. Either they would go to the Soviet Union, which happened to many and ended very badly – the children were separated from their parents and then, in several cases, they did not want to be with their parents anymore; or they went to live with family, grandparents, which was the most usual. [...] If it wasn't for April 25th, such a thing would have happened to ours. And that's one of the terrible things, it's one of the most terrible things, for sure.

However, Rita felt extremely relieved that the April 25th Revolution, which caused the end of the ARA, happened before she had to personally make such a choice. Yet, at the same time she also indicated that she knew that it was something that could have happened and that she would have had to go through with, as her own parents had done in the past.

Rita did not have difficulties returning to life aboveground after the Revolution, because she considered that everything was much easier and that she was still young enough at the age of 25 to adapt to a new reality. At present, she is not politically active, because in the years that followed the Revolution her husband had problems with the PCP and left, never joining another political party again. Rita was not involved directly in the problems, but she was indirectly affected and also distanced herself from the party. Nonetheless, she believes that having grown up within the party marked her life, particularly her position regarding socio-economic inequalities.

## Jaime

Jaime is the youngest of 10 siblings. He considers that his family was poor, however less so when he was born, because a few of his siblings were already working and contributing to the household finances. He started working at age 12 after finishing primary school and was 16 years old when the Revolution took place in 1974. Jaime did not consider that his family had an influence in his political activism, which he attributes to two factors: having been born during the dictatorship and having worked since he can remember. These were the circumstances, in his opinion, that made him become a leftist who cannot live with injustices and inequalities. In order to illustrate the origins of his awareness of political and economic injustices, Jaime told the following story:

> One of the things that struck me the most in my political adolescence – I don't think I was even involved in political activity yet – but something that impressed me deeply was the time right after the April 25th. For four or five months, I went with a group of friends to play soccer in a nearby estate, which was owned by landed gentry. The place had a square, a grocery store, a cafe, a tavern, peasant houses, a GNR [rural police] outpost, and a soccer field. The nearest village was twenty or thirty kilometres away. What happened? The pittance that the workers received was soon spent in the grocery store and in the tavern, and anyone who protested had the GNR to deal with. And the guy, a gentleman, a very highly regarded rural gent, because his workers had soup to eat … the scheme was set up in such a way … that everything would return to him … the added value was always his.

Thus, across the next decade of his life, Jaime's political awareness developed and led him to perceive the new democratic state as the establishment allowing the return of the past – of dominant right-wing forces, of capitalism and even fascism. For Jaime, it was as if the capitalist families had gone on holiday after the Revolution and then came back three or four years later untouched to occupy the same positions in society as before. It is in this context that Jaime started to believe that 'violence is a weapon' that can be used 'according to the political analysis of a certain situation'. Jaime subsequently became involved with the FP-25 (Popular Forces of April 25th), which he saw as 'the armed arm of the workers' against the abuses of the employers. In this context, 'shooting the knee' of an abusive employer would be

> An attempt to convey a practical message for both sides, for the employers and for the victims who had been laid off. If there was a guy who was not paying the salaries, or who had fled to Brazil, that guy needed to realise that he could not do that. And since the state did not act, at least there were some guys that would keep him frightened.

For Jaime, FP-25's victims were in fact perpetrators, because they were responsible for the suffering of others. Ending their life would not just be a response to the bad treatment of a particular individual or group at a particular time, but prevent other similar instances from occurring, conveying a message 'as clear as water'. Jaime highlighted that their struggle also created victims on their side, who were killed by the police, which was quite difficult and painful both personally and for the organisation. Thus, Jaime does not show regret for his actions, but defends the accomplishment of a political choice – a choice that was so important in his life that he even mentioned it in a speech on his own wedding day.

Near the end of the organisation, Jaime was shot by the police and arrested. However, four years before finishing his sentence, in 1996, the government approved an amnesty to all FP-25 militants still in jail, but Jaime did not accept it. For him, the most important thing was to pay his debt to society and only then be able to live unreservedly:

> I am the last prisoner who got out of jail. It closed the inquiry. I am the person who spent more time in jail. And you suddenly see the doors opening, everyone leaving and you stay, because you would not sign a paper, you have your dignity. I owe nothing to society. Therefore, I con-sider myself an activist, a political activist, who was with others in the political struggle until the end of the fight, I risked it all and suddenly I lost. I lost and such a defeat brought about ten years in prison, but I left without owing anything to society, because I served the sentence until the end. I did not get out with a pardon, or with an amnesty, I left with my time served. I served it all, I owe nothing to society.

Jaime cherishes his past very much because it provides him with 'some sense to position things' in the present. It allows him to remember who he was, what he did and why he did it, because he believes that his core values remained the same over time and still define his current political self. Thus, Jaime displays a continuity between his past and his present in terms of his ideals, beliefs and social activism, considering that he has always had a very strong attraction towards civic participation that does not allow him to be passive, and that is simply who he is:

> You are facing someone who, despite everything, maintains the same posture he had 25 years ago regarding his social, ideological and civic participation. I have this need to feel that I am contributing with whatever I do, be it at local political meetings, at the Left Bloc [political party], at work. I'm a leftist man […] I have very strong convictions about social justice and quality of life, which I have kept intact since I've been involved in the political struggle, for 30-odd years, exactly the same thing.

Finally, the continuity of the strong convictions held by Jaime over time also include his radicalised views on how to solve social issues. However, he recognises that his age no longer allows him to take part in politically violent activism:

> Rewinding what I experienced in the 1980s, I do not say that if I was twenty years old today that I would not do the same. Due to my way of seeing society and of being integrated in that society, I am unable to live with injustices, with the arrogance of those who have a uniform or a tie and a pen, I cannot live with it. Now, what will Jaime do? Do you think I'll get away ahead of the police, at fifty seven years-old … I can no longer escape. This is something of which I am completely aware. Now, that does not stop me from looking at the situations that I face every day and saying: what we need here is the FP-25, or something else, to bring at least some justice regarding what we are facing.

## Discussion and conclusion

The concept of 'linked lives' was put forward by Elder (1994, p. 4) and refers to the 'inter-action between the individual's social worlds over the life span'. For this author, the 'social forces' present in the life of different individuals are responsible for the development of their life courses. Within this concept, it is possible to situate one of the most relevant narrative resources which can be clearly observed in the life of Rita: her family narrative environment. From an early age, such narrative resources contributed to the development of her personal political awareness, as well as to later choices in her life, such as supporting the creation of an armed organisation to fight a political system which she perceived as deeply unfair. In Rita's discourse, for instance, the repetition of the word 'normal' is interesting: it was 'normal' to wish to join her clandestine parents, it was 'normal' to remain underground and it was 'normal' to be involved in the process of founding a political organisation to fight the regime. In fact, what Rita considered 'normal' in her personal story represents the choices she made, motivated by the meanings she chose to give her life. These meanings, following Brockmeier (2009, p. 222), enclose three basic characteristics: (1) they are relational – for Rita it all started with the desire to be reunited with her parents, and later her involvement with a political violent organisation was closely related to the fact of being the partner of one of the organisation's founders; (2) they are societal and historical – the need to fight an oppressive and violent regime despite great personal sacrifice strongly influenced Rita's socialisation and (3) they are not deterministic, but set out a variety of possibilities for action – along the way Rita had opportunities to turn in different directions, yet she chose 'continuity'. Thus, Rita, like every human being, was not able to escape the cultural meanings of her environment and had no other 'choice but to choose', setting the course of her unique life story (Brockmeier, 2009, p. 222) and shaping her narrative identity (McAdams & McLean, 2013). Hence, her life story is intensely bound to the time and context she lived in and to her cultural socialisation, mainly led by her family experiences and narratives, which moulded and was moulded by her own personal narrative (Ochs & Capps, 1996; Somers, 1994).

Moreover, people's stories are rooted in the narrative resources of their historical contexts (see, for instance, Plummer, 2017). This is an aspect that can be clearly seen in Jaime's life story, who was born in the last years of *Estado Novo's* regime, which already knew some turbulence. In his early teens, he saw the regime being overthrown, giving place to a period of euphoria and politicisation, which shaped his political awareness and activism. Thus, as an adolescent, Jaime was greatly impacted by the political environment of his time, which from a life course perspective indicates that the impact of social change on the developing individual is in part led by factors associated with their 'life stage [...] at the time of the change' (Elder, 1994, p. 6); a life stage in which they were ready, and in some cases eager, to embrace social and political ideas and ideals (see Sugarman, 2001), seeing themselves and constructing a narrative identity as being a 'product' of the Revolution and of all the intense political activity that followed it. Habermas and Hatiboğlu (2014, p. 33) consider this inclusion of context in constructing the life story as a key feature of adolescence, allowing the personal narrative to become coherent with 'a family constellation, a family history, a socioeconomic and sociocultural situation, and a historical situation'. This perspective builds on Cohler's (1982, p. 218) belief that in adolescence 'persons remodel their histories in a manner analogous to that in which a nation much later rewrites its history, in order to create successive legends about the past relevant to that later point in history'. In addition, Andrews (2007, p. 206), remarking on the relationship between political activism and times of social turmoil, says that individuals' 'starting point is always the political narratives they have inherited'. This is a perspective that was noticeable throughout this article, which explored how different interviewees, in different moments of time and under different political systems, developed a consciousness that shaped their political awareness and framed their subsequent activities. In the first moment of time in my analysis, which is represented by Rita, militants are portrayed as the 'children of the regime' whose discourses, identities and actions were shaped by the way they perceived and related to *Estado Novo*'s dictatorial regime. In the second moment of time, which is represented by Jaime, militants are portrayed as the 'children of the revolution' who were, at a young age, socialised and politicised in the euphoria of the Revolution and who engaged with an armed organisation in the 1980s. These individuals used their different contextual variables as resources to form their narrative identity, as well as to attain meaning to their past experiences, which are dialogically reconstructed and recounted.

Regarding the continuities and discontinuities in terms of political activism in the life of both Rita and Jaime, it is interesting to note that Rita was part of an armed organisation that contributed to the fall of the regime and, consequently, perceived the Revolution as its goal and as the victorious end of their politically violent activism. Thus, in Rita's story, the need to keep fighting cannot be found, which does not diminish the pride she feels in relation to her past. However, Jaime's experience is different, carrying a sense of defeat because of the arrests that caused the dissolution of the armed organisation and the subsquent decision of some militants to accept an amnesty while in prison. Consequently, for Jaime, the struggle is not finished yet, he is still committed, through legal political activism, to the pursuit of social justice. Despite not having changed his mind regarding the use of violence for political purposes, Jaime considers his age and concludes that it is not up to him anymore. Therefore, it is important to note that, as also considered by Horgan (2009), disengagement from a politically violent organisation does not always imply a transformation of personal perspectives. In other words, disengagement is not synonymous with deradicalisation since it is possible that disengaged individuals like Jaime, who, despite not committing violent acts anymore, still hold the same perpectives and activist identities that feed into political violence. Although his body no longer allows his personal engagement, at least in physical terms, he does not rebuke others who choose such political means. In this sense, it is possible to observe two individuals who reconstruct themselves in the present and justify their current political activism (or lack of it) according to their representations of past experiences and events.

In this study, I traced the narrative resources by which two former clandestine militants in Portugal were moulded as subjects through their interactions with the social and political contexts of their time. I identified and analysed the stories that shaped these activists' lives, exploring how such stories impacted their past experiences and choices and how they are put at the service of constructing their present selves. Ultimately, this article demonstrates that the meanings people assign to their autobiographical past shape who they are in the present and constitute the narrative resources that form their life stories, shaping their personal narrative according to the moment in history in which they were living.

## Note

1. The dictatorial period corresponds to *Estado Novo* (New State), which was started by a military coup on the 28 May 1926 and ended by the Carnation Revolution on the 25 April 1974. This Revolution began a process of transition to democracy in the country.

## Disclosure statement

No potential conflict of interest was reported by the authors.

## References

Andrews, M. (2002). Generational consciousness, dialogue, and political engagement. In J. Edmunds & B. Turner (Eds.), *Generational consciousness, narrative, and politics* (pp. 75–88). Lanham: Rowman & Littlefield.

Andrews, M. (2007). *Shaping history: Narratives of political change*. Cambridge: Cambridge University Press.

Arena, M., & Arrigo, B. (2005). Social psychology, terrorism, and identity: A preliminary re-examination of theory, culture, self, and society. *Behavioral Sciences & the Law, 23*(4), 485–506.

Brockmeier, J. (2009). Reaching for meaning: Human agency and the narrative imagination. *Theory & Psychology, 19*(2), 213–233.

Bruner, J. (1986). *Actual minds, possible worlds*. Cambridge, MA: Harvard University Press.

Bruner, J. (2003). Self-making narratives. In R. Fivush & C. A. Haden (Eds.), *Autobiographical memory and the construction of a narrative self* (pp. 209–226). Mahwah, NJ: Erlbaum.

Chase, S. (1996). Personal vulnerability and interpretive authority in narrative research. In R. Josselson (Ed.), *The narrative study of lives: Vol. 4. Ethics and process in the narrative study of lives* (pp. 45–59). Thousand Oaks, CA: Sage.

Cohler, B. J. (1982). Personal narrative and life course. In P. Baltes & O. G. Brim (Eds.), *Life-span development and behaviour (Volume 4)* (pp. 205–241). New York, NY: Academic Press.

Cordes, B. (2001). When terrorists do the talking: Reflections on terrorist literature. In D. Rapoport (Ed.), *Inside terrorist organizations* (2nd ed., pp. 150–171). London: Frank Cass & Co.

Da Silva, R. (2016). *Giving them a voice: Narratives of political violence in Portugal*. Birmingham: University of Birmingham.

Della Porta, D. (2013). *Clandestine political violence*. Cambridge: Cambridge University Press.

Dingwall, R. (1980). Ethics and ethnography. *The Sociological Review, 28*, 871–891.

Elder, G. (1994). Time, human agency and social change: Perspectives on the life course. *Social Psychology Quarterly, 57*(1), 4–15.

Esin, C., Fathi, M., & Squire, C. (2013). Narrative analysis: The constructionist approach. In U. Flick (Ed.), *The Sage handbook of qualitative data analysis* (pp. 203–216). London: Sage Publications.

Frank, A. (2010). *Letting stories breathe*. Chicago, IL: The University of Chicago Press.

Gubrium, J. F., & Holstein, J. A. (1997). *The new language of qualitative method*. New York and Oxford: Oxford University Press.

Habermas, T., & de Silveira, C. (2008). The development of global coherence in life narratives across adolescence: Temporal, causal and thematic aspects. *Developmental Psychology, 44*, 707–721.

Habermas, T., & Hatiboğlu, N. (2014). Contextualizing the self: The emergence of a biographical understanding in adolescence. *New Directions for Child and Adolescent Development, 2014*(145), 29–41.

Habermas, T., & Paha, C. (2001). The development of coherence in adolescents' life narratives. *Narrative Inquiry*, *11*, 35–54.

Horgan, J. (2009). *Walking away from terrorism: Accounts of disengagement from radical and extremist movements*. London: Routledge.

Jackson, M. (2002). *The politics of storytelling: Violence, transgression and intersubjectivity*. Copenhagen: Museum Tusculanum Press.

Jackson, R. (2009). Knowledge, power and politics in the study of political terrorism. In R. Jackson, M. Breen-Smyth, & J. Gunning (Eds.), *Critical terrorism studies: A new research agenda* (pp. 66–84). London: Routledge.

Josselson, R. (2004). The hermeneutics of faith and the hermeneutics of suspicion. *Narrative Inquiry*, *14*(1), 1–28.

Josselson, R. (2007). The ethical attitude in narrative research: Principles and practicalities. In D. J. Clandinin (Ed.), *Handbook of narrative inquiry* (pp. 537–566). Thousand Oaks, CA: Sage Publications.

Kvale, S. (2006). Dominance through interviews and dialogues. *Qualitative Inquiry*, *12*(3), 480–500.

McAdams, D. (1993). *The stories we live by: Personal myths and the making of the self*. New York, NY: William Morrow.

McAdams, D. P. (2008). Personal narratives and the life story. In O. John, R. Robins, & L. Pervin (Eds.), *Handbook of personality: Theory and research* (3rd ed., pp. 242–264). New York, NY: Guilford Press.

McAdams, D. P., & McLean, K. C. (2013). Narrative identity. *Current Directions in Psychological Science*, *22*(3), 233–238.

Mishler, E. (2004). Historians of the self: Restorying lives, revising identities. *Research in Human Development*, *1*(1), 101–121.

Ochs, E., & Capps, L. (1996). Narrating the self. *Annual Review of Anthropology*, *25*(1), 19–43.

Plummer, K. (2002). The call of life stories in ethnographic research. In P. Atkinson, A. Coffey, S. Delamont, J. Lofland, & L. Lofland (Eds.), *Handbook of ethnography* (pp. 395–406). London: Sage.

Plummer, K. (2017). Narrative power, sexual stories and the politics of story telling. In I. Goodson, A. Antikaunen, P. Sikes, & M. Andrews (Eds.), *The Routledge international handbook on life history and narratives* (pp. 280–292). London: Routledge.

Polkinghorne, D. E. (1988). *Narrative knowing and the human sciences*. New York: State University of New York Press.

Polkinghorne, D. E. (2007). Validity issues in narrative research. *Qualitative Inquiry*, *13*(4), 1–16.

Renzetti, C. M., & Lee, R. M. (1993). *Researching sensitive topics*. Newbury Park, CA: Sage.

Sarbin, T. R. (1986). The narrative as root metaphor for psychology. In T. R. Sarbin (Ed.), *Narrative psychology: The storied nature of human conduct* (pp. 3–21). New York, NY: Praeger.

Selbin, E. (2010). *Revolution, rebellion, resistance: The power of story*. London: Zed Books.

Smith, B. (2016). Narrative analysis. In E. Lyons & A. Coyle (Eds.), *Analysing qualitative data in psychology* (2nd ed., pp. 202–221). London: Sage Publications.

Somers, M. R. (1994). The narrative constitution of identity: A relational and network approach. *Theory and Society*, *23*, 605–649.

Spector-Mersel, G. (2010). Narrative research: Time for a paradigm. *Narrative Inquiry*, *20*(1), 204–224.

Stark, L., & Hedgecoe, A. (2004). A practical guide to research ethics. In I. Bourgeault, R. Dingwall, & R. De Vries (Eds.), *The Sage handbook of qualitative methods in health research* (pp. 589–607). London: Sage Publications.

Sugarman, L. (2001). *Life-span development: Frameworks, accounts and strategies* (2nd ed.). New York, NY: Taylor and Francis.

Taylor, M., & Horgan, J. (2012). A conceptual framework for addressing psychological process in the development of the terrorists. In J. Horgan & K. Braddock (Eds.), *Terrorism studies: A reader* (pp. 130–144). London: Routledge.

Tololyan, K. (2001). Cultural narrative and the motivation of the terrorist. In D. Rapoport (Ed.), *Inside terrorist organizations* (2nd ed., pp. 217–236). London: Frank Cass & Co.

Wang, Q., & Brockmeier, J. (2002). Autobiographical remembering as cultural practice: Understanding the interplay between memory, self and culture. *Culture & Psychology*, *8*(1), 45–64.

# Politicisation in later life: experience and motivations of older people participating in a protest for the first time

Jonathan R. Guillemot and Debora J. Price

**ABSTRACT**

With demographic ageing, political activity of older people is increasingly becoming relevant to political science. However, little is known about the possibility of and rationale for politicisation in later life. This article uses in-depth qualitative interviews with older first-time participants in a successful protest against the closure of a charity-run day centre to investigate how and when such politicisation might occur. We find that in response to perceived extreme threat, and provided with high levels of support, frail older people with low levels of early politicisation actively participated in a protest that ultimately prevented closure of their day centre. Furthermore, older people are not a weak population, but were able to use their frailty as political tools for shaming decision-makers. The study reveals that despite low political activity throughout life, politicisation can be triggered for the first time in later life. Three key aspects are highlighted: (1) in spite of poor health, perceived threat seems an essential driver to politicisation; (2) supporters and carers act as an essential determinant to catalyse politicisation in this group; (3) older people are capable of adapting their claim-making performances, including shaming strategies, to achieve the best outcomes, thus illustrating their potential power.

## Introduction

Research into the implications of ageing societies has given insufficient attention to the determinants of later life changes in political behaviour. With the ageing of European populations, political activity of older people is increasingly becoming relevant to political science. Goerres (2009) termed it 'the greying of our democracies', encapsulating fears such as voting power imbalances, increased conservatism and anti-youth tendencies. Little is known about the possibility of and the rationale for politicisation in later life. Percheron, Meyer, and Muxel (1993) defines politicisation as the process whereby individuals adopt sets of knowledge, skills and behaviours which are transmitted by politicising institutions such as the family, the school and the media, among others.

Due to general decreasing physical and mental capability and progressive loss of social role, older people may become progressively disempowered (Goerres, 2009). It is therefore anticipated that the political engagement of disempowered people is unlikely. This paper argues that people in later life can politicise despite an individual history of low political commitment. It investigates the politicisation of people in later life via the participation in a protest. This article describes that, in response to perceived threats, older people who were never politically involved beyond voting, can actively be part of a protest. In-depth evidence from nine older interviewees, all first-time protesters, confirms that politicisation can result from a combination of perceived threat, physiological capability and earlier politicisation but importantly may or even must also be facilitated by external supporters. This research suggests that earlier politicisation is not a necessary feature of later political actions. Furthermore, it supports the view that older people are not the weak population that one could imagine as they are able to use their frailty as political tools for shaming decision-makers.

## Political activity: life course and claim-making performances

### Theories of disengagement and continuation

Political activities of older people are generally conceptualised under two main processes: disengagement and continuation. Under disengagement theory, research has shown that people tend progressively to withdraw from the political activities that require the most energy and resources as they age (Cumming & Henry, 1961; Glenn, 1969), with ill health perceived as a reason to refrain from participating in physically demanding political activities such as protesting (Goerres, 2009). Other than voting, political activities such as being a party member, marching or debating progressively erode from usual activities as people age (Jennings & Markus, 1988); and older people use selective withdrawal to keep doing what matters the most to them (Glenn & Grimes, 1968).

Continuation is an alternative sociological concept also used to understand and explain observed behaviours of older people in the political sphere. Acknowledging the fundamental role of individual determinants of political activity, research has shown that, as people age, they tend to keep doing what they have always done throughout their life (Alwin, Cohen, & Newcomb, 1991; Atchley, 1971, 1989; Krosnick & Alwin, 1989; Tirrito, 2003). According to continuation theory, individuals who have been active members of the political sphere tend to remain active. People who participate in marches at older ages tend to display a lifelong history of protest participation. Voting is also among the strongest and most long-lasting of political activities in older people, where little disengagement is found (Goerres, 2009; Jennings & Markus, 1988).

### Protests and claim-making performances

Political science describes various forms of political participation, ranging from simple layman discussions to active and determined commitments to political roles within society. These activities – or claim-making performances (Tilly, 2006) – extend from being socially acceptable and common, such as voting or debating, to repressible violent political expression modes, such as damaging property (Norris, Walgrave, Aelst, & Url, 2005; Tilly, 2006). This study focuses on protests as one particular political action tool among diverse types of claim-making performances that are used by politically active groups. In Western societies, peaceful demonstrations are mostly regarded as a rightful mean of political expression (Neveu, 2011) but are nevertheless physically and emotionally demanding due to physical constraints and time requirements. Populations attending protests are mainly young and healthy, which suggests a possible association between physical capacity and political engagement (Norris et al., 2005). For these reasons, analyses of politicisation of older people through their first participation in a political demonstration constitute a powerful example of the possibility of politicisation in later life.

### Politicisation: a process of the youth

The lack of research around politicisation of older people may be related to the perception that politicisation is a sociological process, which take place earlier in the life course. The main politicising institutions referred to by Percheron et al. (1993) in their definition of the politicisation process – mainly family and school – suppose that it occurs essentially during upbringing, therefore youth, leaving less for later life politicisation, hence the assumption that politicisation is a process of younger people, and that adulthood and later life are associated with continuation or disengagement on the basis of early political activity patterns. The possibility of politicisation in older age is not envisaged by continuation and disengagement theories which are perceived as universal.

## Political activism and politicisation of older people and other disempowered populations

### Political activism in older people and usage of adapted claim-making performances

In spite of the literature on politicisation of older people being scarce, some research has been conducted around forms of activism of older people. A number of movements have been observed and investigated. The Grey Panthers in the USA gained public fame for demanding the end of mandatory retirement and expanded to Germany and the UK (Walker, 2010). The Raging Grannies in the USA and Canada notably called for social justice for older women (Narushima, 2004). The Argentinean *Jubilados* were older people gathering for years in front of the Buenos Aires National Congress to raise awareness on social issues that older people faced (DuBois, 2013). These experiences are examples of political activism rather than politicisation in older age, but the strategies deployed to be heard via the use of appropriate claim-making performances in a group regarded as disempowered are nevertheless relevant to this study.

Politicisation of disempowered groups is characterised by the use of a specific and adapted claim-making performances. All groups, regardless of their ranking on the scale of social power, use distinctive claim-making performances perceived as the most efficacious to reach a particular goal (Snow, Soule, & Kriesi, 2004). Shaming strategies are typically used by disempowered groups in order to shock the public and therefore gain recognition and leverage by for example publishing videos on social media showing harsh truths hidden behind closed doors such as videos of abuses in slaughter houses. At larger scale, such techniques are used by human rights and environment activists denouncing nature threatening behaviours of industries (Bloomfield, 2014; Jacquet, 2015). Shaming is also a tool known to have been used for political ends by disempowered groups at a smaller scale. For example, Shakespeare (1993, p. 256) described an event during which people in wheelchairs blocked Oxford Street in London. They succeeded by driving the police to a moral dilemma over forcibly removing them in front of the media and witnesses.

### Politicisation of older people: a response to threat

While a number of studies have looked at the politicisation of young people to explain differences in political views and political activities at older ages (Crittenden, 1962; Percheron et al., 1993; Wolfinger & Rosenstone, 1980), much less attention has been given to political behavioural changes in other ages, especially in later life. Political action has been theorised as the product of opportunities for action (specifically, the opportunity to make demands) and threats, with threat conceptualised as 'the probability that existing benefits will be taken away or new harms inflicted if challenging groups fail to act collectively' (Almeida, 2003, p. 347). Since Goldstone and Tilly (2001) argued that the role played by threat in motivating political action had previously been underestimated, threats have been demonstrated to have been important factors in the mobilisation and tactics of a wide range of political actions across time and space (e.g. Almeida, 2003, 2015; Prieto, 2016). However this research considers threats in the context of large-scale political action, and generally theorises threats as a crucial catalyst for protest movements by groups that were already organised but possibly not, or not sufficiently, mobilised. The significance of threats has not been considered on a micro-scale to previously apolitical and uninvolved groups, who had not felt threatened before and were not in any sense organised, nor civically engaged. Few studies have considered the concept of threat in the context of political participation by older people; two studies nevertheless report information relative to the determinants of politicisation of older people (Campbell, 2003; Goerres, 2009).

Campbell (2003) studied the rationale for politicisation of older US citizens for the defence of Social Security and Medicare. Using a multivariate quantitative analysis, she emphasised that perceived threat – in this case the decrease of government benefits – was a significant factor related to politicisation at an older age, and a reason for a modification of the 'normal' political course of individuals. Campbell recognises that 'specific mechanism by which individuals are mobilized by threat cannot be addressed with these data' (Campbell, 2003, p. 41) – a qualitative approach is required.

Goerres (2009) investigated the political participation of older people in Europe through a group of older people having participated in a demonstration. Threat – in this case defined as the risk of losing existing benefits – was identified as an essential reason to mobilise. Furthermore, the author emphasises the role of support from external individuals – experienced and highly politicised individuals – to enable political mobilisation, therefore acting as political catalysts. Despite some participants being first-time protesters, the analysis did not investigate the motivation leading those who politicised. Politicisation of older people is therefore far from being fully understood, particularly with regard to the factors that enable politicisation, however perceived threat and external enablers have been identified as important.

## Politicisation of other disempowered populations: the role of threat and external support

Although politicisation in later life has seldom been investigated, politicisation of other disempowered populations contributes to the understanding of processes underlying politicisation of older people. In a review of unexpected politicisation, Collovald and Mathieu (2009) and Mathieu (1999) compared demonstrations by sex workers, precarious workers and other 'weak' groups. These were characterised by their 'rarity of militant competence, weakness of collective framework, prejudice attached to their collective identity, which is considered inferior or even stigmatised' (Collovald & Mathieu, 2009, p. 120; Mathieu, 1999). In the case of protests by sex workers in Lyon, France, authors gave an account of both the political inexperience as well as the stigma that the group suffered. While perceived threat was outlined as a crucial motivator for politicisation, the authors also found that the support from experienced assistants – political catalysts – was essential to trigger the social movement. Cited in Shakespeare (1993), Klein's (1984) analysis revealed that politicisation in disabled people is the result of society-induced threat: 'Personal problems become political demands only when the inability to survive, or to attain a decent life, is seen as a consequence of social institutions or social inequality rather than of personal failure, and the system is blamed'. In this same analysis of political organisation of disabled people, Shakespeare (1993) cites DeJong (1983) who explains that politicisation of disabled people is the ultimate step after having failed to be heard through other ways. 'When traditional legal channels have been exhausted, disabled persons have learned to employ other techniques of social protest such as demonstrations and sit-ins' (DeJong, 1983, p. 12). This links with a particular characteristic of politicisation of disempowered groups, that is, the use of adapted and specific claim-making performances. Although the literature investigating the politicisation of disempowered people helps bridge the gaps of the literature specific to older people, it is necessary to verify these findings within the specific context of people in later life.

## Aims and methods

The context for this study was a year of heightened unrest and political action in the UK in opposition to austerity-budgets. In May 2010, a Conservative-Liberal Democrat Alliance imposed substantial cuts designed to deal with the aftermath of the 2008 financial crisis. The budget was followed by students and education workers protests against tuition increases. In March 2011 Trade Unions led the largest anti-government protest since the demonstrations against the second Iraq war, followed by a strike in June 2011 (Brown, Dowling, Harvie, & Milburn, 2013). The protest discussed in this article was one of a multitude of small-scale events in response to specific circumstances. The protest, specific to the closure of a charity-run day centre, took place an afternoon of January 2011 and included a small crowd. Following its success, some of the participants went on to participate in larger protests.

This article investigates politicisation of people in later life and its determinants. To this end, it examines a single case of several first-time participants in the abovementioned protest. These first-time participants belong to a larger sample, interviewed as part of a

research looking more broadly at the participation of older people in political demonstrations, regardless of the history of their political activity (Guillemot, 2011). This original
data set also included individuals displaying characteristics of stronger early life political
participation. For the purpose of this article, individuals were eligible if they were participating in a political protest for the first time in their life and if their history of political
participation was limited to, at most, voting.

The nine respondents included in this analysis participated together in one protest in
January 2011. In this case, all respondents were visitors to a charity-run day centre providing lunch and social activities. This centre was supported by public subsidies. Consequence of the budget cuts, many community day centres were due to close in a matter
of months. At the time of the study, one community centre had already closed down in
the Borough and the centre to which the respondents belonged was to be shortly termi-
nated. In January 2011, all the visitors to the centre participated in a protest in front of the
council hall, which lasted several hours. The demonstration was directly aimed at the
closure of that one community centre. Ultimately, the centre was awarded a 12-month
budget extension and was still running early 2017, more than 6 years after these events
took place.

Older participants in demonstrations were identified with the help of a British charity,
who served as a gatekeeper for the recruitment of participants (Heath, Charles, Crow, &
Wiles, 2007). In this subsample, written informed consent was gained from each participant before data collection (Bowling, 2002). Nine in-depth semi-structured interviews
were conducted between 15 June and 7 July 2011. Interviews were audio-recorded
and fully transcribed. Interviewee names used in this article are fictitious to preserve
anonymity. Interviews were conducted according to a discussion guide (Hennink,
Hutter, & Bailey, 2010), which used four categories of information relating to the interviewee's personal history of political commitment, motivators to the participation in
the demonstration, understanding of political issues and personal demographic
characteristics.

Coding and analysis were undertaken using the qualitative analysis software NVivo®,
according to thematic analysis and codes. Codes emerged initially from the discussion
guide and were further elaborated iteratively during the coding process. Interview transcripts were coded according to seven codes, namely history of political commitment, perception of older age, health and demonstrations, personal consequences of the cuts,
description of the mobilisation, the role of the staff in the demonstration and aspects of
disengagement. Each code was reviewed to identify patterns of discourse, which served
as a basis for analytical axes.

## Findings

### Respondents' characteristics and biographical information

Respondents' demographic characteristics are detailed in Table 1. All respondents were
female aged 66–92 years (median age 86) at the time of the interviews. The visitors to
the day centre displayed a broad diversity of physical and mental capacities. The day
centre was not adapted to receive dependent individuals. Though respondents were
often frail and needed physical and mental support, they all lived by themselves and

**Table 1.** Participants' pseudonyms and age.

| Pseudonyms | Age |
| --- | --- |
| Molly | 88 |
| Lauren | 83 |
| Agnes | 92 |
| Regina | 77 |
| Emily | 87 |
| Mary | 66 |
| Francesca | 88 |
| Janet | 86 |
| Laura | 84 |

had a certain degree of autonomy. Some used wheelchairs, others needed walking-assistance devices.

Although respondents had not participated in protests before, they displayed a very committed relationship to voting. All respondents were regular voters and perceived this activity as important. Participating in demonstrations however was not part of their political upbringing or earlier identity. The unexpectedness of their participation was also perceived by the demonstrators themselves. Regina's experience was representative of the feeling.

Regina:     No, [I] never [demonstrated] in my life. I never thought I could be interviewed [on TV], on cameras, [...] on Twitter, that's what it's called, I was on Twitter and that. I never thought I'd do anything like that!

Several other participants explained their history of political commitment through participation in institutionalised behaviours such as voting, as Agnes explained.

Interviewer:     So you haven't demonstrated before?
Agnes:     No, no, no.
Interviewer:     Have you had any kind of political activity?
Agnes:     No, no, I have enough to do on my own, leave the political stuff! No.
Interviewer:     You don't vote?
Agnes:     Oh yes I vote! Of course I vote! You have to vote!
Interviewer:     Have you ever been a political party member?
Agnes:     No, never, I've only demonstrated for here. That's all!

Both Agnes and Regina, like the other protesters from the day centre were not used to taking part in active politics. Molly described her political role according to social classes.

Molly:     I've always voted Labour. Because I'm working class. It's the wrong thing to say, but I'm working class so I voted Labour. That's all.
Interviewer:     Always?
Molly:     No, no, no, I did vote once Conservative, because my husband always voted Conservative. But he was a cinema manager, so I suppose he had different … He was a bit up more than me. So he always voted Conservative and I just voted Labour. That's all. But all my family voted Labour. The nine of us: my mum and dad, eleven of us, we all our life voted Labour.

The above discourse examples from these three participants are evidence of a low early politicisation, associated with consistent voting patterns and low levels of active participation in more demanding political events including demonstrations. Despite these socio-political characteristics, all of them decided to take part in the demonstrations of

2011. The following section describes the protesters' motivations to participate in the protest.

### Motivations to participate in the protest: counteracting the threat of the closure

The apparent reason for people participating was the impending closure of the centre. Although it may not have appeared as a fundamental event to an external observer, the description of the consequences associated with the closure by the centre's visitors took the matter to a different and more dramatic level.

> Molly: Why I did it is because I've always found [council name] very good, very good to the elderly people and, hm, suddenly there's this thing, that they've got to cut things and I thought, why should they? I've worked all my life! Why should they? So, anything that I could help to stop it, I try to do, like going outside the town hall, and raising my voice and shoutin' out [...] Because I think this [the day centre] is a lifesaver for me, for all these people here. It can't close, it can't close. We'd all sit at home and fade away. As I said, I'm not doing it yet, I'm not gonna fade away yet.

Agnes explained her feeling about old age and how the closure of the centre would impact its visitors.

> Agnes: Old age, you got to feel sorry for them. Because most of them, if they close this place, lot of these of people wouldn't get out of bed. They'd be in bed, they wouldn't cook. Now, with me, I have a dinner [here, dinner means midday lunch] down here, I go home and cook in the evening. These people, they only have one dinner here, 'til the next day for them to have another dinner. So what would they do? If this closes, they would rot, I told the eight people in the Council.
> Lauren: That's probably what they want us to do.

These two interviews highlight the grave nature of the threat perceived by Agnes, Lauren and Molly. This interview, where Lauren intervened as she was nearby, details Agnes's point of view on the closure of the centre: a death sentence for many of the visitors. It represented a major threat to her as she explained when asked what would happen if the centre closed. An interesting aspect of Agnes's discourse, however, is the way she referred to older people using the third person, as if she was not part of them. Incidentally, Agnes was the oldest visitor, confined to a wheelchair.

Similarly to Agnes, Lauren explained her view on the consequences of the closure of the centre.

> Lauren: No! [whispers] Please God, no, don't let them shut the place. I know I'd be helped by my daughter-in-law, but she's got her life to live. That is not right. Not right, is it? It's their own life. That's the way I look at it anyway. But I mean, I would willingly go, but I wouldn't push myself. It's just not right. I'm not complaining, I'm quite happy. If I can come here, [employee] is very nice, the people are very nice. We're all different. I'm very happy and I had a good dinner today. For a very reasonable price. I wouldn't go anywhere else. I'm very happy. If this place shut, well ... Really I don't have anywhere else to go. Shame [laughter]. [...] That's going to sound dramatic but to me that would feel like the end of my life. I don't know where else to go.

The centre represented much more to its visitors than just an ordinary location for occasional socialisation. Most of its visitors spent every day at the centre and were fed there. For many, it was like their home was being threatened; the centre appeared as the one thing they looked forward to each morning. This brings a different perspective to the mobilisation of the group: a fight for what was perceived as a right to live. First-time protesters were nevertheless aware of the limitations associated with their physical capacity and were able to perceive these weaknesses as strengths, as the next section describes.

### Consciousness of physical limitations and adaptation of claim-making performances

Participants in the demonstrations were aware of their limited physical capacity. Interviewees explained how their physical frailties, on the contrary, led to the use of previously acquired skills and a selection of adapted claim-making performances, which was more efficient for them; including the use of shaming to gain attention and leverage.

Interviewees described how their physical capabilities slowed them down. Regina recounted the planning of the demonstration and how her health was affected.

> Regina: We made flyers, we made banners and everything else here. I paid for it later. One day we sat in nearly all day doing things and because of the arthritis, when I got home that night I paid for it, my hands and joints were killing me. But we thoroughly enjoyed ourselves when we were making them.

Interviewees were also aware that their physical capabilities were different from crowds usually participating in protests, which can sometimes represent a threat to political institutions. Lauren told of her willingness to fight with a certain irony and wit, showing that her capacity to display strength – and here awareness of it – and physical power were limited.

> Lauren: I am, of course I am [ready to fight]. I would. Wherever I have to go and join the crowd, I would. Oh yeah. I stood outside the town hall. Oh yes. As long as [I am] reminded. Definitely, I would fight for it. Oh yeah. Not that the fist would help, but I would have a go.

By ironically explaining that the 'fist would not help', she acknowledged her physical weakness. The goal was evidently not to display physical force. She describes the contrast between her capabilities and the anticipated threatening appearance of protests. Also, Lauren explained that she suffered from memory loss. When questioned about her motivation, she described both her awareness of her condition but also her determination to fight nevertheless. Later in this interview, when asked about her motivation to demonstrate, she looked suddenly puzzled, then said that she could not remember why they were protesting and casually asked to be reminded the reason why they needed to mobilise; a reminder that the researcher provided. Aware of this situation, carers and other visitors to the centre always made sure to be around Lauren at all times.

Francesca casually presented her willingness to protest despite her physical limitations.

> Francesca: I think I would do anything possible, within my means. I love it here.

Despite their individual and specific physical and cognitive capacities and disabilities, each of the participants detailed their perception of the mobilisation and the different forms it could take. The appropriation of the claim-making performances was interestingly presented.

> Molly: [...] I didn't care anyway. Well there was only a few of us outside [council hall] but I did get lots of people. I stopped them and made them sign the petition, you know. I used to do acting, so I'm not backwards with coming forwards, you know what I mean, so … That's it. I was outside the town hall, and if they ask me to do it tomorrow, I'll do it tomorrow.

Molly's outgoing behaviour to get people to sign the petition showed the use of previously acquired skills for the purpose of this new mission. Regina described her feeling regarding her political behaviour.

> Regina: It doesn't make me feel any different. I can't believe that I've done it! [laughter]. I can't believe that I've done it. [...] Hm, we've only got another year. And if we have to do it next year, to keep it open, I'll do it again. You've got to fight. It's no good sitting back and saying 'oh why has this happened. You know, why don't people do this.' You got to get yourself involved if you believe in something. You can't expect other people to do it all the time.

While a demonstration typically gains success by boasting a large number of people gathered, this small demonstration focused rather on shaming the council as gathering a crowd was unrealistic. Although a demonstration is in many ways a conventional tool within usual claim-making performances, when used by older, frail people, it can be perceived as a deflection of the use and signification of a protest. In fact, several interviewees referred to some aspects of *shaming* decision-makers for pushing older and frail people to protest in the streets on a cold January day and for destroying a key shelter without which visitors feel have nothing. In this perspective, the goal of the demonstration was less to threaten power than to send a message to politicians and utilise a moral strength that their old age provided them. Agnes explained this argument with particular wit.

> Agnes: [manager's name] told us when he got us all together. And we had the councillors, from the council, around here. And we all spoke our mind to them and I said to them, I said, if you close this, I said, this is a red light area, we've got nowhere to go. I said, only prostitutes, pimps and drugies. That's all that's around here. I told them to their face, didn't I?

Agnes was considered by the visitors and the centre's staff as the leader of the movement as she was the oldest but also because she had been interviewed several times by the local media as a result of the protest and her discourse was now well rehearsed.

Francesca put into words the shaming approach, when replying to the question of whether she would protest again in opposition to the centre closing.

> Francesca: I would, yea. 'Cause they took me down in a wheelchair and I'm quite happy with that. And I think it's to see a few people in wheelchairs, it does help. Yea. 'What do you want to go down there for? It wouldn't do any good'! I say, how do you know? If you don't go and don't try, you won't know. You've got to give it a try! Yea. [...] If it's for the benefit of the centre, yes. I never say no to things like that, if it's for the good.

Although all respondents participated in the protest by the Town Hall, most did not participate in another much larger protest, which took place in central London in March 2011 against cuts more generally. Respondents explained their choice in light of their physical limitations, as Mary's discourse illustrated.

Mary: There was a big one, but I didn't go to that, because sometimes, these demonstrations, I know you got to fight for things, sometimes there is fighting and all of that, there is a lot of funny people out there, but I didn't go to that, you're with me? There was a demonstration, a while back, I didn't attend to that. [… B]ecause sometimes there is a lot of hateful people and they can do something and sometimes they involve horses, you know, so that one I didn't go. But to the town hall outside I went.

While this study investigates the motivators to politicisation, Mary points out one reason why older people refrain from participating in protests, which is fear of threatening behaviours, regardless of the actual existence of the behaviour or the threat that they bring. Janet and Laura contributed to this view that they could not be part of a larger event, when asked if they participated in the large-scale protest.

Laura: No we didn't [go to the large demonstration].
Janet: They started off from here, didn't they? And they marched through, didn't they? For hours.
Laura: It was a long time, a long way.
Janet: You couldn't really cope with it.
Laura: Some in wheelchairs, they took some wheelchairs as well.
Janet: But they had some people to push them didn't they? I mean, I couldn't have walked that far. Hours and hours.

The physical difficulty and the risks associated with protesting show a distinctive constraint applying to these visitors to the day centre. To an extent, it seems nearly impossible that they could have achieved even the participation under investigation here by themselves, hence the question to which we turn next: the role of their environment in their participation.

### Catalysts of the protest: empowerment by the staff

There are indications that the day centre's visitors received strong support from the centre's staff. The charity social workers acted as political educators contributing to a later politicisation and also as physical assistants. For this reason, the centre's staff can be regarded as a catalyst: an agent enabling and precipitating a reaction. Regina's description of the decision-making process for marching attested of the role of the charity.

Regina: I didn't really make a decision. Just we talked here and that … And we talked this and we talked that and we just went and suggest we were gonna do it. There was no hesitation about, no we're gonna do it. We just all said yes, we're gonna do it! There was no … No real thinking about it. [...] Over here we decided we weren't gonna sit back and then …
Interviewer: Who spoke about it?
Regina: [manager's name] and [social worker's name], they talked to people here and they were telling about it and asked if we'd … I think it was [another social worker] … And we said we weren't gonna let it happen. And the day … We heard the day we were going somewhere and we decided we weren't gonna let it ruin our day and when we come back

here, the following day, we sat back and it was all sorted that we'd do what we would do.

Although Regina presented the decision of participating as an obvious choice initiated among the visitors themselves, she then explained that it came from the staff. Naturally, the staff were the first to be informed of the imminent closure and were expected to communicate the information to the visitors. However, when she explained that 'it was all sorted that [they]'d do what [they] would do' it became clear that the staff positively encouraged the people to protest.

Interestingly, the nuance between the centre's visitors and the centre's staff became blurred when a close look at the vocabulary was given. The way 'we' was used in this extract to refer to both the staff and the visitors emphasised that little difference between both groups existed, in this domain at least.

The role of the charity workers as physical assistants was described by Agnes when she recalled the day of the demonstration.

> Agnes: [I went] in a wheelchair, I was ill, with bronchitis … It was so good. We've got the best manager in the world with [manager's name], who you've just seen, he's our manager, he's wonderful. He got hot water bottles on me, blankets, eight o'clock at night, we was [sic] around that town hall, demonstrating and I was ill.

The protest outside the Town Hall took place in January in deepest winter, in the evening. An aspect of senescence is the degeneration of the body's thermoregulation. Older people get colder more easily and tend not to feel the cold. Protesting in the cold is tiring and can be seen as hazardous for older people if someone is not looking after them. The manager's role was fundamental in Agnes' ability to protest. By warming her up with hot water bottles and with blankets, he *enabled* her political action.

One can question whether this political action would have taken place without the central role of the staff. Although the aim of this study was not to question the motivations of the staff to participate in the demonstration, it became clear that the jobs of the centre's social workers were also put at risk by the closure of the centre. This demonstration was the result of the combined motivations of the staff and the visitors rather than the visitors only. The discourse by Regina brought this aspect into perspective.

> Regina: We live life from day to day. But we're not going to sit back and let the council take away the bit of enjoyment we've got here. On top of which these people that help run these places are marvellous people. They go over the 100% to look after whoever is in need. Why should they lose their jobs as well? 'Cause it's not just the club that's being closed down, it's people who are going to lose their jobs as well. And this is one other reason we all fight, for what we believe in.

The goal of the staff may be to protect their jobs but is also the result of strong defiance towards a social policy perceived as destructive and life-threatening. The charity staff acted as extensions of the visitors and provided them with the necessary support for them to develop their capability to act as rightful citizens.

## Discussion

This study confirms pre-established determinants to politicisation of older. As described in Campbell (2003) and Goerres (2009) and confirmed with other peripheral studies (Shakespeare, 1993), perceived threat – described by respondents as indirect death due the closure of a day centre providing meals and social interaction – is a key determinant to the politicisation of older people, even when in poor health. Despite emphasised as a barrier to politicisation, this study shows that poor health is a potential barrier but insufficient to prevent politicisation if individuals are appropriately supported.

This study establishes two other determinants, which have been demonstrated in other disempowered populations and therefore fills a gap in the literature. The adaptation of claim-making performances to increase political impact as emphasised by Shakespeare (1993) is evidenced in this study through the intention of shaming authorities. Finally, the importance of catalysts highlighted by Collovald and Mathieu (2009) and Mathieu (1999) and to a lesser extent Goerres (2009) is demonstrated in this study by the crucial role played by the staff.

This study shows that in response to threat and provided with support, older people with low levels of politicisation can participate in a protest. It confirmed earlier findings that political mobilisations are generally a function of perceived threat, physiological capability, earlier politicisation but also external support. Furthermore, this study contributes to the view that older people are not the weak population subgroup that one could imagine: older people can use their frailty as shaming tools to communicate their claims.

Nine respondents were included in this analysis. While this sample appears small, it is not unusual considering the specificity of the study population. In a qualitative study analysing the experience of older people protesting in England in 2004/2005, Goerres (2009) interviewed 22 individuals, 14 of whom were protesting for the first time and only four of whom had never been politically active before. Because such late politicisation is rare, larger samples could only be identified with great difficulty.

Because it is a case study looking at a very specific group of people in the very specific context of the closure of a day care centre, the case may not be representative of older people in Britain generally. However, a case study rarely aims to gather representative people, but rather aims to understand generalities from the perspective of unusual situations. The significant role of the charity in the politicisation of the respondents is undeniable. It nevertheless sheds light on political behaviours in later life in a unique manner.

While this case study shows the possibility of politicisation in later life and its determinants, it does not of itself contradict nor falsify theories of continuation and disengagement. This paper shows that there are exceptions to these rules and proves that specific circumstances can lead to unusual outcomes.

## Conclusion

The main contributions of this study are that politicisation, despite low political activity throughout life can be triggered for the first time in later life. Four key aspects are highlighted: in spite of poor health, which acts as a barrier, though surmountable, perceived threat seems an essential driver to politicisation. Catalysts, whether they are supporters or carers, act as an essential determinant to politicisation. Finally, older people are capable of adapting their claim-making performances, including shaming strategies, to achieve the best outcomes, thus illustrating their potential power.

Evidence from this study both supports and challenges theories of political engagement in later life, namely that of continuation and disengagement. It shows that these theories do not fully describe the political activity older people and that politicisation in later life is possible. These findings are valuable and innovative contributions to theories of social unrest genesis. A closer look at specific 'hard to politicise' population subgroups may inform us of profound social processes in the construction of social movements. Was this case an epiphenomenon, or, on the contrary, do these mobilisations occur in other contexts? These preliminary results call for a broader assessment of the capability of older people to politicise, to gain control over specifically designed claim-making performances, especially in the current context of reforming social policies in Western countries.

## Ethical approval

All procedures performed in studies involving human participants were in accordance with the ethical standards of the institutional and/or national research committee and with the 1964 Helsinki declaration and its later amendments or comparable ethical standards. King's College London Ethics Committee reviewed and approved the methodological and ethical approach used in this research.

## Disclosure statement

No potential conflict of interest was reported by the authors.

## References

Almeida, P. D. (2003). Opportunity organizations and threat-induced contention: Protest waves in authoritarian settings. *American Journal of Sociology*, 109(2), 345–400.

Almeida, P. D. (2015). The role of threats in popular mobilization in Central America. Social movement dynamics. In M. von Bülow & F. M. Rossi (Eds.), *Social movement dynamics: New perspectives on theory and research from Latin America* (pp. 105–126). Farnham: Ashgate.

Alwin, D. F., Cohen, R. L., & Newcomb, T. M. (1991). *Political attitudes over the life span: The Bennington women after fifty years*. Madison: University of Wisconsin Press.

Atchley, R. C. (1971). Retirement and leisure participation: Continuity or crisis? *The Gerontologist, 11* (1), 13–17.

Atchley, R. C. (1989). A continuity theory of normal aging. *The Gerontologist, 29*(2), 183–190.

Bloomfield, M. J. (2014). Shame campaigns and environmental justice: Corporate shaming as activist strategy. *Environmental Politics, 23*(2), 263–281.

Bowling, A. (2002). *Research methods in health: Investigating health and health services*. Buckingham, UK: Open University Press.

Brown, G., Dowling, E., Harvie, D., & Milburn, K. (2013). Careless talk: Social reproduction and fault lines of the crisis in the United Kingdom. *Social Justice, 39*(1(127)), 78–98.

Campbell, A. L. (2003). Participatory reactions to policy threats: Senior citizens and the defense of social security and medicare. *Political Behavior, 25*(1), 29–49.

Collovald, A., & Mathieu, L. (2009). Mobilisations improbables et apprentissage d'un répertoire syndical. *Politix, 86*(2), 119–143.

Crittenden, J. (1962). Aging and party affiliation. *Public Opinion Quarterly, 26*, 648–657.

Cumming, E., & Henry, W. E. (1961). *Growing old, the process of disengagement*. New York, NY: Basic Books.

DuBois, L. (2013). Activist pensioners, a contradiction in terms? Argentina's Jubilados. *Anthropology & Aging Quarterly, 34*(2), 170–183.

Glenn, N. D. (1969). Aging, disengagement, and opinionation. *Public Opinion Quarterly, 33*, 17–33.

Glenn, N. D., & Grimes, M. (1968). Aging, voting, and political interest. *American Sociological Review, 33* (4), 563–575.

Goerres, A. (2009). *The political participation of older people in Europe: The greying of our democracies*. Basingstoke, UK: Palgrave Macmillan.

Goldstone, J. A., & Tilly, C. (2001). Threat (and opportunity): Popular action and state response in the dynamics of contentious action. In Ronald R. Aminzade (Ed.), *Silence and voice in the study of contentious politics* (pp. 1–266). Cambridge: Cambridge University Press.

Guillemot, J. R. (2011). *Motivations of people in later life to take part in demonstrations* (M.Sc. Gerontology dissertation). King's College London.

Heath, S., Charles, V., Crow, G., & Wiles, R. (2007). Informed consent, gatekeepers and go-betweens: Negotiating consent in child- and youth-orientated institutions. *British Educational Research Journal, 33*(3), 403–417.

Hennink, M., Hutter, I., & Bailey, A. (2010). *Qualitative research methods*. London, UK: SAGE.

Jacquet, J. (2015). *Is shame necessary?: New uses for an old tool*. New York: First Vintage Books Edition.

Jennings, M. K., & Markus, G. B. (1988). Political involvement in the later years: A longitudinal survey. *American Journal of Political Science, 32*(2), 302–316.

Krosnick, J., & Alwin, D. F. (1989). Aging and susceptibility to attitude change. *Journal of Personality and Social Psychology, 57*(3), 416–425.

Mathieu, L. (1999). Une mobilisation improbable: l'occupation de l'église Saint-Nizier par les prostituées lyonnaises. *Revue Française de Sociologie, 40*(3), 475–499.

Narushima, N. (2004). A gaggle of raging grannies: The empowerment of older Canadian women through social activism. *International Journal of Lifelong Education, 23*(1), 23–42.

Neveu, E. (2011). *Sociologie des Mouvements Sociaux* (5th ed.). Paris: La Découverte, Collection Reperes.

Norris, P., Walgrave, S., Aelst, P. V., & Url, S. (2005). Who demonstratesAntistate rebels, conventional participants, or everyone? Who demonstrates? *Comparative Politics, 37*(2), 189–205.

Percheron, A., Meyer, N., & Muxel, A. (1993). *La socialisation politique*. Paris: A. Colin.

Prieto, G. (2016). Opportunity, threat, and tactics: Collaboration and confrontation by Latino immigrant challengers. In *Narratives of identity in social movements, conflicts and change* (pp. 123–154). Bingley, UK: Emerald.

Shakespeare, T. (1993). Disabled people's self-organisation: A new social movement? *Disability, Handicap & Society, 8*(3), 249–264.

Snow, D. A., Soule, S. A., & Kriesi, H. (Eds.). (2004). *The Blackwell companion to social movements.* Malden, MA: Wiley-Blackwell.

Tilly, C. (2006). *Regimes and repertoires.* Chicago, IL: The University of Chicago Press.

Tirrito, T. (2003). *Aging in the new millennium.* Columbia: University of South Carolina Press.

Walker, A. (2010). Aging and politics: An international perspective. In R. H. Binstock, L. K. George, S. J. Cutler, J. Hendricks, & J. H. Schulz (Eds.), *Handbook of aging and the social sciences,* 6th ed. (pp. 339–359). Cambridge, MA: Academic Press.

Wolfinger, R. E., & Rosenstone, S. J. (1980). *Who votes?* New Haven, CT: Yale University Press.

ACADEMY
of SOCIAL SCIENCES

# Talking politics in everyday family lives

Sevasti-Melissa Nolas, Christos Varvantakis and Vinnarasan Aruldoss

**ABSTRACT**

How do children encounter and relate to public life? Drawing on evidence from ethnographic fieldwork conducted between 2014 and 2016 for the ERC-funded Connectors Study on the relationship between childhood and public life, this paper explores how children encounter public life in their everyday family environments. Using the instance of political talk as a practice through which public life is encountered in the home, the data presented fill important gaps in knowledge about the lived experience of political talk of younger children. Working with three family histories where political talk was reported by parents to be a practice encountered in their own childhoods and one which they continued in the present amongst themselves as a couple/parents, we make two arguments: that children's political talk, where it occurs, is idiomatic and performative; and that what is transmitted across generations is the practice of *talking* politics. Drawing on theories of everyday life developed by Michel de Certeau and others we explore the implications of these findings for the dominant social imaginaries of conversation, and for how political talk is researched.

## Introduction

The paper addresses the ERC-funded *Connectors Study*'s concern with the relationship between childhood and public life, and how an orientation towards social action emerges (or not) in childhoods that are located in different national cultural contexts, over time, and during a historical moment of global economic precarity (Nolas, 2015; Nolas, Varvantakis, & Aruldoss, 2016). The analysis draws on three family histories composed through longitudinal ethnographic research carried out between 2014 and 2016 with families living in Athens (Greece), Hyderabad (India), and London (England). We focus on the phenomenon of political talk as that is encountered across generations (families of origin, current families). Political talk has been defined as 'a specific type of social interaction, [which] manifests itself in the form of discrete events where two or more people engage in exchanges of meaning with reference to politics' (Schmitt-Beck & Lup, 2013, p. 514), and as 'conversations about public concerns that take place in private, semi-public, and public settings … and have an informal and spontaneous character, in contrast to formally arranged and goal-orientated discussions and deliberation' (Ekström, 2016, p. 1). We argue that these three families, in which parents reported growing up with political talk as part of the discursive repertoires of their families of origin and in which we observed the children, aged between 5 and 7 years, experimenting with political talk, provide an opportunity to explore the much understudied 'phenomenology of political talk' (Schmitt-Beck & Lup, 2013) at the same time as raising questions about what aspects of political talk are transmitted intergenerationally.

Responses to the question of how children encounter public life and with what consequences have preoccupied political scientists, sociologists, and psychologists since the 1950s (Almond & Verba, 1963; Hyman, 1959; Niemi & Sobieszek, 1977). In line with trends across the social sciences, and because of the close relationship between political science and psychology, the early study of political socialisation focused on the learning and transmission of political knowledge, attitudes, and behaviours where such knowledge and attitudes were often narrowly confined to matters of government, elections, and other legislative procedures (see Sapiro, 2004 for an excellent review). At the same time, the role of early experience itself in the formation of politically knowledgeable, politically partisan, and politically active subjects was, and continues to be, contested (Dinas, 2013; Marsh, 1971; Niemi & Hepburn, 1995).

Underpinning these studies were behavioural models of socialisation (e.g. social learning theory) in which children, our main focus here, were conceived as passive recipients of adult, expert knowledge. As Moran-Ellis and Sünker (2008) argue, the longstanding dominance of developmental psychology, functionalist sociology, and education in studying childhood in the twentieth century resulted in an emphasis on questions concerning what children would *become* as adults, how that becoming would happen in order for children to take up pre-assigned roles, and how adults might intervene in children's lives to ensure the 'right' trajectories were in place for those roles to be attained. While the 'preparatory view' of childhood has stood alongside more agentic views of children held in anthropology (Hardman, 1973), social psychology (Mead, 1934), and psychoanalysis (Freud, 1966), it was not until the arrival of the sociology of childhood (James & Prout, 1990) on the one hand, and socio-legal changes on the other (e.g. UN Convention on the Rights of the Child), that views of children's agency and capabilities in socio-cultural reproduction started to be mainstreamed.

As disciplinary spaces for the study of political socialisation start to be permeated by scholars from outside the political science and psychology nexus, social imaginaries of the child have begun shifting. In particular, the introduction of a communicative research paradigm where talk is foregrounded marks a break with the aforementioned passive view of the child in the study of political socialisation (Buckingham, 1999; McDevitt & Chaffee, 2002; Ojeda & Hatemi, 2015; Sapiro, 2004). For instance, McDevitt and Chaffee's (2002) family study of primary school children in California finds that children are co-creators of family communication and political talk, a finding that is further corroborated by George (2013) who focuses on the linguistic strategies that Californian children use in order to draw their parents into political conversations. The importance of political talk is also encountered in the findings of longitudinal cohort studies which suggest that political talk mediates the transmission of civic practices across the life course (Pancer, 2015). As such, the study of political talk has been pursued as a route to understanding children's political socialisation, the latter understood as interpretative reproduction (Corsaro, 1992) in which 'children are not only acted on by adults but [are] also agents of political change and cultural interpretation and change' (Bluebond-Langner & Korbin, 2007).

The research presented in this paper joins existing communicative research in understanding children as active meaning makers and participants in intergenerational political talk. It contributes to the identified lack of knowledge in the phenomenology of political talk (Schmitt-Beck & Lup, 2013) and extends current understandings in two significant ways. Using ethnographic data with children, further contextualised through parental biographical interviews, we make the case that the phenomenology of political talk in childhood is largely idiomatic and performative. At the same time, we argue that what is transmitted across generations is not so much political talk, a noun which suggests the transmission of substantive political knowledge and values, as it is the practice of *talking* politics, as a verb, a collaborative activity between generations. These findings have implications for reconfiguring the social imaginaries of political talk and its transmission, imaginaries which are often unwittingly reproduced in research methodologies that focus exclusively on interviews and focus groups. We address these issues in the discussion section of the paper.

## Encountering political talk

The Connectors Study takes place in two European cities (Athens and London) and one Indian city (Hyderabad). These cities were originally chosen for the different narratives of economic boom and bust that they afforded, and the extent to which their different economic fortunes offered a historical moment in which to think about the relationship between childhood and public life, and an emergence (or not) of social action in childhood. One aim of the study is to extend the evidence base beyond the typical North American and Northern European contexts which underpin a large part of the literature on children's and young people's participation in public life, and to engage in cross-cultural and cross-national conversations in understanding the meanings and practices at the intersections of childhood, activism, and public life. A second aim of the study is to create theory from the bottom up on the relationship between childhood and public life.

To this extent, we did not start the research anticipating to focus on political talk, and indeed the formulation of exploring 'the relationship between childhood and public life' was purposely broad in order to enable a sociological imagination to take root and unfold. In this sense, the emergence of political talk as a fruitful line of inquiry may be likened to the walking practice of creating *desire lines* across urban and rural landscapes. A desire path is the consequence of landscape erosion as walkers veer off the beaten path creating new transit lines across the city and the field. De Certeau (1984) has argued for the link between 'the chorus of idle footsteps' found across the city and the acts of speaking and writing, arguing that 'turns of phrase' can be likened to composing a path (p. 100). Given the study's aims of re-theorising children's participation, the instance of political talk in family life enables us to compose a first path through a large, multimodal data set and to enunciate one of a number of instances in which children may encounter public life.

The family is a highly suitable context for the study of political talk. Survey and interview research on political talk suggests that trust and intimacy, often found in close family and friendship relationships, are necessary for political talk to emerge between people

(Bennett, Flickinger, & Rhine, 2000). Some research suggests that young people find political talk desirable but also dangerous and risky, and so will sometimes avoid it (Ekström, 2016). Where children and young people engage in political talk with significant others they often take an active role in initiating conversations about politics while parents differ in the degree to which they respond and engage with their children's questions (George, 2013). This suggests that children's questions may require parents to educate themselves in order to reply with confidence. The frequency of political talk in everyday life also varies according to levels of confidence and knowledge (Bennett et al., 2000), as well as varying cross-nationally (Schmitt-Beck & Lup, 2013). As such, according to the existing knowledge base, political talk, despite being about highly public issues, appears to be a very private social interaction practiced in the safety of the home and/or the comfort of known and trusted significant others.

The literature on children's encounters with public life, variously described as children's participation and political socialisation, while espousing a perspective of children as active meaning makers has been slow to embrace the idea that younger children are participants of political and cultural change. It is more typical, and historically has been the case (Niemi & Hepburn, 1995), that adolescence is seen as a key moment in the life course for studying young people's political encounters. Yet, as Sapiro (2004) convincingly argues, political and social scientists, we would add, should abandon childhood at their peril. Established literature on identity and social categorisation demonstrate unequivocally that younger children (5–6 years) display the tendencies to respond politically to the world around them as they navigate social-group categories and identities of gender, race, and ethnicity (Bennett & Sani, 2003 cited in Sapiro, 2004; Lloyd & Duveen, 1990), as well as the inequalities and injustices that such differences often entail. At the same time biographies and autobiographies of people who have been civically and politically active, committed to publicly engaging with issues of common concern during their lifetime, suggest that encounters with public life can and do happen early (Andrews, 1997; Nolas et al., 2016). As such, in the Connectors Study we recruited children who were between 5 and 8 years old at the time of joining the study.

A total of 45 children (split more or less equally in terms of gender), and their families, took part in the study. The within-city and between-cities sample captured socio-economic, class, religious, racial, ethnic, and political diversities as relevant to each city. The research also engaged children whose families bring a diversity of experiences to the study in terms of family composition, parental levels of education, parental occupational groups, employment status, parental civic/political engagement, and city geography.

The sub-sample of three ethnographic family histories analysed for this paper was selected for two reasons. Firstly, we observed children experimenting with political talk during our fieldwork which was unprompted by us. Secondly, during parental interviews, when asked, their parents reported that they had grown up with political talk in their families of origin and continued to talk politics with their partner and significant others in the family. As such, political talk was part of family communicative repertoires across generations offering an opportunity to study the phenomenology of political talk as that related to children (a key focus on the study) and to raise questions about what is transmitted across generations (a key theme in the political socialisation literature).

The three families we draw on have a number of commonalities despite their geographical and national-cultural differences. They are all middle class and professional families where both parents work (with one exception). The parents are educated to degree or post-graduate level and there is one advanced degree (PhD) holder in each of the families. All three sets of parents identified as aligned to a greater or lesser extent with progressive politics, and parents demonstrated a high degree of confidence in talking about politics and social issues. In terms of family dynamics participant observation suggested that authoritative and democratic parenting styles were employed by the parents. In this respect, these families can be described as embodying something of the Habermasian ideal of communicative action as a means to negotiate and make family decisions, and of high awareness, and at times direct engagement, with issues of a social and political nature and concern. Other families in the study also fit these broad descriptions but did not indicate a continuity in political talk. We return to this observation in the discussion.

At the same time, there were a number of differences amongst the families which are significant and worth noting. For the family in Athens, it is important to understand that while both parents were politically active in their youth (rally attendances, party memberships), identifying with extreme left groups and political parties, each parent responded to the present historical moment and political situation in Greece differently. Having voted for the current government, 18 months into their administration, Ioulia,[1] the mother, barely concealed her disappointment and anger describing the government as 'traitors'. Conversely Nikos, the father, trying not to be overly pessimistic, would often in conversation identify the positive aspects in the government's policies. For the family in Hyderabad, both parents, Vijaya and Kailash, were actively involved in the separatist Telangana movement which in 2015 resulted in the split of the State of Andhra Pradesh into Andhra Pradesh and the new Indian state of Telangana. The parents described themselves as having been ideologically attracted to each other in their youth, with their partnership itself considered a highly political union in so far as they came from different castes and married against their parents' wishes and prevalent social norms. Vijaya and Kailash regularly organised and attended political gatherings and/or held gatherings in their home which took place in earshot of their daughter, Asha. Finally, the family in London is a European migrant family. Alessandra is from Italy and Manolis is from Greece, although Alessandra grew up in London. In Manolis's family of origin there is a tradition of involvement in local politics. His father was the mayor of the small town the family lived in when Manolis was growing up. Alessandra has been involved in community-related matters such as setting up an Italian speaking playgroup and lobbying the local MP to visit her son's school as a way of bolstering the school's fragile reputation.

Multimodal ethnography (Dicks, Soyinka, & Coffey, 2006) was used in developing the family histories. As well as participant-observation in everyday family life which happened through seven documented visits to each family over an 18-month period, a range of methods were also used to find out more about children's life worlds: playing (introduced by the children in the study), photography, neighbourhood tours and drawing of maps, mapping of significant relationships, biographical interviews (children and parents), and a children's creative workshops. The initial ethnographic fieldwork with children and their families took place between October 2014 and May 2016. Previous research suggests that political talk in everyday life is largely elusive (Schmitt-Beck & Lup, 2013) making it hard to document through participant observation. Our study joins a small number of ethnographic studies on the topic (Eliasoph, 1998; George, 2013) and in the discussion, we will return to the possibilities and limitations of using ethnographic methods in the study of political talk.

## The phenomenology of political talk

Taking up the challenge to shed light on 'the phenomenology of political talk', we draw on an assemblage of cultural theories that focus on peoples' lived experiences and the social practices that emerge in and through everyday day times and spaces. In this paper, we mobilise the interdisciplinary thinking of De Certeau (1984; De Certeau, Giard, & Mayol, 1996) and Seremetakis (1994) whose combined scholarship draws on an impressive and international range of sources to build a picture of everyday life that is both familiar and strange, reproduced at the same time as it is also altered and evaded, and in which meaning is sedimented in objects, gestures, and memories. Here the everyday is both the repository of age-old wisdom, as well as the location of inventiveness. Both approaches are much less cultural *theory*, as they are epistemological approaches for engaging with the rich and messy tapestry of the ordinary through close, empirically driven analysis of everyday life and its narrative production (Nolas, 2014).

In particular, we draw on what in French de Certeau calls *récits*. In French, *récits* refers to a short piece of writing, with just one storyline, real or fictitious, and as a verb (réciter) connotes the telling of a story that relates to the teller alone (e.g. 'le récit de mes vacances', 'le récit de mon enfance').[2] The word *récits* has been translated into English as stories. In Greek, its meaning encompasses the Greek words μύθος (mythos/myth) and the polysemous word ιστορία (istoria) meaning both story and history (Herzfeld, 1991). In several other European languages, the translation of *récits* (German: erzählung; Danish: fortælling) also connotes a relation(ship); while in Telugu the translation is closer to the English stories as well as being used to mean tall tales and excuses.[3] What this means is that *récits* are not just the recounting of a real or imagined event, as the English definition of a story suggests. Instead *récits* are carriers of past and present public and private selves, of history and biography, and of the self's relationships across time.

In this section, we present three such *récits* as each researcher/author encountered them in the field. The *récits* were chosen for their illustrative power of how children encounter, make sense of, and reproduce political talk in their everyday family spaces and times. These are not the only forms of political expression encountered in the fieldwork, but in line with previous research on the topic they are the most recognisable as 'political talk' at the same time as they subvert the very category of political talk through their particular and distinctive 'turns of phrase' (De Certeau, 1984).

### *'I don't believe that the Bermuda triangle is a gateway to other dimensions'*

We start our journey in Athens with brothers Alexandros, aged 7, and Yiannis, aged 5, who live in a middle class suburb in the southeastern region of the Attica basin. Alexandros has a profound interest in mathematics and physics, as well as aspirations of becoming an inventor – when he talks about his microscope his eyes light up. Yannis, his younger brother writes stories and aspires to be an author. Both brothers dislike doing their homework, and their preferred pastime, of watching cartoons and playing videogames, is the source of endless family negotiations in which Alexandros emerges as a skilled negotiator.

During the fourth visit to the family home, Christos found himself present during a political discussion between Alexandros and his brother. At the time of the research in Greece, Syriza, a left-wing party had been in government for about nine months. Following the June 2015 referendum result and the outcome of the negotiations with the IMF and Eurozone for a bailout deal, Syriza called for a new election to be held, in which the party ran on a more centrist agenda.

The conversation below started off with a discussion about family routines which were to be interrupted by the forthcoming elections. The mention of elections offered the siblings an opportunity to extensively discuss the current political scene in Greece. The siblings refract current affairs through religious, scientific, fantasy, and historical discourses as a way of navigating the political, raising ethical questions, and creating a moral order. Their analysis also departs considerably from what 'mama said' suggesting the potential for agency in making sense of politics:

| | |
|---|---|
| **Alexandros**: | There were riots downtown? Yesterday or a few days ago? [He asked the researcher]. |
| **Yannis**: | Yes, because Tsipras quitted. |
| **Alexandros**: | They quited him, he didn't quit. |
| **Yannis**: | Yes, they did, because he started becoming like Samaras. |
| **Alexandros**: | No, that's lies. |
| **Yannis**: | Yes, mama said so too. |
| **Alexandros**: | No, he tried to give money to the people. |
| **Yannis**: | Yes, he did. He is just. I believe he will go to Heaven when he dies |
| **Alexandros**: | Hitler, certainly went to hell. But I don't believe in Hell and in Heaven. And neither do I believe in God, and not in Adam and Eve. |
| **Yannis**: | I think there is Heaven. |
| **Alexandros**: | If there are aliens, why should God be only in our planet? And why in our dimension only, since there are more dimensions? I believe there are more dimensions, but I don't believe that the Bermuda triangle is a gateway to other dimensions. |
| **Yannis**: | I don't believe that too. |
| **Alexandros**: | But there are flying saucers. [he smiled] Tiny, super tiny alien flying saucers: Viruses! |
| **Yannis**: | There are no Aliens, and the infinite is in fact finite! |
| **Alexandros**: | Yes, universe is just a huge milky way, that has an end. |
| **Yannis**: | But, I believe in Jesus, I just don't believe that he was the son of God. |
| **Alexandros**: | He was a man. |
| **Yannis**: | And he will not return on earth. He was just a man who did extraordinary good deeds. |
| **Alexandros**: | He wasn't that good, this is a myth, he was as good as other men are. He was probably fair (δίκαιος/just). But other men are fair, and brave. Kolokotronis was brave, he did good deeds … Tsipras is fair too. Samaras is not fair, he gives most of the money to the Germans and to the rich guys. |
| **Yannis**: | It would be fair [Samaras] to die, I could kill him. |
| **Alexandros**: | No, it wouldn't be fair. |
| **Yannis**: | No. |
| **Alexandros**: | And Germany must take back all the money we owe them. But we don't owe them that much as they say we do! |

**Figure 1.** Photograph taken by Alexandros (6 June 2015) as part of the visual methods brief of taking pictures of 'things that matter to me'.

**Yannis**:      In the referendum, everybody voted No, which meant to not pay the Germans. But nothing happened, and the money [in Greece] didn't finish [run out] after all.

**Alexandros**:   No country can go bankrupt, ever. Because all the money are circulated in all countries. Except Africa. (Dialogue reconstructed from fieldnotes, Athens, 18 September 2015)

The issues raised by this exchange capture a number of ongoing preoccupations for Alexandros and Yannis, who regularly try to make sense of social inequalities as they encounter these in their environment. For example, Alexandros often talks to Christos about money with a sophisticated understanding of the economic dimensions of consumption, production, exchange, and capital. Similarly, the imaginary aspects, the metaphysical concerns, the economy, and the modern-day politics are all themes that surfaced and re-surfaced in Christos's discussions with the two brothers (Figure 1). Discussions around these issues are quite characteristic of the talk within this family, as Christos has experienced it. Finally, as previously mentioned, Alexandros's and Nikos's parents hold different views about the current political situation. As such, the family discursive repertoires vis-à-vis current political realities could be described as oscillating between hope and despair (Hoggett & Randall, 2016). This oscillation is reflected in the boys' dialogue as they improvise off each other never quite settling on one position or another.

### 'Kondalu Pagalesinaam'/'we break the hills'

The next récit comes from Asha, aged 6, who lives on one of Hyderabad's university campuses with her parents. Asha likes outdoor play, and regularly watches cartoon programmes. She is passionate about drawing and likes to watch films on television. Her parents, in line with contemporary popular beliefs about the negative relationship between screen time and childhood, discourage her from doing so. Asha is inspired by her father to write Telugu poems and, at one point during the fieldwork, wrote a four-line poem for Vinnarasan and our local researcher Madhavi Latha, entitled 'Peacock'. She aspires to become an Indian Administrative Officer, a top ranking civil servant in order to serve people, an echo of an earlier dream her father harboured for himself.

Data collection took place following the May 2014 elections in which the right-wing Bharatiya Janata Party (BJP) swept to power nationally, and the Telangana Rashtra Samithi (TRS) regional political party, which spearheaded the Telangana Movement for more than a decade, formed the maiden government in Telangana.

During visits to the family, Vinnarasan often heard political discussions take place between Asha's father and visitors, many within earshot of Asha. During the first visit to the family, Asha wanted to accompany her father to a school function where he was invited to give a talk. Discussing other times when she had accompanied her father to public events, Asha recounted her recent attendance at a meeting to commemorate the anniversary of Indian social reformer B. R. Ambedkar's birth during which the organisers screened a documentary about his life. Asha informed Vinnarasan that she has also watched on-campus screenings of documentaries on revolutionaries Bhagat Singh and Che Guevara, noting that she was the only child in the room. During another field visit, Asha tells Vinnarasan that she likes accompanying her parents to meetings because she can play in a different place, and besides the food is always good.

In the fourth field visit to the family, Asha wanted to share with the researchers her experiences of revolutionary songs encountered at a political event she had attended. She explained to the researchers that she had accompanied her parents to a political event in the auditorium during where she sang a particular song which she then, without much encouragement, went on to perform for the researchers:

| | |
|---|---|
| **Vinnarsan**: | How do you know the song, whose choice is that? |
| **Asha**: | Nana (father), he taught us the song. |
| **Madhavi**: | Do you still remember the entire song? |
| **Asha**: | Yes! Asha responds and begins singing the song that starts with *kondalu pagalesinaam/we break the hills* …. When she's finished Vinnarasan asks her; |
| **Vinnarsan**: | Do you know the meaning of the song? |
| **Asha**: | No, I just by-heart the song. |
| **Madhavi**: | What was the response you got after singing the song? |
| **Asha**: | They clapped. |
| **Vinnarsan**: | Do you know or understand what people [adults] spoke on that day in the meeting? |
| **Asha**: | Hu hum [meaning no]. I have seen some banners in Telugu but I don't know what they are for. [She said she can read Telugu but she is not good at it as English is the first language in her school]. (Dialogue reconstructed from fieldnotes, 7 November 2015). |

*Kondalu pagalesinaam/we break the hills* is a song about worker's plight that talks about the lived experiences of toiling the land, the labour of production, and the eventual revolution. The song was composed by Gummadi Vittal Rao, popularly known as 'Gaddar', a revolutionary poet singer who emerged as a powerful and popular cultural icon of post-independence India. Gaddar's songs express the struggles of Indian society, and especially of Telugu society. The song has four stanzas and Asha sings the complete song without fumbling. In recounting where she encountered the song, Asha was specific about the date of the meeting and her demeanour with the researchers communicated elation about her experiences on that day and her ability to perform *Kondalu pagalesinaam* for them.

### A game of voting: 'maybe my dad couldn't live in the United States'

Finally, in a north London neighbourhood on a broad, tree-lined street with terraced housing we meet Alessio, aged 6. Alessio is fascinated by videogames and takes an active interest in the word around him. He also takes a keen interest in the study and from the outset asked Melissa many pertinent and probing questions that scrutinised the study design and his involvement.

The fieldwork described below takes place a month after the 7 May 2015 General Election in the United Kingdom that dissolved the Conservative-Liberal Democrat Coalition government which had been in power from May 2010, giving way to an outright, and unexpected, Conservative majority. Asked about national or international news that has resonated over the last 12 months at the time of the biographical interviews (March 2016), both parents talked at length about being moved by the refugee crisis, and financially supporting relief organisations, as well as exploring their concerns about the upcoming referendum on the UK's EU membership.

During the second visit to the family, Melissa spent the day with Alessio which included going to Italian school with him and then to a children's play in the afternoon. After lunch, and as they waited to leave the house for the theatre, Alessio invents a game which makes little sense at the time. Alessio explains that this is a made-up game of 'voting'. He takes the scrabble pieces and throws them up in the air. Once they have landed he selects the ones that are either face up or face down (this changes each time) and tells Melissa they are 'candidates'. The game goes on for a good 20 minutes in which scrabble pieces are tossed up in the air, sorted, and tossed up again, until there is only one piece left. Melissa remembers watching from the sidelines in bemusement, taking a few photographs, and reflecting on her ineptitude at making sense of what she was observing:

> After we've played noughts and crosses a number of times Alessio wanders over to the box of
> toys as if looking for something else to play. He takes out a banana pouch containing lots of

**Figure 2.** Photograph taken by Sevasti-Melissa Nolas of Alessio playing his 'voting game'.

scrabble pieces. We play a made-up game of 'voting' using the scrabble tiles. We had to throw them up in the air, the ones that landed face up/letter up could be 'candidates'. In the end, we took all the tiles and put them in two long lines. Alessio walked between the tiles and those tiles that didn't get disrupted could be voted for. In the end the letter A tile won. I didn't quite understand this game, other than it's fun to throw tiles in the air and to separate and sort tiles. I recognise this as a 'homegrown' game a bit like Eleanor's [another child in the study] button game. I also thought it was interesting that Alessio called it a voting game, though not sure I could draw any significance from that at this point. (fieldnotes, London, 6 June 2015) (Figure 2)

Nine months later in March 2016, Melissa interviews Alessio. During the interview, she asks him if there is anything that has happened recently that he considers to be unfair. Alessio starts to talk about the UK referendum on EU membership. He worries that his father, who does not hold a British passport, may not be allowed to stay in the country, 'Maybe Daddy, my Dad would not live in the United States. You know that voting thing?' (child biographical interview, London, 21 March 2016). Brexit is a recurrent topic of conversation in the family, and a topic that was discussed at length in both parental interviews. Manolis had told Melissa that he had spent some time explaining Brexit to Alessio in 'how do you say, a neutral way' and that 'as usual, as Alessio does, he doesn't answer anything, he takes it and then he comes to me after a couple of weeks. He always does that' (father biographical interview, 3 March 2016). While Alessio's comments contain inaccuracies (e.g. USA instead of UK) the exchange mirrors a number of public debates and concerns pre- and post-referendum regarding European citizens' right to remain in the UK and the freedom of movement of people across Europe.

## Talking politics in everyday family lives

Our encounters above echo findings in the emerging body of qualitative literature cited earlier that suggests that children can be initiators of political talk. As Nikos, Alexandros's father, also observes: 'of course, they ask, it makes sense, if they ask you have to respond' (Nikos, biographical interview, Athens). At the same time, children's political talk, at least in the ways we encountered it, brings something of the uncanny (Highmore, 2002) into our understanding of how talking politics happens in everyday family life. Our experience was that children's 'political talk' was largely idiomatic and did not, on first hearing, conform to received notions of the political even when children were talking about institutional politics as in the examples above.

In both the Athens and London excerpts, we find current events refracted through other familiar *récits* and everyday objects. A host of deeply gendered and racialised human, non-human, and abstract characters (God, Adam and Eve, Kolokotronis, Samaras, Jesus, Tsipras, the Germans, aliens, Africa) are mobilised as part of a series of complex plotlines (morality, religion, cosmology, and nationalism) and complicating actions (Bermuda triangle, riots, death, voting) with everyday objects (scrabble pieces) deployed as props. It took several months to start to imagine Alessio's scrabble voting game as a meaningful activity. In Hyderabad, by contrast, we find that Asha's performance of a political song taps into 'cultures of memories' (Rao, 2014) that bring together regional and political traditions of cultural transmission (Kaplan & Shapiro, 1998; Muthukumaras-wamy & Kaushal, 2004; Seymour, 2006). In embracing both the ordinary and the strange, children's practices of talking politics serve to de-familiarise our social imaginaries of political talk and to introduce an everyday aesthetic (Highmore, 2002) into our understanding of talking politics in family life. As de Certeau argues, narration (*réciter*) by way of the past and by way of quotation, provides a detour that serves to disrupt established ways of knowing and doing. All *récits* presented served to disrupt children's everyday activities (playing, talking, waiting) as well as disrupting scholarly ideas of political socialisation in which reproduction happens without mediation and change, and in which conversation is orderly.

Social imaginaries of communication in general and political talk in particular continue to rest on an idealised and exclusive notion of conversation as carried out in cafes and parlours, amongst seated adult men engaged in turn-taking conversation (cf. Habermas, 1981/1984). Children's political talk jolts such imaginaries enmeshed as it is in other activities, occurring as it does without prelude or postscript, and embedded as it is in motion and commotion. For example, one should not imagine the exchange between Alexandros and Nikos as taking place between two seated and perfectly concentrated-in-the-act-of-dialogue children. The brothers were entirely mobile throughout the duration of the short exchange. Alexandros was playing with the head of a Lego figure as he was talking and Yannis was walking along the back of the sofa, a tight rope walker in the middle of a balancing act. The exchange was preceded by play, and gradually dissolved into play once again. In Hyderabad, Asha burst into song largely unprompted by the researchers. The performance took place in the middle of a conversation where Vinnarasan and Madhavi had been asking Asha about changes in her life since they had last seen her five months previously. The researchers and Asha had been sitting on a wooden sofa for the interview, when Asha stood up with gusto, and performed the song. Finally, a child's constant sweeping movements across the living room floor as he roamed the perimeter of the carpet sorting and collecting scrabble pieces that were repeatedly tossed up in the air and fell undeterred to the floor punctuated Alessio's rendition of talking politics.

Parental interviews and our own participant observation further develop a sensory appreciation of the times and places of political talk within everyday family life. The London excerpt of Alessio playing voting-scrabble took place on a Saturday afternoon, post-lunch, and in-between organised activities, Italian school in the morning and a visit to a children's theatre performance in the afternoon. It suggests that spaces in which children might talk politics are largely unstructured, and lurk on the edge of adult activities: Alessio's parents were sorting the clean laundry as he played. At the same time, all three sets of parents, in their separate interviews, invoked more communal family spaces and times, such as the kitchen table and meal times, in their descriptions of political talk in their families of origin and in their current families. Their descriptions of political talk reinforced the idea, also captured by survey research, that political talk emerges in intimate, safe, everyday informal environments. Here the phenomenology of political talk differs for parents and children but is not unrelated. While adults may be sitting around a table 'talking in very loud voices with their friends over dinner about politics' (Alessandra, London), children might on occasions 'be sitting along with us' (Kailash, Hyderabad) or 'they've eaten, they're watching TV' in the background while parents 'end up talking politics' (Ioulia, Athens).[4] Such overlapping adult-child spaces give children the opportunity to both tune-in and tune-out of political talk as necessary and in response to their own playful activities.

These observations about the phenomenology of talking politics in everyday life lead us to suggest that what is transmitted across generations is not necessarily the substance of political talk as much as it is its practice. In her biographical interview, Ioulia describes at length how she would have 'clashes' with her own father as a teenager over their opposing political views. But the term 'clashes' did not carry a negative connotation for her. Instead it was a valued conversational (discursive) practice which she continued in her own family. Similarly, Kailash talks about the intertwining of family and regional histories of involvement in the labour movement which he credits for his own biographical 'habit of participating' (Kailash, biographical interview, Hyderabad) in progressive social change (cf. Andrews, this issue; Pedwell, 2017).

In particular, through the exploration of the phenomenology of political talk we start to see a sonic landscape of multiple and overlapping past and present voices (grandparents, parents, children, the television, researchers) in which talking politics might unfold in everyday life. The practice of talking politics is mediated by both the mundane and ordinary (playing on a Saturday afternoon), as well as by other family practices of communion and commensality. Of eating together, Giard (1996) and Seremetakis (1994) have both argued that sensory acculturation and the materialisation of historical consciousness occur through the preparation and consumption of food in families. Enmeshed as talking politics is in these practices of remembering and feeling together, political talk is not just a way of encountering public life in the private sphere. Evoking the full multilingual meaning of Michel de Certeau's term *récit*, it is also a way of relating and of creating relationships (Ekström, 2016) between past and present selves, current interlocutors, orators, and audiences.

## Conclusion

The paper has theorised encounters between childhood and public life through the phenomenon of talking politics in family life. We have argued for a view of political talk as a social practice that is embedded in everyday times and spaces and in which meaning is sedimented in objects, gestures, and memories. In this sense, children's political socialisation, to use the language of the political science literature, and the transmission of political cultures across generations is an embodied, sensory experience mediated by particular *récits* that are both familiar and strange, in which biography and history become sedimented at the same time as the telling of stories disrupts taken for granted meanings (De Certeau, 1984).

The analysis has implications for how we understand continuity and change in practices (Shove, Pantzar, & Watson, 2012) of talking politics across generations. It has been argued that theories of childhood are overly reliant on cognitive, conceptual, and rational models of an idealised form of communication that ignores the everyday, embodied, and lived experiences of 'sentiment devices' (Oswell, 2012), or idioms, of childhood. In this paper, we have engaged with childhood idioms as those relate to talking politics and with the absurdist, imaginative, playful, and repetitive social interaction that the children shared with us.

These ethnographically generated observations have implications for future research on talking politics in family life and other social milieus characterised by high degrees of trust (e.g. close and old friendships). The data, and their analysis, trouble the ways in which 'political talk' has been imagined and reproduced in research studies to date

(Bhavnani, 1990; Ekström, 2016; Stevens, 1982). Idealised social imaginaries of political talk and its transmission are unwittingly reproduced in research methodologies that focus exclusively on interviews and focus groups. Future research will need to think creatively about the possibilities of spending time and building trusting relationships with interlocutors, young and old, in the field. It is our experience that such investment, while resource intensive, pays off empirically in generating rich data that takes us beyond the idea of political conversation, especially in childhood, as a sit-down, turn taking, quiet and polite activity.

Finally, it is worth remembering that this paper only focused on a small number of families who reported continuity of talking politics across generations, and whose initial definitions of politics aligned with an institutional understanding of the political. Further analysis will explore discontinuities in the practices of talking politics across generations as well as inventions of traditions of talking politics where those were not experienced in families of origin – both further patterns in the overall sample. Equally, subsequent analysis will also need to explore the full breadth of the meaning of the political in families' everyday lives, what matters to children and parents and their relationships of concern to the world (Sayer, 2010), and how differences in socio-economic experiences intersect with children's experiences of encountering public life in everyday familial contexts.

## Notes

1. All names appearing in this manuscript are pseudonyms.
2. Holiday stories, childhood stories; with thanks to Louisa Zanoun for the semantic clarifications.
3. With thanks to Madhavi Latha for her assistance with this translation.
4. All quoted texts are from parental biographical interviews.

## Acknowledgements

The authors would like to thank the anonymous reviewer and Charles Watters for their feedback on earlier drafts of the paper.

## Disclosure statement

No potential conflict of interest was reported by the authors.

## Funding

The research was supported by a European Research Council Starting Grant [ERC-StG-335514] to Sevasti-Melissa Nolas.

# References

Almond, G. A., & Verba, S. (1963). *The civic culture: Political attitudes and democracy in five nations.* Princeton, NJ: Princeton University Press.

Andrews, M. (1997). *Lifetimes of commitment: Aging, politics, psychology.* Cambridge: Cambridge University Press.

Bennett, S. E., Flickinger, R. S., & Rhine, S. L. (2000). Political talk over here, over there, over time. *British Journal of Political Science, 30*(1), 99–119.

Bhavnani, K. K. (1990). *Talking politics: A psychological framing for views from youth in Britain.* Cambridge: Cambridge University Press.

Bluebond-Langner, M., & Korbin, J. E. (2007). Challenges and opportunities in the anthropology of childhoods: An introduction to 'children, childhood and childhood studies'. *American Anthropologist, 109*(2), 241–246.

Buckingham, D. (1999). Young people, politics and news media: Beyond political socialisation. *Oxford Review of Education, 25*(1/2), 171–184.

Corsaro, W. (1992). Interpretive reproduction in children's peer cultures. *Social Psychology Quarterly, 55*, 160–177.

De Certeau, M. (1984). *The practice of everyday life.* Chicago, IL: University of Chicago Press.

De Certeau, M., Giard, L., & Mayol, P. (1996). *The practice of everyday life (Volume 2: Living & Cooking).* Chicago, IL: University of Chicago Press.

Dicks, B., Soyinka, B., & Coffey, A. (2006). Multimodal ethnography. *Qualitative Research, 6*(1), 77–96.

Dinas, E. (2013). 'Opening "openness to change": Political events and the increased sensitivity of young adults'. *Political Research Quarterly, 66*(4), 868–882.

Ekström, M. (2016). Young people's everyday political talk: A social achievement of democratic engagement. *Journal of Youth Studies, 19*(1), 1–19.

Eliasoph, N. (1998). *Avoiding politics: How Americans produce apathy in everyday life.* Cambridge: Cambridge University Press.

Freud, A. (1966). *Normality and pathology in childhood: Assessments of development.* Hampstead: Karnac Books.

George, R. (2013). 'What's a vendetta?' Political socialization in the everyday interactions of Los Angeles families. *Discourse & Society, 24*(1), 46–65.

Giard, L. (1996). Part II: Doing-cooking. In M. De Certeau, L. Giard, & P. Mayol (Eds.), *The practice of everyday life (Volume 2: Living & Cooking)* (pp. 151–246). Chicago, IL: University of Chicago Press.

Habermas, J. (1981/1984). *Theory of communicative action, volume one: Reason and the rationalization of society* (Book). (Thomas A. McCarthy, Trans.). Boston, MA: Beacon Press.

Hardman, C. (1973). Can there be an anthropology of children? *Journal of the Anthropological Society Oxford, 4*(1), 85–99.

Herzfeld, M. (1991). *A place in history: Monumental and social time in a cretan town.* Princeton, NJ: Princeton University Press.

Highmore, B. (2002). *Everyday life and cultural theory: An introduction.* London: Routledge.

Hoggett, P., & Randall, R. (2016, December 12). Sustainable activism: managing hope and despair in social movements. *Open Democracy*. Retrieved April 19, 2017, from https://www.opendemocracy.net/transformation/paul-hoggett-rosemary-randall/sustainable-activism-managing-hope-and-despair-in-socia

Hyman, H. H. (1959). *Political socialization: A study in the psychology of political behaviour*. Glencoe, IL: Free Press.

James, A., & Prout, A. (1990). *Constructing and reconstructing childhood: Contemporary issues in the sociological study of childhood*. London: Routledge.

Kaplan, J., & Shapiro, L. (Eds.). (1998). *Red diapers: Growing up in the communist left*. Urbana: University of Illinois Press.

Lloyd, B., & Duveen, G. (1990). A semiotic analysis of the development of social representations of gender. In G. Duveen & B. Lloyd (Eds.), *Social representations and the development of knowledge* (pp. 27–46). Cambridge: Cambridge University Press.

Marsh, D. (1971). Political socialisation: The implicit assumptions questioned. *British Journal of Political Science*, *1*(4), 453–465.

McDevitt, M., & Chaffee, S. (2002). From top-down to trickle-up influence: Revisiting assumptions about the family in political socialisation. *Political Communication*, *19*(3), 281–301.

Mead, G. H. (1934). *Mind, self and society*. Chicago, IL: University of Chicago Press.

Moran-Ellis, J., & Sünker, H. (2008). Giving children a voice: Childhood, power and culture. In J. Houtsonen & A. Antikainen (Eds.), *Symbolic power in cultural contexts: Uncovering social reality* (pp. 67–83). Rotterdam: Sense Publishers.

Muthukumaraswamy, M. D., & Kaushal, M. (2004). *Folklore, public sphere, and civil society*. New Delhi: Indira Gandhi National Centre for the Arts.

Niemi, R. G., & Hepburn, M. A. (1995). The rebirth of political socialisation. *Perspectives on Political Science*, *24*(1), 7–16.

Niemi, R. G., & Sobieszek, B. I. (1977). Political socialisation. *Annual Review of Sociology*, *3*(1), 209–233.

Nolas, S.-M. (2014). Towards a new theory of practice for community health psychology. *Journal of Health Psychology*, *19*(1), 126–136.

Nolas, S.-M. (2015). Children's participation, childhood publics, and social change: A review. *Children & Society*, *29*(2), 157–167.

Nolas, S.-M., Varvantakis, C., & Aruldoss, V. (2016). (Im)possible conversations? Activism, childhood and everyday life. *Journal of Social and Political Psychology*, *4*(1), 252–265.

Ojeda, C., & Hatemi, P. K. (2015). Accounting for the child in the transmission of party identification. *American Sociological Review*, *80*(6), 1150–1174.

Oswell, D. (2012). *The agency of children: From family to global human rights*. Cambridge: Cambridge University Press.

Pancer, S. M. (2015). *The psychology of citizenship and civic engagement*. Oxford: Oxford University Press.

Pedwell, C. (2017). Transforming habit: Revolution, routine and social change. *Cultural Studies*, *31*(1), 93–120.

Rao, D. V. (2014). *Cultures of memory in South Asia: Orality, literacy and the problem of inheritance*. New Delhi: Springer.

Sapiro, V. (2004). Not your parents' socialisation: Introduction for a new generation. *Annual Review of Political Science*, *7*(1), 1–23.

Sayer, A. (2010). *Why things matter to people: Social science, values and ethical life*. Cambridge: Cambridge University Press.

Schmitt-Beck, R., & Lup, O. (2013). Seeking the soul of democracy: A review of recent research into citizens' political talk culture. *Swiss Political Science Review*, *19*(4), 513–538.

Seremetakis, C. N. (1994). The memory of the senses, Part II: Still acts. In N. Seremetakis (Ed.), *The senses still: Perception and memory as material culture in modernity* (pp. 23–43). Chicago: University of Chicago Press.

Seymour, S. (2006). Resistance. *Anthropological Theory*, *6*(3), 303–321.

Shove, E., Pantzar, M., & Watson, M. (2012). *The dynamics of social practice: everyday life and how it changes*. London: Sage.

Stevens, O. (1982). *Children talking politics: Political learning in childhood*. Oxford: Martin Robertson.

# Digital citizens? Data traces and family life

Veronica Barassi

**ABSTRACT**

In the last decades, different scholars have focused on how political participation has been transformed by digital media. Although insightful, current research in the field lacks a critical understanding of the personal and affective dimension of online political participation. This paper aims to address this gap by looking at the interconnection between digital storytelling, identity narratives and family life. Drawing on an ethnographic research, the paper shows that activists construct their political identities online through complex practices of digital storytelling that involve the reinterpretation of early childhood and family life. These processes of digital storytelling have an un-intended consequence: they enable the political profiling of different family members. The paper argues that these digital practices, which produce politically identifying digital traces, are transforming political socialisation in family life and introducing new ways in which we can think digital citizenship across the life course.

## Introduction

Over the last 10 years, the relationship between digital technologies and political participation has been a key area of research. Scholars questioned and analysed the different ways in which political activists were appropriating and using digital technologies to organise and partake in collective actions and mass protests (Barassi, 2015; Barassi & Treré, 2012; Cammaerts, Mattoni, & Mccurdy, 2013; Castells, 2012; Gerbaudo, 2012; Kavada, 2015; Mattoni, 2012; Postill, 2014; Wolfson, 2014). They also investigated the complex relationship between technological affordances and the emergence of new political repertoires of protest (Gerbaudo, 2012; Wolfson, 2014). Current research in the field of digital activism is of central importance as it highlights the fact that political participation and civic engagement have been radically transformed by digital technologies. Yet, what is missing from this body of literature is an attention towards the personal and affective dimension of online political participation.

This paper position itself within the field of media anthropology (Askew & Wilk, 2002; Brauchler & Postill, 2010; Ginsburg, Abu-Lughold, & Larkin, 2002) and argues that scholars have much to gain if they start reflecting not only on the relationship between political participation and digital storytelling, but also on how activists' online identity narratives are tightly interconnected to family life. Drawing on a comparative ethnography amongst activists in Italy, the UK and Spain, the paper will show that activists construct their political identities online through complex practices of digital storytelling that involve a political appropriation and reinterpretation of early childhood and family life. These practices of self-construction through digital storytelling, it will be shown, enable the political profiling of different family members, including children. Acknowledging these micro-practices can enable us to appreciate not only that political socialisation in family life is being transformed by digital practices but also that these digital practices are transforming current understandings of digital participation and digital citizenship. The argument will be structured as follows. In the first part of the paper, I will explore the role family life plays in the construction of activists' identity narratives. In the second part of the paper I will proceed to explore how digital storytelling within the family is introducing new ways in which we can re-think digital participation.

## Identity narratives, family life and the everyday construction of political subjects

### Political socialisation and family life: the problem of cognitive models of value transmission

On a winter day in 2007, I was interviewing Katie[1], who at the time was in her mid-30s and had been involved with the British Trade Union Movement since she was in her early 20s. We sat down for a long chat about her understanding of British politics and about her experience of the relationship between media technologies and political participation, which was the direct focus of my research. During the interview Katie talked about her middle-class upbringing, and told me that from a very early age she identified with working class struggles and the Labour movement:

> [When I was a young girl] I asked my father what was the difference between the higher classes and the working classes, and he replied that an easy way to think about it was by looking at the difference between the Sheriff of Nottingham and Robin Hood. Since then, I knew on which side to stand.

The research with Katie and the British Trade Union Movement was part of a much larger research project, which took place between 2007 and 2013, and which consisted in a cross-cultural ethnographic analysis of three different activist groups. After working with Katie's political organisation, which was involved in the Labour movement in the UK, I carried out research with two other organisations: one embedded with the Italian Autonomous movement and one with the Spanish Environmental movement. My research was largely influenced by the field of media anthropology (Askew & Wilk, 2002; Ginsburg et al., 2002; Brauchler & Postill, 2010). As argued elsewhere (Barassi, 2015) the field of media anthropology distinguishes itself for three main reasons. In the first instance, it draws on the ethnography of media to understand how people negotiate with communication technologies. Subsequently, it is defined by scholars' commitment to theorise and understand media as everyday practice and as social processes (not merely as text, technologies or organisational structures). Finally, it challenges ethno-centric and techno-deterministic understandings of media's social impacts by looking at cultural variation. It was for this reason that I decided to investigate how three largely progressive and left-wing political groups, which came from very different political cultures, related to web technologies. I was especially interested in the ways in which they dealt with issues of online identity construction and with the surveillance of the data they produced (Barassi, 2015).

Since the very early days of my research work, as Katie's interview shows, I had to come to terms with the ways in which activists understood and defined their political identity in relation to family life. This finding was of course not new. In the last 50 years, within the social sciences, different studies have argued that political beliefs are transmitted and constructed within family life (Acock & Bengtson, 1978; Baker, 1974; Connell, 1972; Hess, Torney-Purta, & Valsiner, 2005; Jennings, 1984; Liebes & Ribak, 1992). Departing from different disciplinary traditions, these works were based on a variety of methodologies, which span from the use of qualitative interviews with children and parents (Connell, 1972; Liebes & Ribak, 1992) to large-scale national surveys amongst children in school age (Hess et al., 2005). In recent years we have seen the emergence of new works in the field, which drew from the earlier insights on children and political socialisation to explore the discursive construction of party politics in family life (Gordon, 2007) or the relationship between environmental activism and family values (Pettifor, 2012). All these works are of fundamental importance. It is in this body of literature that we can start appreciating how political socialisation is tightly interconnected to family life, and shed light on the fact that the political values of the family are the first cues that children learn in the shaping of their own political beliefs.

Although insightful in highlighting critical questions about political socialisation, these works remain, however, only marginally important in the study of the lived experience of political activism. Part of the problem lies in the fact that this literature focuses too much on the cognitive/rational dimension of political formation. By investigating the way in which political participation is shaped by values and beliefs, these scholars explore how political values are transmitted through the family.

There is no doubt that one important dimension of the making of political subjects needs to be found in political values and beliefs, and the way in which activists develop a sense of social justice that it constructed within the family. My interview with Katie revealed precisely that: Katie had developed her own political values following the teachings learned from her father. However, my own research also revealed that there is much more to 'the making of political subjects' in family life, which has less to say about the transmission of 'political values' from parents to children, and more to say about the very subjective and affective dimension of 'being political' (Fenton, 2016). Of course, the study of the 'affective dimension' of political participation involves acknowledging the complexity of emotions that are triggered by one's own sense of the political. These include anger, solidarity, nostalgia, fear and many other different emotions, which could lead to very different political consequences. When talking about the 'affective dimension' of political participation, the aim of this paper is not to shed light on the complexities of political emotions or their consequences. Rather the aim of this paper is to highlight how political identities are often constructed through affective processes of meaning construction in relation to early childhood and family life. The paper will thus show not only that political identities are tightly interconnected to the construction of biographical narratives that emerge within the family (Nolas, Varvantakis, & Aruldoss, 2016) but also how these biographical narratives are shaped by messy and affective processes of storytelling.

### Identity narratives and family life

The relationship between political identity, biographical experiences and narrative construction was a key element of my research design. My own research methods were influenced by the belief that one particular problem of ethnographic research relates to the fact that – as DeWalt and DeWalt (2002) mentioned – with participant observation alone it is unlikely that the ethnographer will gain historical depth. Hence I enriched my ethnographic work with 87 semi-structured interviews, which were all based on the *life history* method (Alleyne, 2000; Hastrup & Davis, 1992). My intention was to understand activists' biographical experience and path to political involvement, and to explore the way in which they experienced technological change. The choice of focusing on activists' life narratives was motivated by the belief that the *life histories* approach in the study of activism is particularly important, as it can provide the researcher not only with a historical dimension, but also with insights concerning the way in which people internalise *collective repertoires* of the past (Tilly, 1994, p. 244).

It was thanks to the life history method that I collected a variety of testimonies that highlighted the social complexities that define the relationship between family life, political identity construction and biographical narratives. Over and over again when asked to explain how they became politically involved, the activists I interviewed not only mentioned the importance of family life in their political development, but also seemed to assume that the connection between one's own family life and political identity was inevitable. One day in 2011, I sat down for an interview with Marta[2] in the garden of the 'Autonomous Zone Milan' (Zona Autonoma Milanese). Marta, who was in her late 20s, described her path to political involvement, departing from her family:

> My father was a trade unionist, my mother a politically engaged teacher. I grew up feeling politics, breathing politics, and believing that politics is not about parties, and institutions but rather about social experience and commitment. If you look at my family, and my past, it's obvious why I am politically engaged.

Marta's interview was interesting, as it highlighted the fact that 'being political' – as Fenton (2016) rightly argues – does not only relate to rational political values, but it is a complex experiential process defined by an affective dimension. Marta, in fact, did not share the same political values of her family. In contrast to her father who was a Trade Unionist, she identified much more with forms of grassroots politics, and she was deeply influenced by the autonomists and anarchist discourses that emerged during the global justice movements in the 1990s (Day, 2005; Holloway, 2002). However, she believed that she had inherited from her family a 'sense of the political' and she constructed her political identity through a complex biographical narrative, which started precisely from that 'feeling of the political' acquired during childhood. In order to investigate the affective role family life plays in the construction of one's political identity, therefore, we need to appreciate the intricate interstices of biographical narratives and political identity construction.

Here the concept of 'political identity' as discussed in the anthropology of social movements (Escobar, 2004; Pratt, 2003) is particularly insightful. According to Escobar political identity needs to be detached from fixed notions of 'identity politics' that dominate early social movements research, and instead needs to be understood as a relational concept, a concept which defines both self-consciousness and participation to communities of imagination and practice (Escobar, 2004). Identity is, therefore, not something carried as a definer of the individual, but a process of self-imagination, which is constantly constructed through the everyday practice in the encounter of groups (Escobar, 2004, p. 252).

This process of self-imagination and identity construction is tightly interconnected to the process of storytelling. In the anthropology of social movements, Pratt (2003) was perhaps one of the first to highlight this relationship. He argued that in the study of social movements and political activism, we have much to gain if we approach the understanding of identity as *narrative* and appreciate how this narrative develops on two different, albeit interconnected, axes. On the one hand, identity narratives are constructed through the *hierarchical axis*, which suggests who 'we' are, through opposition and the creation of the *other*. On the other hand, identity narratives are constructed through the *biographical axis*, which establishes who people are through the medium of time (2003, p. 10). The biographical axis is thus the process whereby activists, like Marta or Katie, construct themselves by reflecting on their experience of the political since early childhood.

In Pratt's (2003) work, therefore, it becomes clear that biographical narratives, which emerge within the family, are a fundamental aspect of political identity. Yet within the social movements literature there is little exploration of this relationship. Most of the works on political identities focus on the *hierarchical axis* of identity narratives, hence on the multiple ways in which activists define their sense of belonging to a group in opposition to 'other' groups. The works of Alleyene on black activists (2000) and of Nolas et al. (2016) constitute perhaps the major exceptions to this trend. In fact, within their work the scholars insightfully explore the lived experience of activism, by looking at the interconnection between family life and biographical narratives.

### Identity narratives and family life: identification, distancing and social tensions

One particular element that emerges in the work of scholars like Alleyne (2000) or Nolas et al. (2016) is the understanding that identity narratives are a product of social tensions and personal contradictions. Identity narratives are problematic and messy; they relate to how activists understand the influence of early childhood and family life. At the same time these narratives are shaped by activists' perception of a wide variety of political cues that emerge in their encounter with others throughout their life. These cues can be drawn from their experience of the historic and political context, the institutions they cohabit or the lived experience of specific – and often traumatic – political events.

During my research amongst the Autonomous group in Italy, for instance, all these different dimensions came into life as activists discussed their life histories in relation to their political development. What surprised me was the fact that activists' identity narratives were often very similar. In fact, after discussing the influence family life played in the shaping of their political selves, they would reflect on the social injustice they felt as they were growing up within an Italian political context, whose democratic promise had been hacked by the neoliberal and hegemonic monopoly of Silvio Berlusconi. They also talked about the first political experiences within 'institutional' settings such as high-school and universities or recalled traumatic experiences – such as the police brutality of the Genoa 2001 G8 demonstrations. Consequently, activists referred to different political experiences and social contexts when defining themselves politically, which included and situated family life within a broader political-historic context.

The understanding that identity narratives are shaped by messy and complex processes of narrative construction – which not only bring together elements of family life with other key social experiences but also include forms of self-recognition and self-distancing from specific relationships – shares some similarities with Hegel's understanding of the making of political identities. As Moland (2011) has suggested, Hegel believed that political identity develops from within the family and within civil society. He also argued that if we look at the role of the family in processes of identity construction we need to appreciate the fact that individuals develop the capacity to decide, which inherited traits or qualities they want to endorse (2011, p. 37). Therefore, in order to understand the complexity of the making of political subjects we need to take into account how activists continuously shape their identity narratives through open-ended processes of approximation and distancing from the political values learned in the family as they reflect on these values in relation to other values and social experiences learned through civic engagement.

These open-ended and complex processes of self-construction are not linear, rational and conscious, but rather are affective and contradictory. Once we understand this complexity, we can turn our attention to an important transformation that is impacting on family life at the moment: the rapid proliferation of digital storytelling practices and the everyday construction of political identities online. The next part of the paper will thus explore the nuances and complexities of these processes and will argue that scholars have much to gain if they turn their attention on how digital storytelling within family life is raising new questions about digital participation and the making of digital citizens.

## Digital storytelling: between self-construction and the political profiling of others

### Digital activism and the construction of the online political self

In understanding the relationship between political identities, digital storytelling and biographical narratives we are faced with two fundamental problems. On the one hand, within the study of digital activism different scholars have focused mostly on processes of collective identity construction (Kavada, 2015; Milan, 2015; Treré, 2015) and very little attention has been placed on the relationship between political self-construction, digital storytelling and family life.. On the other hand, within communication research we have seen the emergence of different studies that have focused on digital storytelling in a variety of ways, yet they have overlooked the complex relationship between the lived experience of political activists and digital storytelling. The edited collection by Lundby (2008), for instance, brings together different approaches to digital storytelling with some scholars focusing on how digital storytelling has emerged in collective offline contexts whilst others look at more individualised forms of storytelling on live blogs and social media. Within the collection little attention is placed on the relationship between political activism and digital storytelling. One exception to this is the chapter by Couldry (2008), whose article explores the relationship between political participation and digital storytelling. Through the concept of 'alternative publics' (Bennett & Toft, 2008), Couldry reflects on the relationship between 'voice' and democratic emancipation. This is to the detriment, however, of a careful analysis of the relationship between political activism, self-construction and digital storytelling.

In this regard, the work of Vivienne (2016) is particularly insightful. Vivienne (2016) shows not only that activists engage in digital storytelling as a powerful way of building their political identities but also that they use different platforms to make different identities coexist. This understanding emerged very clearly from my own research. During my research, I carried out a digital ethnography of activists' Facebook profiles, and analysed how activists' Facebook timelines enabled practices of self-construction through digital storytelling. The digital ethnography also highlighted the fact that there was a bound relationship between these online practices of self-representation and family life. Through the digital ethnography, I realised that there were two different, yet interconnected ways in which activists referred to early childhood and family life as a way to construct their online political identities.

On the one hand, activists uploaded old images of childhood, and created a textual narrative around these images that was highly political. On their Facebook profiles, therefore, photos of themselves attending demonstrations or direct actions were at times juxtaposed with images of themselves as smiley toddlers and faces covered in chocolate. What fascinated me about this digital practice is the fact that through posts and playful interactions with friends and social networks, these early childhood images were often framed in political terms. The black and white photograph of a three-year-old wearing denim dungarees, and standing with her legs apart is read by those commenting on the photo as an example of political determination. The image of a group of boys (probably 10 or 11 years old) standing on a rock near a lake in what looks like the open countryside is followed by different social media interactions on the importance of environmental activism at a very young age. What was surprising about these digital practices was the fact that when specific political references were missing, comments mentioned the 'style' of the time and would refer to the political-historical context, such as Thatcherism and the miner strike, or the terrorism of the 1980s in Italy.

If on the one hand activists framed childhood images in political terms to construct their identity narratives, on the other they posted images of their family members and discursively constructed these images by presenting their family members as political and moral agents. Mothers, sisters, and uncles were captured during demonstrations and political rallies, and framed with comments that related to their political commitment. Photos of grandmothers or great uncles were often followed by comments on the role they played in the resistance movement in Italy during the Second World War. Again, when explicit political references were missing, activists discussed the moral qualities of their family members, their social commitment and engagement with the community or other socially significant activities. What is particularly interesting about these practices is the fact that these processes of self-construction with reference to family ties are not linear and simple, but involve a series of social tensions. In fact, often activists used these platforms to negotiate the political tensions emerging with family bonds. On the Facebook profile of an activist, for instance, there is the image of a group of elders sitting in a hospice. She has titled the image 'visiting granny' and in the caption, she criticises her grandmother and her friends for their racist remarks. Another activist, instead, used the social media platform to reflect on the loss of his grandparents and to make public the fact that despite their clear political differences he perceived them as key agents in his political formation.

### Digital storytelling and the political profiling of family members

Both examples shed light on the fact that the digital construction of early childhood and family life, therefore, played a fundamental role in the shaping of activists' online identity narratives through storytelling. These processes of online negotiation through digital storytelling are a vivid example of what has been discussed above in relation to the complexity of identity narratives, and the fact that these narratives are shaped by a dual process of self-recognition and self-distancing from family bonds. Yet they also shed light on the fact that the construction of one's own political identity on social media with reference to family life involves the construction of the political identity of others. This is particularly evident if we consider the representation of children. Over and over again during the digital ethnography I had to come to terms with the fact that activists' Facebook timelines were filled with images of their own children or the children of other family members and friends. By sharing images and personal identifying information of these children, activists constructed their political profiles by making visible their family of origin's political history and the political values. In addition to this, activists discursively constructed these children as political agents. On the Facebook profile of Paul[3], an activist involved in the British Trade Union Movement, for instance, there is a picture of his toddler son sitting on the floor together with another boy. The caption of the image reads: 'discussing the details of their vanguard party'. This is not an isolated example. During my research, I came across posts of children at demonstrations holding banners and flags, children playing together and being described as 'plotting the next revolution', children with signs openly criticising the current government or supporting specific political campaigns. It is clear that there is a playful and joking dimension in the posts. However, critical questions emerge about these 'political' associations.

Activists' digital practices, in fact, revealed that through digital storytelling they not only constructed their political identities but they also constructed the political profiles of other family members by sharing personally identifying political data. These digital micro-practices, as the next and final part of the paper will show, shed light on the fact that we need to create new theoretical models that enable us to understand the making of digital citizenship across the life course and re-think existing models of political participation.

### The making of digital citizenship: from the engaged citizen to the datafied self

One particularly problematic element that emerges in the construction of online political identities, today, through digital storytelling is represented by the notion of 'web presence' as developed by Leaver (2015), who has rightly argued that one of the key problems of current discussions on online identity is the assumption that users have an agency in the shaping of their digital profiles. Yet this is not entirely true. The notion of 'web presence' therefore is particularly useful in the context of family life because it enables us to appreciate the fact that digital identities are not only constructed by the subject/user, but are often constructed by others.

As argued above, my research revealed that activists not only share personal identifying information of their family members online, but discursively construct them as political and moral agents. Through the sharing of posts and tagging of images therefore, they play an active role in the definition of the digital profiles of their family members. These digital interactions that are widespread within family life, and which appear to be harmless and playful, may be transforming the lived experience of digital participation and hence the making of digital citizens across the life course. This is not only because being able to appropriate personal data flows means being able to represent ourselves in public but also because the production of digital traces within family life needs to be understood with reference to broader processes of surveillance and archiving of citizens' personal data.

Within the social sciences, digital citizenship has often been defined as an empowering, positive concept, used to describe how humans participate in society through digital media (Barron, Gomez, Martin, & Pinkard, 2014; Mossberger, Tolbert, & McNeal, 2007; Ohler, 2010). However, in the last years, a growing body of research has shown that with the rise of big data the concept of digital citizenship is increasingly becoming more problematic. From social media to mobile apps, from institutions to governments, citizens are forced to digitally participate in society because their personal information is digitised, shared, stored, analysed and exploited for them by others. In this context digital citizenship is often constructed by the different digital traces that we willingly or unwillingly leave behind in our everyday digital interactions, or that others create for us (Dencik & Hintz, 2016; Isin & Ruppert, 2016; McCosker, Vivienne, & Johns, 2016). At present, therefore, key questions are emerging on how the concentration, organisation and storage of personal identifying information are leading to the construction of citizens as quantified selves (Lupton, 2016). The aim of this paper was to start addressing these questions. As it has been shown, activists' everyday social media practices talk directly about the experiential and relational processes of data production. Through practices of digital storytelling activists did not only construct their own political narratives, but also constructed the political narratives of others. Shedding light on these relational processes and on how digital traces may be defining the civic and political profiles of generations to come, therefore, has become a key priority in research on political participation and civic engagement across the life course.

## Conclusion

This paper aimed to shed light on political activists' complex processes of identity narrative construction. Drawing on Pratt's (2003) notion of identity narratives, the paper has shown that activists often construct their online political biographies with reference to early childhood and family life. These practices of digital storytelling on social media are particularly important to the study of political activism. This is because they not only highlight how activists' identity narratives today are often negotiated on these platforms, but also how these digital constructions enable the digital profiling of different family members. We do not know whether the personal data that we produce today on social media are going to be available in the future. Yet, it is reasonable to assume that the digital production of personal data will continue to be an aspect of our societies in the next decades, and that the digital surveillance of citizens will be strengthened by new practices of governance (Lyon, 2014). Therefore, starting to question how everyday digital practices build the data futures of generations to come is, today, more important than ever, as it can shed light on how digital participation and digital citizenship are being transformed by our complex data cultures.

## Notes

1. Fictional name to protect the interviewee's anonymity.
2. Fictional name to protect the interviewee's anonymity.
3. Fictional name to protect the participant's anonymity.

## Disclosure statement

No potential conflict of interest was reported by the authors.

## Funding

This work was supported by British Academy [grant number SG 2009-10].

## References

Acock, A. C., & Bengtson, V. L. (1978). On the relative influence of mothers and fathers: A covariance analysis of political and religious socialization. *Journal of Marriage and the Family*, *40*(3), 519–530. doi:10.2307/350932.

Alleyne, B. (2000). *Personal narrative & activism: A Bio-ethnography of 'life experience with Britain'.* London: Goldsmiths College.

Askew, K., & Wilk, R. R. (Eds.). (2002). *The anthropology of media: A reader.* Malden, MA: Wiley-Blackwell.

Baker, K. L. (1974). The acquisition of partisanship in Germany. *American Journal of Political Science*, *18* (3), 569–582. doi:10.2307/2110632.

Barassi, V. (2015). *Activism on the web: Everyday struggles against digital capitalism.* New York, NY: Routledge. Retrieved from http://www.bookdepository.com/Activism-on-Web-Veronica-Barassi/9780415717915

Barassi, V., & Treré, E. (2012). Does Web 3.0 come after Web 2.0? Deconstructing theoretical assumptions through practice. *New Media & Society*, *14*(8), 1269–1285. doi:10.1177/1461444812445878.

Barron, B., Gomez, K., Martin, C. K., & Pinkard, N. (2014). *The digital youth network: Cultivating digital media citizenship in urban communities.* Cambridge, MA: MIT Press.

Bennett, W. L., & Toft, A. (2008). Identity, technologies and narratives: Transnational activism and social networks. In A. Chadwick & P. N. Howard (Eds.), *Routledge handbook of internet politics* (pp. 246–258). London: Routledge.

Brauchler, B., & Postill, J. (2010). *Theorising media and practice.* Oxford: Berghahn Books.

Cammaerts, B., Mattoni, A., & Mccurdy, P. (2013). *Mediation and protest movements.* Bristol: Intellect.

Castells, M. (2012). *Networks of outrage and hope: Social movements in the internet Age*. Cambridge: Polity Press.

Connell, R. W. (1972). Political socialization in the American family: The evidence re-examined. *Public Opinion Quarterly, 36*(3), 323–333. doi:10.1086/268014

Couldry, N. (2008). Digital storytelling, media research and democracy: Conceptual choices and alternative futures. In K. Lundby (Ed.), *Digital storytelling, mediatized stories: Self-representations in new media* (pp. 41–61). New York: Peter Lang.

Day, R. J. F. (2005). *Gramsci is dead: Anarchist currents in the newest social movements*. London: Toronto: Pluto Press.

Dencik, L., & Hintz, A. (2016). *Digital citizenship in an Age of mass surveillance*. Berlin: Re:Publica. Retrieved from https://re-publica.com/de/file/republica-2016-lina-dencik-arne-hintz-digital-citizenship-age-mass-surveillance

DeWalt, K. M., & DeWalt, B. R. (2002). *Participant observation: A guide for fieldworkers*. Lanham, MD: Rowman Altamira.

Escobar, A. (2004). Identity. In D. Nugent & J. Vincent (Eds.), *A companion to the anthropology of politics* (pp. 248–267). Malden, MA: Blackwell.

Fenton, N. (2016). *Digital, political, radical*. Malden, MA: Polity Press.

Gerbaudo, P. (2012). *Tweets and the streets: Social media and contemporary activism*. London: Pluto Press.

Ginsburg, F. D., Abu-Lughold, L., & Larkin, B. (Eds.). (2002). *Media worlds: Anthropology on new terrain*. Berkeley: University of California Press.

Gordon, C. (2007). 'Al Gore's our guy': Linguistically constructing a family political identity. In D. Tannen, S. Kendall, & C. Gordon (Eds.), *Family talk: Discourse and identity in four American families*. Oxford: Oxford University Press.

Hastrup, K., & Davis, J. (1992). History and the people without Europe. In *Other histories* (pp. 1–14). London: Routledge.

Hess, R. D., Torney-Purta, J. V., & Valsiner, J. (2005). *The development of political attitudes in children*. New Brunswick, NJ: Aldine Transaction.

Holloway, J. (2002). *Change the world without taking power: The meaning of revolution today*. London: Pluto Press.

Isin, E., & Ruppert, E. (2015). *Being digital citizens*. London: Rowman & Littlefield International.

Jennings, M. K. (1984). The intergenerational transfer of political ideologies in eight western nations*. *European Journal of Political Research, 12*(3), 261–276. doi:10.1111/j.1475-6765.1984.tb00088.x

Kavada, A. (2015). Creating the collective: Social media, the occupy movement and its constitution as a collective actor. *Information, Communication & Society, 18*(8), 872–886. doi:10.1080/1369118X.2015.1043318

Leaver, T. (2015). Born digital? Presence, privacy, and intimate surveillance. In J. Hartley & W. Qu (Eds.), *Re-orientation: Translingual transcultural transmedia. Studies in narrative, language, identity, and knowledge* (pp. 149–160). Shanghai: Fudan University Press.

Liebes, T., & Ribak, R. (1992). The contribution of family culture to political participation, political outlook, and its reproduction. *Communication Research, 19*(5), 618–641. doi:10.1177/009365092019005004

Lundby, K. (2008). *Digital storytelling, mediatized stories: Self-representations in new media*. Bern: Peter Lang.

Lupton, D. (2016). *The quantified self*. San Francisco, CA: John Wiley & Sons.

Lyon, D. (2014). Surveillance, Snowden, and big data: Capacities, consequences, critique. *Big Data & Society, 1*(2). doi:10.1177/2053951714541861

Mattoni, A. (2012). *Media practices and protest politics How precarious workers mobilise*. Oxford: Routledge.

McCosker, A., Vivienne, S., & Johns, A. (2016). *Negotiating digital citizenship: Control, contest and culture*. Lenham, MD: Rowman & Littlefield Publishing Group.

Milan, S. (2015). From social movements to cloud protesting: The evolution of collective identity. *Information, Communication & Society, 18*(8), 887–900. doi:10.1080/1369118X.2015.1043135

Moland, L. L. (2011). *Hegel on political identity: Patriotism, nationality, cosmopolitanism*. Evanston, IL: Northwestern University Press.

Mossberger, K., Tolbert, C. J., & McNeal, R. S. (2007). *Digital citizenship: The internet, society, and participation*. Bellingham, WA: The MIT Press.

Nolas, S.-M., Varvantakis, C., & Aruldoss, V. (2016). (Im)possible conversations? Activism, childhood and everyday life. *Journal of Social and Political Psychology*, 4(1), 252–265.

Ohler, J. B. (2010). *Digital community, digital citizen*. Newbury Park: Corwin Press.

Pettifor, H. (2012). *Do parents affect the early political priorisation of nature in their children?* Institute for Social and Economic Research. Retrieved from http://s3.amazonaws.com/academia.edu. documents/30494411/2012-11.pdf?AWSAccessKeyId=AKIAJ56TQJRTWSMTNPEA&Expires=14780 27402&Signature=6I56%2FOH3s%2FYxkIzfUzIt34WPHkY%3D&response-contendisposition=inline %3B%20filename%3DDo_parents_affect_the_early_political_pr.pdf

Postill, J. (2014). Democracy in an age of viral reality: A media epidemiography of Spain's Indignados movement. *Ethnography*, 15(1), 51–69. doi:10.1177/1466138113502513

Pratt, J. (2003). *Class, nation and identity: The anthropology of political movements*. London: Pluto Press.

Treré, E. (2015). Reclaiming, proclaiming, and maintaining collective identity in the #YoSoy132 movement in Mexico: an examination of digital frontstage and backstage activism through social media and instant messaging platforms. *Information, Communication & Society*, 18(8), 901–915. doi:10. 1080/1369118X.2015.1043744

Tilly, C. (1994). Afterward: Political memories in space and time. In J. Boyarin (Ed.), *Remapping memory: The politics of TimeSpace* (Minnesota Archive Editions edition, pp. 241–257). Minneapolis: University of Minnesota Press.

Vivienne, S. (2016). *Digital identity and everyday activism: Sharing private stories with networked publics*. New York, NY: Springer.

Wolfson, T. (2014). *Digital rebellion: The birth of the cyber left*. Urbana: University of Illinois Press.

# Welfare mothers' grassroots activism for economic justice

Sheila Marie Katz

**ABSTRACT**
Several events during the course of this research – including the
Great Recession, Barack Obama's election and presidency, and the
Occupy and student protests – increasingly focused media
attention and public interest on social justice and economic
inequality. Given the 2016 US elections interest continued to grow
on these topics and sparked new attention to the role of
organising and activism on social policy issues such as on health
care, the economic conditions of working families, access to
higher education, and the deteriorating social safety net. Through
ethnographic research in the San Francisco Bay Area, this paper
examines how mothers who pursued higher education while on
welfare engaged in grassroots activism to reform social safety net
policies. This project explores how they became grassroots
activists, how they developed an oppositional consciousness and
participated in grassroots anti-poverty activism, and the
consequences of that participation.

## Introduction

In the San Francisco Bay area of California, a former welfare mother founded LIFETIME, a
grassroots welfare-rights activist organisation, in 1996, the same year as the US welfare
reform, to assist parents on welfare pursuing higher education after these policy
changes. This paper examines how welfare mothers mobilised through grassroots activism
to fight welfare reform and for economic justice. Through ethnographic observation, qualitative interviews, and focus groups, I find that LIFETIME participants developed an oppositional consciousness (Mansbridge, 2001) through welfare rights organising. This paper
explores how they became grassroots activists, developed an oppositional consciousness,
participated in grassroots activism, and the consequences of that participation for their
lives.

## Policy background: US Welfare reform

In August 1996, United States President Bill Clinton signed the Personal Responsibility and
Work Opportunity Reconciliation Act (PRWORA), which ended federal welfare for low-
income families as an entitlement programme and 'reformed' the welfare system. The
Temporary Assistance for Needy Families (TANF) programme was created. The central fea-

96

tures of the welfare reform law required states to create new state-implemented welfare programmes emphasising a 'work-first' approach that required work for participants, placed lifetime limits on public assistance, and implemented punitive sanctions for non-compliance with regulations. Under the new TANF programme, the 'work first' approach required half of adult welfare participants to work or engage in activities that directly promoted work (job search, on-the-job training, or community service work). The 'work first' goal was to get participants quickly off welfare, yet no attention was paid to ending poverty or finding jobs at livable wages.

The policy's punitive aspects focused on 'ending government dependency' based on false stereotypes of poor women. Negative stereotypes of welfare recipients and the 'welfare queen' caricature of the 1970s and 1980s drove welfare reform policies (Katz, 2012). Luna (2009) explains, 'because of the negative social constructions associated with welfare, to many, the punitive nature of the policy seems justified' (p. 442). Kelly (2010) agrees, finding the controlling image of welfare mothers consists of racist stereotypes that represent women on public assistance as childlike, hyperfertile, lazy, and bad mothers. The construction of this controlling image from sexist and racist stereotypes, myths, and moral judgements served to publically justify the dismantling of public assistance programmes and institute increased regulations on recipients (p. 77).

Consequently, 'work first' welfare reform policies restricted participants' access to higher education. Even though other aspects of American culture value higher education and recognise the necessity of education for upward mobility, for mothers on welfare education is actively discouraged. Despite the 'pull yourself up by your bootstraps' discourse, the TANF programme devalues and severely limits higher education. Therefore,

> because of statues that limit their access to education and training, particularly at the post-secondary level, millions of would-be students have been blocked from these programs, making welfare one of the few contexts in modern American life in which education is explicitly discouraged. (Ratner, 2004, pp. 45–46)

Welfare reform's 'work first' focus also ignored the deteriorating conditions in the US of low-wage work. Full-time minimum wage work no longer pays enough for an adult with dependent(s) to escape poverty. Women's wages in the US are generally so low that for women with children to earn enough to support their families, most need at least a bachelor's degree. Considerable research finds that higher education for women on welfare leads to increased wages, more employment opportunities, and better chances at economic self-sufficiency (Gittell, Gross, & Holdaway, 1993; Kahn, Butler, Deprez, & Polakow, 2004; Mathur, 2004; Shaw, Goldrick-Rab, Mazzeo, & Jacobs, 2006). However, pursuing a bachelor's degree was no longer possible in most states after the welfare reform. California implemented TANF through the California Work Opportunity and Responsibility to Kids (CalWORKs) programme, in January 1998. Although the national TANF programme discouraged higher education, CalWORKs was among the few state programmes allowing higher education (Kahn et al., 2004). Advocates and activists across the country were concerned that welfare reform's focus on punitive sanctions, lifetime limits of receipt of aid, and low-wage work would reduce welfare rolls without addressing the underlying reasons people were in poverty; which is exactly what happened (Katz, 2012). Therefore, in this policy context, LIFETIME was founded.

## LIFETIME

A mother on welfare finishing her bachelor's degree at the University of California Berkeley founded Low-Income Families' Empowerment through Education, LIFETIME, as a non-profit grassroots community organisation in 1996. While in community colleges and at UC Berkeley, she networked with other student parents, formed support groups, designed and conducted student-led classes, and created student parent resource centres on various local college campuses. She became an activist and a grassroots organiser. She graduated from UC Berkeley the same year the welfare reform was passed nationally. Since many of the student parents she knew were single mothers who either had or were receiving welfare, she founded LIFETIME focused on fighting welfare reform policies that were demeaning, based on disparaging stereotypes of poor women, and restricted access to higher education. The core of LIFETIME's organising strategy was to empower parents to fight for rights in the welfare system and to work collectively to change punitive policies. LIFETIME used a three-step sequence aimed at developing participants' oppositional consciousness to challenge welfare policy. First, help people through immediate personal crisis with advocacy services; second, engage in leadership development and issue training; and third, mobilise for grassroots political action to change policies that caused the crisis.

To accomplish this, first, LIFETIME provided peer-advocacy for welfare participants to pursue higher education. The organisation conducted outreach workshops at community colleges and universities across the Bay Area, and eventually across California, to teach student parents how to advocate for themselves, how (or when) to reach out to LIFETIME or other advocacy organisations for support, or when to file a state appeal. The focus of this step was to help parents resolve their individual problems with the welfare system so that they can stay in college.

The second step was to empower student parents to work collectively on grassroots campaigns to change welfare policies. The organisation focused on developing participants' oppositional consciousness by building leadership skills, teaching the structural aspects of welfare reform policy, and empowering political participation. The organisation held Parent Leadership Trainings to inform about welfare policy, upcoming policy changes, and becoming involved in political advocacy. Those who participated in LIFETIME's leadership trainings were designated 'Parent Leaders' and were the most active in LIFETIME's grassroots political work and actions.

## Literature review: welfare rights organising and developing oppositional consciousness

LIFETIME's welfare rights organising created an 'oppositional consciousness' among participants. Mansbridge (2001, p. 5) explains that oppositional consciousness 'is usually fueled by righteous anger over injustices done to the group and prompted by personal indignities and harms suffered through one's group membership' and defines it as a matter of 'identifying with members of a subordinate group, identifying injustices done to that group, opposing those injustices, and seeing the group as having a shared interest in ending or diminishing those injustices'. This paper contributes to two literatures in gender, social movements, and activism – first, the literature on developing oppositional consciousness, and second, the welfare rights literature. LIFETIME's approach contributes to the literature on how an organisation supported their development of an oppositional consciousness.

The strategy LIFETIME used, as Abramovitz (1999) points out, is an organising strategy more often used by groups led by marginalised women than men, especially poor and working class women. Hardy-Fanta (1993, p. 3) found, in her study of Latina/Latino politics, that women in her study were particularly good at 'making connections' between their individual problems and how those related to social structural issues – through organising, the women's connections of 'private troubles and public issues' got them involved politically in the public issues that contributed or caused the private troubles. LIFETIME helped parents make similar connections between their problems with the welfare system and how the system was intentionally designed to demean their experiences in poverty. Therefore, making the link between their 'private troubles and the public issues', is a process which could also be referred to as 'radical social services', a description that comes from a history of radical social work. Although there are many ways to define radical social work, one is:

> (1) a belief that the institutional structure of society is the source of the personal problems of the clients; (2) a focus on economic inequality as a central concern and cause of other social and individual problems; (3) a critical view of social service agencies as instruments of social control, co-optation, and stigmatization; (4) a focus on both structural and internalized oppression; and (5) a linkage of cause and function of private troubles and public issues. (Reisch & Andrews, 2002, p. 6)

These elements correspond to how LIFETIME developed an oppositional consciousness with participants – helped them solve their personal troubles and then engaged them politically to challenge the structures that caused the oppression.

The foundation of LIFETIME's work acknowledges that US society unfairly shames those who use welfare – and the welfare system creates personal indignities and harm to them. The organisation worked to funnel women's 'righteous anger' into political action. LIFETIME's development of parent leaders echoes the definition of oppositional consciousness by Mansbridge (2001). LIFETIME raised the consciousness of mothers on welfare to identify with each other, worked to stimulate their awareness of the sources of economic injustice, and mobilised them to combat the injustice. As the experiences below illustrate, the lived experiences of mothers on welfare tell a very different story from the rhetoric used by administrators and politicians in the welfare debate. LIFETIME believed listening to the voices of those affected by policies is a critical step in making policies that improve women's lives.

Second, LIFETIME, the grassroots activist organisation researched, fought for welfare rights at the county, state, and federal levels. Therefore, their work is best understood alongside welfare rights research such as on the National Welfare Rights Organization (Piven & Cloward, 1979) or Reese's work about welfare rights organising after welfare reform (2011). Reese observes that welfare rights campaigns of the late 1990s were 'fairly small-scale' and that 'welfare rights activism did not gain such wide popularity' as the movement did during the 1960s (p. 42). LIFETIME's strategies and goals were also similar to those explored by Naples' research on community activist mothers and the War on Poverty. She examines how activist mothers organised communities to fight poverty. In her research, activists conceptualised democratic citizenship 'as something achieved in community and in benefit of the collectivity rather than as an individual pos-session' (1998, p. 3), which was similar to LIFETIME's frame in their organising.

## Methods

I conducted ethnographic research in the San Francisco Bay Area of California through in-depth qualitative interviews, focus groups, and participant observation with single mothers pursuing higher education while participating in the CalWORKs welfare pro-gramme, half of whom were participants with LIFETIME. The primary focus of this paper is the women's activism with LIFETIME; therefore, it centres on this common aspect of their lives. The broader project covers many facets of the participants' complex lives, explored through their rich narratives about their pathways into higher education and onto welfare, their experiences in the labour market and the Great Recession, and in other areas of activism (see Katz, 2008).

In the overall project, research participants were recruited through the community col-leges and universities and through LIFETIME. I focused my recruitment through the office on each campus that serves students on welfare or the centres for student parents. I sought participants at each location by sending emails to the offices list-serves or groups, posting flyers in the offices or centres, attending workshops to hand out flyers and introduce myself, and hanging around. I interviewed 45 women from November 2005 until December 2006. I conducted three focus groups in June 2007 with 19 additional women, including a separate focus group for LIFETIME parents (4). I conducted second interviews with 25 of 45 interview participants in August and September 2008. In Spring 2011, I conducted follow-up interviews with 35 of 45 participants (78% retention rate). In 2006, when I first met participants, just over half of the interview participants were involved at some level in LIFETIME's activism (24) and the rest had no or minimal involvement (21). Their participation in activism changed over the course of the research, which is explored in my forthcoming book. Participants' racial and ethnic backgrounds reflected the diversity of single mothers on welfare in 2006 in San Francisco and Alameda Counties. In 2006, interview participants in my study ranged in age from 18 to 51, with median age of 33. The median number of children interview participants had in 2006 was 2.

My involvement with LIFETIME was multi-faceted. I first met LIFETIME's directors in June 2003, at a feminist policy conference in Washington, DC when they spoke on a panel about welfare reform and grassroots activism. I moved to the San Francisco area a few months later – for family reasons – and I approached the organisation to allow me to volunteer while I developed my doctoral dissertation about activist welfare mothers in college. In November 2003, I observed my first event with LIFETIME, a weekend-long 'Parent Leadership Training'. Thereafter my involvement with the organ-isation deepened; my volunteer work developed into a part-time paid staff position helping the executive director with research and grant-writing. I was not an organiser or on the advocacy staff, but occasionally all staff helped in various capacities with events. Between being in the office for paid work and observing events outside of my paid time, from March 2005 through December 2006, I observed or participated in most of LIFETIME's grassroots protests, parent leadership meetings, special events, and policy briefings.[1] The findings discussed below come from both my ethnographic field notes and interview data about the experiences of welfare mothers participating in grassroots poverty activism.

Interviews and focus groups were audio recorded, transcribed verbatim, and entered into ATLAS-ti qualitative data software for coding and analysis. Using longitudinal and ethnographic methods working with a marginalised population, I utilised a grounded theory (GT) approach to recruitment, data collection, coding, and analysis (Charmaz, 2006) to understand participants' experiences, narratives, and meanings. I moved back and forth between the field and my analysis (see Katz, 2008; Charmaz & Katz, in press, for a thorough discussion of how GT was used in this study). I developed codes through 'in vivo coding' by using participants' terms for phenomena as code names, which 'preserves participants' meanings of their views and actions in the coding itself' (Charmaz, 2006, p. 55). Through focused coding, I developed more specific categories of coded data, guided by the interpretations and analysis of participants. I used grounded theory particularly because the population was suspicious of outsiders – especially bureaucrats or academics – asking invasive personal questions insensitive to people's stories or how they framed experiences. Using grounded theory allowed me to conduct a few interviews or field observations, analyse and reflect on the process, adjust questions or methods to be more sensitive, inclusive, and understanding of the narratives and complex experiences of participants. Several times during the research, participants introduced me to prospective participants on campus or at LIFETIME events (snowball sampling). These introductions were invaluable and usually involved the past participant conveying how much she enjoyed participating in the interview and how I 'get it' when discussing welfare issues. This was very important, especially when recruiting those with complicated experiences, because many were cautious about participating in academic research about welfare.

## Interview findings

Jasmine, a 39-year-old white/Latina mother of three and domestic violence survivor, graduated in 2006 with her Associate's Degree and finished her bachelor's degree in 2010. I met Jasmine at the June 2003 conference in Washington; we came to know each other well over the next several years and we still keep in touch. We travelled together to Washington and Sacramento, and she was my first interview in November 2005. Jasmine was an active LIFETIME parent leader. She first heard about the organisation in a town hall meeting organised by the food bank she used while her family was homeless. She recounted

> being stopped from [attending] school and being homeless, because that was the main thing, we were living in a filthy store front illegally which didn't have a bathroom or a kitchen for three and a half years. One of the LIFETIME people was there and heard my testimony and they came up to me and introduced themselves and I got in touch with them and basically that's how it all started. That was like in April 2001.

She continued,

> LIFETIME came up to me because they heard me talk about quitting school as I was speaking, about being forced [by my caseworker to quit school], and from that time on I filed an appeal and I won my appeal in early 2002. I went back to school in August 2001 even though the

county told me not to, I did anyways ... with LIFETIME's advice. I would have never done this had I not met LIFETIME because I had no idea that they [caseworkers] were breaking the law because I was already going to school and they made me quit. And that's against the law in California.

Jasmine traced her trajectory with the organisation:

I came to LIFETIME as a client about my case, being forced to quit school. And from that time, my development with LIFETIME has been a really positive and uplifting for me, in the sense that I got on the parent leadership committee which is comprised of groups of CalWORKs parents who help LIFETIME form decision making about laws or policies that affect our life because we are the ones living our life. And part of that meant going to Sacramento on [legislative] visits, and in some cases to Washington, D.C. to do the same and be involved in briefings. (interview, November 2005)

Jasmine felt her involvement with the organisation

opened up a really big door for me in every way. It kind of brought me out of my shell, I didn't feel like I was the only one in the world and isolated in this situation, it showed me that there are other people out there facing similar barriers and challenges like myself, and a lot of people at that.

Jasmine related how she developed an oppositional consciousness:

[LIFETIME] showed me how the resources in the system were not being given to me and how the social system had been dropping the ball basically and failing parents like myself who are really truly trying and who have good intentions in every way to get out of poverty. Nobody wants to be in poverty, and poverty doesn't have a time limit on it, so why does welfare, and LIFETIME seemed to understand all these things.

In addition to learning the dynamics of poverty and welfare policy through the organisation's trainings, Jasmine worked with the organisation to change them: 'LIFETIME has also been integral in helping to form and change law and policy in California that affects families, like mine, and I've been a part of that change by being involved with LIFETIME'.

Seventeen participants in this study identified as activists and parent leaders. Twelve were very engaged, while five occasionally participated. Nine of the 12 most active parent leaders connected with LIFETIME through workshops and presentations at community colleges or university campuses. Parent leaders were also active on their own campuses, and made announcements at meetings or in classes to let others know about the organisation. Of the nine leaders who found LIFETIME on campus, five got involved because of a personal connection made during the workshop or an introduction by a college staff member. Jasmine's narrative about how she came to be involved with the organisation illustrated a common thread in many of the LIFETIME mothers' narratives. She thought she was alone in her experience of pursuing higher education while on welfare. However, when she met a member of the organisation, she found out she was not alone, became involved in LIFETIME, and active in grassroots politics. As we see in Jasmine's narrative, her trajectory to involvement with LIFETIME followed the organisation's strategy for engaging parents in grassroots politics and developing an oppositional consciousness. She met a LIFETIME parent leader who helped her with personal welfare issues, she attended a parent leadership training, and joined the parent leadership committee.

LIFETIME's parent leaders got involved in several ways, but as Jasmine's narrative illustrates, a personal connection with a staff member or parent leader is a critical first step.

LIFETIME's presentations often resonated with student mothers and inspired them to become involved. The resonance could be an issue they were interested in or a reminder of a forgotten aspect of their personality, which was triggered by the organisation's way of engaging parents to advocate for themselves. Involvement escalated because women connected with LIFETIME's work. For mothers like Jasmine, political engagement, although a time commitment, gave strength and support to persevere in school while on welfare and motivated them to fight for that right.

Although many parent leaders became involved with LIFETIME through college workshops, mothers also got involved through referrals for LIFETIME's advocacy services from other social service organisations. D, a 46-year-old black mother of three and community college student, related how she found out about the organisation in a time of crisis. Because the organisation helped her through that crisis, she became part of the parent leadership committee:

> I found out about LIFETIME, my youngest daughter was a hell raiser, she really was, and because I stayed in [domestic violence shelter] transitional housing, I didn't have the power to deal with it the way I wanted to deal with it ... the social worker for the intervention handed me the LIFETIME card ... I picked up the phone, I called and they gave me an earful, I went back to the caseworker, and I said, 'they said that I have the right to get aid for my emotional, mental problems. I had the right to seek remedy for my health and that is the law and therefore I am demanding to get relief.' And she got all nervous (laughs) and she said let me check on it, let me talk to my supervisor, I said I'm not going anywhere. When she came back she said you have a six-month waiver, and I said, thank you ... They didn't have to sell me, I went to their parent leadership summit, and I sat through that, and I called them and I said I'd like to volunteer.

D's narrative outlines LIFETIME's central strategy of engaging women in grassroots politics. The organisation helped mothers meet their immediate needs by empowering parents to advocate for themselves at the welfare department through a system of peer-mentoring and support. Usually done over the phone, as D illustrated with 'and they gave me an earful', she got the information she needed to legally challenge caseworker demands. LIFETIME effectively met the immediate needs of mothers, helped them through their crisis, and invited them to learn to change the system that contributed to the crisis in the first place. D's journey of escaping domestic violence to testifying about welfare policy in front of lawmakers in Sacramento, although unusual for most welfare mothers, was almost typical for parent leaders. LIFETIME engaged parents politically, developed their oppositional consciousness, and trained them to engage the policy-making process. The organisation's strategy of grassroots political engagement also builds on creating relationships between parent leaders; mothers further along their educational journeys mentored the parents just starting.

LIFETIME engaged both in institutional politics – such as participating in legislative briefings, hearings, and visits with policymakers, and also in extra-institutional grassroots politics such as sit-ins, political theatre, and protest marches. One strength of LIFETIME's approach to grassroots political engagement was training mothers on welfare to address the legislators who determine welfare policy. Most of the parent leaders gave testimony about welfare policies in Sacramento or in Washington. Sometimes mothers brought their children with them. Often, policymakers did not know or have never even met a woman on public assistance. LIFETIME's strategy was to make the matter personal; mothers on welfare testified about their own experiences and dispelled myths about welfare mothers. On more than one occasion, however, LIFETIME's directors (themselves former welfare mothers) were told not to bring welfare mothers (and especially their children) to state hearings or to meet with politicians because the mothers' testimony discomforted the policymakers. The LIFETIME directors interpreted this request as evidence this strategy worked and used the request as impetus for more grassroots work.

## Ethnographic research: grassroots poverty activism

In March 2005, a small group of mothers on welfare from New York, Ohio, and California, along with LIFETIME's Executive Director and I, met with Andrew Bush the top TANF administrator in the country, at the Office of Family Assistance, part of the US Department of Health and Human Services, in Washington, DC The Office of Family Assistance administers the TANF programme, which, along with the Violence Against Women Act (VAWA), was up for reauthorisation. Mr Bush was a George W. Bush Administration appointee (but no relation) and the administration focused on marriage promotion policies for low-income families. LIFETIME joined nationwide advocates in Washington for the National Coalition Against Domestic Violence's lobby week to advocate for domestic violence survivors, and the LIFETIME mothers also advocated for TANF to expand women's access to higher education.

The meeting started on a hopeful note but ended in an impasse. At the start, each mother introduced herself and explained she was a survivor of domestic violence, and in the aftermath relied on the welfare system. Yet none of them received domestic violence counselling, services, or waivers from welfare work requirements. Moreover, all had been sanctioned off welfare because of repercussions from domestic violence. They only recovered their welfare benefits with advocates' help who also helped them secure safe housing, and enrol in higher education. The mothers informed Mr Bush that surviving or experiencing domestic violence is the most common characteristic of women on welfare, more so than any other demographic characteristic such as race/ethnicity, age, level of education, or number of children. Furthermore they explained that three of them were escaping severely abusive marriages, one was escaping an abusive partner who was a veteran, and one recently moved several states away to escape an abusive boyfriend. The central message the women conveyed was that 'family violence is NOT an option' and they advocated the Office of Family Assistance make the Family Violence Option of welfare reform mandatory for states and require states to give accommodations to domestic violence survivors on welfare. Throughout the meeting, Mr Bush repeated one phrase: 'we are going to have to agree to disagree'. He went on to explain the priorities of the Office of Family Assistance under the Bush Administration, the primary was marriage promotion policies. The mothers, wanting to find common ground with Mr Bush, suggested the marriage promotion policies include safeguards or exemptions for survivors of domestic violence. Again, Mr Bush repeated 'we are going to have to agree to disagree'. 'Okay', one of the mothers said, trying to take yet another step back and find common ground to lay a foundation for the discussion; asked 'well, can we agree that domestic violence is a major issue for mothers on welfare?' Again, Mr Bush repeated 'we are going to have to agree to disagree'. The meeting ended when one of the mothers asked in exasperation, 'well, I know that you want us to agree to disagree, but can we at least agree that domestic violence is bad?' In response, Mr Bush abruptly stood up, politely thanked us for coming, and quickly excused himself. His departure disheartened the mothers because their strategy of finding common ground from which to start their discussion of welfare, domestic violence, and higher education proved fruitless.

During the meeting debrief, the mothers emphasised over and over that they did not fully understand why he was so cold and unwilling to discuss possible TANF policy changes. Although they knew going into the meeting it would be the toughest one of the week, no one understands why he was so obstinate. Through other conversations with progressive and conservative policymakers, no one had experienced such a cold shoulder. The mothers had been meeting on Capitol Hill all week with legislative staffers and members of Congress, all listened attentively, even if, although they never directly said it, they disagreed with what they advocated. Their encounter with Mr Bush left the mothers wondering, why did he even take the meeting if he was going to treat them that way?

In response, in June 2005, LIFETIME returned to Washington with a larger group of welfare activists to raise awareness of poor women's experiences with domestic violence ahead of the VAWA and TANF reauthorisation. The purpose of the trip was two-fold: hold a grassroots research briefing on Capitol Hill featuring the testimonies of three welfare mothers about domestic violence, welfare, and higher education along with research presentations by LIFETIME's director, a well-known DC welfare researcher, and myself. In preparation, that spring, LIFETIME worked with welfare rights and domestic violence organisations across the country to have low-income domestic violence survivors make t-shirts with their picture, story, and message to policymakers. They gathered over 100 t-shirts. LIFETIME intended to deliver the shirts to the Assistant Secretary of Health and Human Services, Dr Wade Horn, who was the director of the Administration for Children and Families, the agency that administered TANF.

LIFETIME also organised a protest outside the US Department of Health and Human Services. The protesters included grassroots activist welfare mothers from across the country assembled under an overpass a block from the HHS offices. They quickly clipped t-shirts to clotheslines attached to six 8-foot tall wooden poles to assemble a portable 'clothesline project' exhibit.[2] The group chanted as they marched 'Family Violence is *Not* an Option' and planned to deliver t-shirts and LIFETIME's research brief about domestic violence and welfare reform to HHS. For over an hour, they stood on the sidewalk in front of HHS and chanted, with LIFETIME's executive director leading the group and shouting the group's demands.

The protest was loud and visible on an otherwise calm street filled with sedate federal office buildings. Office workers in the HHS building told protesters (later by email) they could hear the chanting inside the offices all the way up the building. Eventually, a top assistant to Dr Horn came down to chat with the group on the sidewalk. This conversation was short, he declined allowing anyone, even a smaller group, to enter the building. He finally accepted the research report and a couple of t-shirts and quickly went back into the building. The group, less than fully satisfied with the interaction, agreed it was probably the best to be hoped for, and marched back down the sidewalk to under the overpass where they started to debrief and disassemble the clotheslines.

## Consequences of their participation

Being involved with LIFETIME's political activities and developing an oppositional consciousness characterised parent leaders. One of the women in the room in March 2005 at the US Department of Health and Human Services was Jasmine. Jasmine celebrates the impact of the organisation on her life:

> It's had a tremendous impact on me in a very positive way and it's one of the key components and pillars in my life that really holds me together when I really feel despair … Otherwise it is so easy to give up in this kind of situation because it's extremely challenging on a person, and organizations like LIFETIME, they really know how to hold people together to keep moving forward. And that's just been a really important part of my life more than anything else, because LIFETIME is my life, what LIFETIME does, is my life … I'm proud of it, and even when I graduate I intend to continue with the work because I am LIFETIME.

Her proclamation 'I am LIFETIME' exemplified the identity and oppositional consciousness developed as activists with the organisation.

LIFETIME participants' narratives differed significantly from the narratives of the mothers who did not participate in activism in the way they framed their participation in the welfare system. LIFETIME participants used the oppositional consciousness they developed and discussed use of welfare as a right they have as citizens, rather than as something shameful. They cited their rights under the welfare system; and in many cases, through grassroots political engagement, they fought for those rights. Although this difference sounds explicit, it came through their narratives in subtle ways. The best way to illustrate this point is by examining the way mothers discussed their shame about welfare. Mothers not involved with LIFETIME discussed this shame in internalised ways.

For example, Misha, a 29-year-old black mother of one and community college student, explained that she does not talk about welfare because it is embarrassing. She worried what others around her would think if they knew she was on aid:

> I don't talk about that. That's embarrassing. I don't talk about that. And I don't know, I just no, I don't … I would feel very ashamed if somebody asked me, you know, ohhhh, you're on welfare, I would feel ashamed because they are going to keep that in their head.

Misha's perspectives about shame were typical among mothers and suggests how the welfare system and society made women feel ashamed using welfare assistance. The shaming of welfare mothers is well researched (Hays, 2003 ; Mitchell, 2003). Along these lines, Newman (1999), in *No Shame in My Game*, explores how low-wage workers created identities in their work not based on this culture of shaming the poor. Creating a culture of shame for welfare mothers and low-wage workers highlights how society attempts to blame poor individuals for their economic circumstances.

However, LIFETIME mothers through their oppositional consciousness were more likely to resist internalising shame. Sometimes, they explicitly externalised shame, and explained how American society tried to create a culture that overtly shames mothers on welfare. Critical of this culture of shame, they outlined how the welfare system – and caseworkers specifically – shame women who used social programmes. Their stance attempted to shift the responsibility off individuals who were poor, and to uncover the structural dynamics of poverty. They pointed out the political advantages to blaming poor individuals, specifically single mothers, for their need to use welfare. Part of the resistance of shame is accomplished through explaining how mothers believed they earned the right to use a necessary resource. For instance, Jasmine countered people who tried to make her feel ashamed that she was on welfare by pointing out the realities of her life, and her self-actualisation as a productive member of society:

> A lot of people say that I shouldn't be using their tax dollars to go to school on, that I should go and get a job, a lot of people think that I'm wasting my time, a lot of people think that I'm taking on school just as an excuse not to go to work. (Laughs) ... I've worked for 15 years in the service industry paying taxes, and now my taxes are paying for me to get back into the work industry to pay more taxes, and even more than I did before. So this is a springboard and a fair exchange in every way. So I look at it this way, I'm really paying for my school at the end of the day because I did my part out there.

By stating that she was an active participant in working society and paying taxes, she refused to accept the conservative rhetoric that produced shame. Jasmine's perspective was akin to those LIFETIME used in trainings.[3] Through the parent leadership trainings, LIFETIME encouraged mothers to reclaim the identity of 'welfare mother' and externalise or recognise shame they felt was not their fault, but was a product of the conservative framing of the welfare debate. Tony, a 33-year-old black mother of two and recent UC Berkeley graduate, also linked the shaming with assumptions by policymakers about what families on welfare need, instead of focusing on what citizens want in their country. Tony explained:

> More than anything, the women that are on CalWORKs ... are raising children and are trying to get a better education are already dealing with a life situations that are very challenging ... to pigeonhole people into your own preconceived notions of what a social policy should look like, based on what you want your city to look like or whatever, just doesn't make any sense. Because people are individuals and their lives are complex, and their issues are complex ... If the top had a different conceptual view of what their country should look like, who its citizens are, what they want their state, or county, or cities to look like, and kinda have a humanistic or holistic view of it, things would be much better. People are very arrogantly creating policies that have absolutely nothing to do with any research or anything but their own life experience, basically only along with their own biases about others out there. There is a huge disconnect between policy and practice.

Tony's assessment of how policymakers 'pigeonhole' participants into what they expect welfare parents to be like is challenged by her work as a LIFETIME parent leader. Tony attributes her perspective to her participation in LIFETIME and the organisation's framing of the welfare debate. Mothers who were involved with LIFETIME adopted some of these perspectives. The framing of shame is the best overt example of how LIFETIME helped mothers use their oppositional consciousness to move from an internal analysis of welfare use to an external one.

## Discussion and implications

LIFETIME developed participants' oppositional consciousness, which resulted in less internalisation of the shame associated with being on welfare. Participating with LIFETIME in grassroots activism gave them a voice in the policy-making process and helped them see themselves as 'experts' about living in poverty. Their ideas for social policy change were more structural. LIFETIME's work in welfare rights' activism illustrated a central concept about democracy – decisions should be made by those affected by them.

The process by which LIFETIME developed participants' oppositional consciousness is an under-used method for mobilising marginalised populations. Furthermore, this method worked with participants from 18 years old to 51 years old – women at many ages responded to this process. LIFETIME worked with low-income parents on welfare to meet their immediate needs, helped them through their personal crisis or urgent problems, then worked to empower participants to connect personal issues with broader structural inequalities. LIFETIME facilitated participants to feel empowered to challenge the social policies that affected their lives. This research shows how other types of grassroots organising can use this method like LIFETIME to develop an oppositional consciousness among marginalised populations.

## Notes

1. I tried balancing being a researcher and working for the organisation – a balance many researchers have navigated. My project was broadly about these issues, and studying activism of LIFETIME was part of the project, but not the entire study. LIFETIME participants knew I was both a part-time staff or volunteer (depending upon when) and a graduate student doing research. Most also knew I was married with no children, and had no experience on welfare. Not all participants in my research were active with LIFETIME, and not all who were active with LIFETIME volunteered to be part of my interviews.
2. Our event was not connected to this organisation, but this is the basic idea: http://www.clotheslineproject.org.
3. Based on a conversation with one of LIFETIME's directors, some self-selection to this perspective is possible. She felt that some mothers who get most involved were those who resisted the shaming before getting involved. LIFETIME's frame of shame resonated with them and they became more involved as a consequence.

## Disclosure statement

No potential conflict of interest was reported by the authors.

## Funding

This work was supported by the Directorate for Social, Behavioral and Economic Sciences [grant number SES-0727624]; National Poverty Center [grant number 1 U01 AE000002-03].

# References

Abramovitz, M. (1999). Toward a framework for understanding activism among poor and working-class women in twentieth century America. In G. Mink (Ed.), *Whose welfare* (pp. 214–248). Ithaca, NY: Cornell University Press.

Charmaz, K. (2006). *Constructing grounded theory*. London: Sage Publications.

Charmaz, K., & Katz, S. (in press). Subjective stories and social issues: Strategies for making connections. *Qualitative Methods in Psychology Bulletin*.

Gittell, M., Gross, J., & Holdaway, G. (1993). *Building human capital: The impact of post-secondary education on AFDC recipients in 5 states*. New York, NY: Howard Samuels State Management and Policy Center at the City University of New York.

Hardy-Fanta, C. (1993). *Latina politics Latino politics*. Philadelphia, PA: Temple University Press.

Hays, S. (2003). *Flat broke with children: Women in the age of welfare reform*. Oxford: Oxford University Press.

Kahn, P., Butler, S., Deprez, L., & Polakow, V. (2004). Introduction. In V. Polakow, S. Butler, L. Deprez, & P. Kahn (Eds.), *Shut out: Low income mothers and higher education in post-welfare America* (pp. 1–17). Albany, NY: SUNY Press.

Katz, S. (2008). *Pursuing a "reformed" dream: CalWORKs mothers in higher education after "ending welfare as we know it"* (Unpublished doctoral dissertation). Vanderbilt University, Nashville, TN.

Katz, S. (2012). TANF's 15th anniversary and the great recession: Are low-income mothers celebrating upward economic mobility? *Sociology Compass, 6*(8), 657–670.

Kelly, M. (2010). Regulating the reproduction and mothering of poor women: The controlling image of the welfare mother in television news coverage of welfare reform. *Journal of Poverty, 14*, 76–96.

Luna, Y. (2009). Single welfare mothers' resistance. *Journal of Poverty, 13*, 441–461.

Mansbridge, J. (2001). The making of oppositional consciousness. In J. J. Mansbridge & A. Morris (Eds.), *Oppositional consciousness: The subjective roots of social protest* (pp. 1–19). Chicago, IL: The University of Chicago Press.

Mathur, A. (2004). *From jobs to careers: How California community college credentials payoff for welfare participants*. Washington, DC: Center for Law and Social Policy.

Mitchell, T. (2003). If I survive, it will be despite welfare reform: Reflections of a former welfare student. In V. C. Adair & S. L. Dahlberg (Eds.), *Reclaiming class: Women, poverty, and the promise of higher education in America* (pp. 113–118). Philadelphia, PA: Temple University Press.

Naples, N. (1998). *Grassroots warriors: Activist mothering, community work, and the war on poverty*. New York, NY: Routledge.

Newman, K. (1999). *No shame in my game*. New York, NY: Vintage Press.

Piven, F. F., & Cloward, R. A. (1979). *Poor people's movements: Why they succeed, how they fail*. New York, NY: Vintage Books.

Ratner, L. (2004). Failing low income students: Education and training in the age of welfare reform. In V. Polakow, S. Butler, L. Deprez, & P. Kahn (Eds.), *Shut out: Low income mothers and higher education in post-welfare America* (pp. 45–74). Albany, NY: State University of New York Press.

Reese, E. (2011). *They say cut back, we say fight back: Welfare rights activism in an era of retrenchment*. New York, NY: Russell Sage Foundation.

Reisch, M., & Andrews, J. (2002). *The road not taken: A history of radical social work in the United States*. New York, NY: Routledge.

Shaw, K., Goldrick-Rab, S., Mazzeo, C., & Jacobs, J. (2006). *Putting poor people to work: How the work first idea eroded college access for the poor*. New York, NY: Russell Sage Foundation.

# Play as activism? Early childhood and (inter)generational politics

Rachel Rosen [ID]

**ABSTRACT**

Both young children and imaginative play are often considered to be fundamentally apolitical. Such views have been increasingly challenged, however, as both 'the political' and activism are being reconceptualised in more expansive ways. In seeking to critically build upon these efforts, I draw on ethnographic data generated in an early years setting in a super-diverse low-income community in London to highlight the space of imaginative play as a resonant site for investigations of the political. However, whether or not something is considered a 'political' matter is a political struggle in itself, and one that players may neither desire nor achieve. I make a case for both distinguishing between play and activism, and considering ways to foster connections between them. Imaginative play has the potential to enrich an intergenerational politics where adults and children engage together for a more just future.

Referring to the ubiquitous image of 'the child' in political posters, historian Dubinsky suggests that: 'Children appear, so that adults can act' (2012, p. 8). Ruddick (2007) meanwhile worries about the possibility for neoconservative 'ventriloquism' when adults claim to speak for the speechless foetus or child. What is most striking is that the affective force of 'the child' – as object for intervention or incitement to action – resonates across political lines. The 'young child' is a powerful trope, symbolising a bundle of adult anxieties, hopes, and attempts to control uncertain futures. Yet, the actual beings called young children in everyday parlance are largely understood and treated as being fundamentally apolitical. Their action is represented as learning, development, and newness to the world or, in less generous accounts, as pathology and manipulation.

In response, a small body of scholarship and practice has arisen, countering the relegation of early childhood in popular discourse and social theory to a 'private' and sequestered realm away from 'the political'. This literature has a dual concern: on the one hand, attending to the politics of early childhood (Moss, 2007) and, on the other, considering the politics of young children. In this latter approach, 'the political' is seen to be far more than formal structures of governance and rational, verbal acts – conceptualisations which exclude very young humans on both developmental and social grounds (Oswell, 2009). Instead, these approaches draw on more expansive ways of understanding what is political. They highlight the diversity of spaces where contestations take place over power, injustice, and the ways in which people seek to define and meet their needs (Brown, 2002; Fraser, 1990). Rather than assuming a priori which sites, modes, and speech count as political, Kallio and Häkli (2011) argue that we should begin by looking at children's experiences and lived worlds with these understandings in mind. The turn to children's politics has also prompted examination of young people's activism, with Nolas, Varvantakis, and Aruldoss (2016) staging an '(im)possible conversation' across these categories and pointing to a view of activism as both contesting the status quo and prefiguring new social relations, and likewise both the potential for action and action itself.

In the main, efforts to rethink the political in light of insights gleaned from research about children's lives do not intersect with the large body of cross-disciplinary scholarship about children's imaginative play. This increasingly focuses on play in developmental and educational terms, grounded in what Sutton-Smith (1997) refers to as a rhetoric of 'play as progress'. There is, however, a small, but significant, body of work which draws attention to the relationship between play, subjectivities, and social inequities (e.g. see discussion in Rosen, 2016). Notwithstanding that it focuses more on *social* than *political* subjectivities and agency (Kallio & Häkli, 2011). Insights therein provide the basis for rethinking the relationship between play and the political, and even play and activism, given play's possibility for imagining and enacting new ways of being (Bosco, 2010; Lester, 2011).

Bringing together these bodies of literature on play, politics, and childhood prompts the questions: When can play be considered political? If we accept that there is a potential for political agency to be enacted in and through imaginative play, can this be understood as a form of activism? What are the promises and risks of such conceptual moves? In taking up these questions in the discussion which follows, I advance three main arguments. Drawing on ethnographic data, I begin by highlighting imaginative play as a resonant site for investigations of the political. Then, I suggest that whether or not something is considered a 'political' matter, rather than intimate or educational, for example, is a political struggle in itself, and one that players may neither desire nor achieve. Finally, I consider these points in light of broader efforts in the social sciences to rethink the boundaries of activism, arguing that it is important to both distinguish, and consider ways to foster the connections, between play and activism.

## Play and the political

By way of entry into these arguments, I offer the story of a quest to stop an insatiable monster. I was about one year into an ethnographic study[1] at Westside Nursery, based in a super-diverse low-income community in London, UK, when Peter, a charismatic – and contentious – pre-schooler, waved me over. Cecilia also responded to his wave, but Peter pushed her and yelled: 'No! This is just for boys!' Cecilia pushed back, and the tension escalated, a full-blown physical fight about to erupt. Standing next to me and looking on, Kaltrina – a fellow pre-schooler – shouted at the two: 'The monster! Come over!' The fight between Peter and Cecilia stopped as quickly as it had begun and they ran with the others who had joined us to hide from the 'monster'. Sabir wiped his brow and Cecilia breathed rapidly as Kenza whispered: 'We have to trap the monster in there.' She pointed to a set of fenced-in stairs. Peter exclaimed: 'No! He's the hulk. He'll just jump out. We have to get him with our guns.' A cacophony of voices responded, shouting conflicting strategies. 'Let's cut his head off with the sword!' 'Let's put ropes across the top so he can't get out.' 'We need more children to help us', Kenza pronounced authoritatively. 'The monster is so big. He is eating all the fish. We have to save them.' Seeming to concur, the group set off in search of assistance. The assembled group of nine players gathered around Kaltrina as she insisted: 'OK. We need many plans', moving her hands up and down as if to show the magnitude of tactics necessary to stop the voracious beast.

This imaginative activity was not at all unusual at Westside Nursery where vampires, beasts, and other horrific creatures roamed the outdoor space with impunity during the parts of the daily schedule which were organised into 'free play' blocks. To call this imaginative play, however, is not to indicate how such activity was understood by the participants, nor is it intended in any way to minimise its importance. Play is not just 'fun and games' but is very 'real' in experience and effect, and as I will go on to suggest, intricately bound up with questions of the political, or indeed the political economy.

As has been well documented, play has become a site of big business (Cook, 2014; Hughes & Mac Naughton, 2001), ranging from commercial products to specially designed spaces and activities. The play described above was no different. We hid from the insatiable monster behind a wall of blocks purchased from Community Playthings, a multi-million-dollar corporation with a global 'reach' expanding across seven world regions. The themes and characters in this and many other moments of imaginative play I observed involved narratives which drew on monster-saturated media directed at a market of child viewers. To give a sense of this scope, Disney's *Monsters Inc* film grossed US$590 million and the four *Shrek* Films grossed a total of US$2.9 billion (FindTheData, 2012).

Play is also one way that people orient and position themselves and others. Central preoccupations for players at Westside Nursery included who could play and who could not, as well as what each character could do and what they were unable or forbidden to do. Play, then, is implicated in the formation of subjectivities and social relations (Rosen, 2016). Although such engagements are not always discussed in the academic literature in relation to political subjectivities, they certainly resonate with contemporary descriptions of 'the political' as sites where 'injustice is possible' (Nakata, 2008, p. 19), where social relations are profoundly shaped by capital, and where power and value(s) are negotiated and contested (Brown, 2002). Peter's initial refusal to allow girls into play, for instance, reinforced gender binaries by using characteristics associated with dominant forms of masculinity – strength, agility, and physicality – as a basis for exclusion. More broadly, play is increasingly used to make distinctions between 'adults' and 'children', with certain playful activities consigned to childhood which were previously common across generational orders[2] (Aries, 1962/1996). Indeed, play has become synonymous with an idealised childhood, such that young children, on an increasingly global basis, spend numerous hours engaged in activity which is, at very least, named as play.

In many cases, play has also become a site of surveillance and regulation. Framed as a way to promote progress and development, it has become 'an almost hallowed concept for teachers of young children' (Pellegrini & Boyd, 1993, p. 105). The point here is that young children's play in early childhood settings – including the violently themed play about the insatiable monster – takes place within highly structured settings, largely designed and ordered by adults in order to achieve certain instrumental ends (Ailwood,

2003). Despite the terminology of 'free play', neoliberal pedagogies of play are primarily concerned with producing certain types of human capital: 'school-ready' learners and employment-ready future adults (Dahlberg & Moss, 2005). At Westside Nursery, an exhaustive national reporting structure and ranking system created the conditions where educators watched, documented, and evaluated children's play based on prescriptive developmental milestones. When children were deemed to be 'stuck' and unable to meet these teleological goals, educators also intervened to 'move them on' (Rosen, 2015a).

Finally, play often surfaces complex ethical and political questions. Peter's initial rejection of 'girls' raised political questions about possible ways to disrupt and challenge sexist practices. The story of the insatiable monster, devouring the fish for its own individual benefit, has resonances with overtly political questions about private appropriation and accumulation. Indeed, the monstrous has often been used as a cultural trope to signify political concerns, including hyper-consumption, unbridled expansionism, and the destruction of non-renewable resources (McNally, 2011). What's more, the confrontation with the enormous, ravenous, and growing monster which not only existentially threatened the fish population but also the players themselves raised a series of questions about what sort of action is possible, ethical, and even necessary in the face of such horror. The players confronted questions about whether death or imprisonment would offer an effective and satisfactory response, as well as the relative benefits of individual and collective action.

It is for these reasons that I am arguing that play *may* be understood as a highly political space. It is also one in which players have the potential for political agency, understood here as 'participation and engagement with discourses and taking action designed to change life situations (political, economic, social and cultural practices)' (Skelton, 2010, p. 147). Players in the monster tale 'engaged' with hegemonic discourses and inequitable social relations such as attempted gendered exclusions. They 'took action' against the greedy monster, albeit primarily within the cultural reality of play.

## Play as a 'political' matter

Taking seriously Kallio and Häkli's (2011) suggestion that we start investigations of the political by attending to *how* something becomes political (or not), here I consider how investigations of play speak to this question. I argue that whilst play may certainly be understood as a politicised site, as noted above, whether or not this occurs is an empirical question.

This necessitates addressing what makes something 'political'. 'A matter is "political"', argues Fraser, 'If it is contested across a range of different discursive arenas and among a range' of people (1990, p. 205). Fraser's point here is that beyond 'official' structures of governance, there is a 'discursive politics' and part of what happens in this space is contestation over whether a matter is one of official political concern rather than domestic, educational, or economic. Something is not essentially political in content but whether it is viewed as political is a matter of struggle itself. Extending this point, Kallio and Häkli (2011) contend that in some cases struggles to politicise a matter may move it from the 'private' into the official political where it becomes institutionalised.

Both these distinctions between the official and discursive political, and the emphasis on *how* something becomes political rather than *if* it is political, provide an important extension to my previous point that play can be understood as a site of the political. These distinctions suggest that there is a significant potential that the matter of play may be considered leisure or educational not only due to definitional differences. Whether play is considered political also relates to the relative degree of contestation about it and the themes it raises. Put slightly differently, a number of factors pose serious limits to the potential of young children's play in the contemporary moment being seriously considered as a site of the political.

To illustrate this point, it might be helpful to share a brief anecdote. I was recently discussing our website tagline 'Researching and teaching the politics of children and childhood at UCL' with a senior childhood scholar. She commented: 'I'm glad you put this on the site. I'm so tired of the focus on play in childhood studies rather than on important political issues.' Such a statement might not be surprising coming from a political scientist largely concerned with the official politics of adults. But why might a knowledgeable and respected childhood scholar make such comments – particularly someone who has dedicated a great deal of her scholarly life to recognising children's contributions and working for their improved status and well-being?

Certainly, I think this academic was countering the relegation of children to the realm of play, and indeed the more widespread age-based segregation of young children into 'islands' (Zeiher, 2003), separated into institutions and activities away from others in their communities. At the same time, however, such comments reflect and reproduce dominant Rousseaunian-inflected imaginaries of play as innocent, fun, and free – entirely Other to the political. Yet, as I have discussed above, the insatiable monster narrative makes short work of any such conceptualisations of childhood play. More pressingly, by dislocating the potential for play to have political import, such comments effectively set young children outside of the political given that this is how their activity is organised and understood on an increasingly global scale. This positions play, and the matters raised in playful activity, at the margins, not seen or heard as potentially political issues or acts to be contested 'across a range of different discursive arenas and among a range' of people.

A second relevant factor here relates to players' uses of hidden spaces. Given the extent of adult control over when, where, and how children are expected to engage in early childhood settings, it is not unsurprising that many studies have documented the ways in which children find or make hidden spaces to play away from adult surveillance and intervention (Albon & Rosen, 2014; Skanfors, Lofdahl, & Hagglund, 2009). Children may make use of the physical affordances of spaces which limit the presence of larger (typically adult) bodies. They may take play to spaces where adult sight lines are restricted or engage in mobile play that adults are not able to follow. Indeed, much of the monster saga described above took place in a hidden space behind a large tree, off to the side of the outdoor space with very limited sight lines from other parts of the nursery. When taken into the open, the play moved rapidly across the boundaries of the specific spaces which adult staff members were placed and required to monitor. The point here is that such use of hidden space limits the range of people amongst whom contestations can take place, restricting the extent to which play and the concerns explored within it can become politicised. My intention here is not to hold children responsible for being deemed inherently apolitical, but to note that whether play and its themes become a political matter or not is achieved through struggle, and processes of politicisation, and this may be neither desired nor achieved by child players.

## Play as activism?

So far, I have argued that play is a relevant site for investigation of the political. I have tempered my claims by suggesting that the historical location, context, and visibility of play effect if and how it becomes politicised and a site where political agency is exercised. Invoking political agency moves the discussion into the terrain of social change, social action, and even activism, and it is to this that I now turn. I consider whether young children's potential for political agency in and through imaginative play can be understood as a form of activism, as well as the promises and risks of such a conceptual move. In what follows, I do not deny the possibility that imaginative play can be part of, or involved in, activist efforts, but I contend that there are dangers to conflating play and activism. I tread a cautious path between denying play a space within/as activism and broadening definitions of activism to include everything and anything.

This intervention speaks with, but also against, accounts critical of the ways in which 'activism', which broadly speaking can be understood as collective efforts at transformation actualised through political agency (Nolas et al., 2016), has been reduced to the spectacular, the programmatic, the national, or global; separated from people's quotidian lives; and tied to self-aware intentionality. Indeed, there have been various attempts to question the boundaries between activism and the everyday, opening up the tenor and type of action typically considered activist by both social scientists and participants in social movements (Martin, Hanson, & Fontaine, 2007). This scholarship draws attention to the 'cautious, modest, pragmatic, experimental, stuttering, tentative' practices of a minor politics or activism (Rose, 1999, p. 280). To give one such example, Horton and Kraftl (2009) argue that stated intentions and sentiments for change, expressed in terms of 'I should do X in order to achieve Y', but not necessarily combined with action, can be understood as 'flickering' activist dispositions and 'implicit activism'. They consider responses of parents to the threatened closure of a neighbourhood Children's Centre, which take this projective, but not necessarily actualised form of action. They argue that 'everyday, affective bonds and acts ultimately constituted *politicised activism* and commitments' (Horton & Kraftl, 2009, p. 15; my emphasis).

Without doubt, there is a need to question on both epistemological and political grounds the limitations of current doxa which offer impoverished characterisations of activism (Bobel, 2007). By focusing only on large-scale mobilisations, iconised by the highly visible solitary hero or charismatic leader, the arduous work of building and nurturing activism is obscured. This can limit understandings of how political movements are sustained emotionally and practically. Such concerns are particularly urgent when activism may feel impossible, futile, or risky, which are symptomatic of the pervasive sense that 'there is no alternative', either viable or imaginable, to capitalism and its exploitative social relations (Fisher, 2009). Furthermore, as feminist scholarship has pointed out, the cooking, caring, and emotional labour – including relationship building and the cultivation of dissenting subjectivities – which are so central to activist efforts continue to be deeply gendered (Martin et al., 2007).

More expansive notions raise a question as to whether play can be seen as a form of activism where players may 'seek to engender a small reworking of their own spaces of action' (Rose, 1999, p. 280). Such reworkings are, for example, evident in Cecilia's refusal to be excluded from the physically active and heroic play on the basis of spuriously gendered assertions. Similar instances were apparent throughout the ethnography such as a time when children and an adult-educator playfully swapped institutional roles, as a succession of children usurped the 'teacher's chair' and commanded others in a way that simultaneously claimed, and poked fun at, institutional authority. In many ways, the characteristics of play would seem to not only lend themselves to such reworking but can be understood *as* fundamentally transformative interjections in the world. Imaginative play, as Henricks (2006) puts it, involves pulling apart and building the world anew. Players operate in the subjunctive mode: 'as if' they were someone else or 'what if' the world was otherwise. Play makes it possible to refuse accepted meanings and create new ones: as in the critical moment which began this article, a fence can become a prison, the wind can become a greedy monster, and antagonisms between individual children can be reshaped into a collective endeavour. In play, participants experiment with varying ways of being and acting, and can overturn the status quo, at least within the confines of the play: small bodies and children – who are subordinated and regulated in ways justified by their positioning as children – became more powerful than an enormous, domineering and monstrous enemy. In other moments, child players used the trope of dying and death in a variety of ways including, as I have argued elsewhere, as a way to provoke caring touch *from other children* (Rosen, 2015c). The recognition that players can make different worlds in play is suggestive of the social constitution of our quotidian lives, and therefore its possible reconstitution (Katz, 2004). Indeed, Katz explains that having 'a vision of what else could be' is central to any radical politics (2004, p. 253).

Building on such understandings, Bosco argues that children's play and 'playful becoming' should be considered as activism insofar as it 'contributes, both directly and indirectly, to political and social change' and allows for 'experiment[ation] with political relations' (2010, pp. 385–386). Lester (2011) puts forward a similar argument. Although he does not use the term activist, it is implied. Lester (2011, p. 13) contends that children's play 'can be seen as full (*political*) participation' and that play is necessarily an exercise of children's 'collective agency to appropriate available times/space for their desires'. He goes on to suggest that by offering moments of hope and providing children with the opportunity to control aspects of their own lives, playing 'becomes a political and ethical movement for both adults and children' (Lester, 2011, p. 21).

My concern here is that collapsing emotional labour, sentiments for change, individual 'acts of defiance' (Bobel, 2007), or indeed imaginative play into activism – regardless of intent or actual enactment – does a disservice to efforts aimed at understanding and working towards social, political, and economic transformation. I take intent to be an essential defining feature of activism, albeit that the form of activity could just as easily be cooking for a group meeting or speaking at a demonstration and need not be identified by participants as activism at all. Conflating play and activism also limits the ability to evaluate political impact (both intended and not) and efficacy (in terms of both practical changes and formation of new alliances or solidarities) of various forms of action. It also limits the development of movements which might bring about social change. Histories of worker and civil rights struggles, as well as those against slavery and imperialism, point to the 'efficacy' and necessity of collective movements in the face of injustice, domination, and exploitation, albeit that there are diverse ways of understanding collectivities.

My apprehensions take a particular form in relation to claims that play is a space of activism. To acknowledge play as a site for considering the political, and to point to the possibility of contestation of the status quo around, or via play, is not the same thing as arguing that this will *necessarily* happen. Play also reproduces and amplifies injurious social relations (Rosen, 2016). While Peter's initial exclusion of girls was challenged in the monster saga above, there were many other instances at Westside Nursery where ascriptions of gender, 'race', ability, and class were used to police the boundaries around play groups, assign play characters, and imagine ludic worlds. For instance, girls were denied roles as superheroes, while boys racialised as Black were told that they could only be the troubled character of 'Black Spiderman', effectively re-constituting the iconic saviour role as one of privileged White masculinity. Play often reinforced hegemonic practices in their narratives: for instance, play stories revolved around 'mothers' cooking, caring, and cleaning for others reflecting traditional gendered divisions of labour or included shopping, buying, and consuming as ways to build up stores of material posses-sions (both symbolic and imaginary) as the basis for achieving power and social status. Play in these instances bypasses debates over values, power, and injustices. Furthermore, there is no guarantee that new imaginings in play will necessarily become everyday ways of being and living. The point I am making here is that it is important not to essentialise play as fundamentally change-oriented and activist despite its contestive and subjunctive characteristics.

Moves towards more expansive notions of activism are important, in that they connect the deeply intimate to the political. However, even Rose (1999, p. 280), in forwarding 'minor politics' as activism, pays significant attention to the ways 'small reworkings' join up 'with a whole series of other circuits and cause them to fluctuate, waver and reconfi-gure in wholly unexpected ways'. Even if political agency exercised in the 'cramped spaces' of play can combine into something more, the opposite is just as likely. By collap-sing play into activism, we limit our theoretical resources for considering why such con-nections do or do not happen. One question to ask then is: what is it about the characteristics of (young children's) playful activity which might constrain/enable such wider reconfigurations? What conditions allow, and what preclude, new commonalities to be forged through play? To simply replace the programmatic and spectacular with the intimate and tentative is effectively a reversal of the feminist slogan 'the personal is political'. It has risky implications given the exploitative continuity of inequities which extend beyond the local. Although the monster saga was a particular and localised instan-tiation of gendered exclusions and their contestation, it bears marked similarity to narra-tives in other nursery settings. Furthermore, the ongoing ethnography suggests that it did not cause more than very momentary flicker beyond this particular moment nor was there any indication that such action was motivated by, or intended to challenge, hegemonic formations of gender or relations of exploitation.

## The place of play in (inter)generational activism

In this article, I suggest that play is a resonant site for investigations of the political but argue that whether play and its themes become political matters is both an empirical question and a matter of struggle itself. I contend that the possibility of exercising political agency within and around play is different from suggesting that play is a space of activism. Crucially, however, I have rejected developmental arguments which render young chil-dren, and their imaginative play, essentially outside the realm of political contestation as well as concurring with arguments that the sites and activities of politics, and indeed activism, cannot be determined *a priori*. Instead, my emphasis on distinguishing between play and activism has focused on attending to the ways in which political change occurs and characterising activism as fundamentally bound up with concerns of social, political and economic transformation.

Nevertheless, these points of distinction do not mark an incommensurability between play and activism, and in these concluding comments, I highlight the value of fostering connections between them for (inter)generational activism. In bracketing the 'inter' of intergenerational, I seek to keep two slightly different points in view. First, this construction nods to the possibility of thinking 'intergenerationally' about activism, moving political contestation out of an adult-only realm and stressing the importance of social memories across generations in forging political solidarities (Nolas et al., 2016). Second, I highlight the necessity of contesting generational orders which reify a sharp binary between childhood and adulthood; essentialise 'the child', ascribing her/him with, often deficit, characteristics, normative activities such as the contemporary bourgeois conflation of play and childhood, and marginal social status; and lead to the subordination of children, *inter alia*, as a generational group.

Taking such an (inter)generational approach by attending to the politics of and in children's play can contribute to more inclusive and diverse communities committed to social justice. Transformations will be fundamentally limited if almost one-third of the world's population, those under 18,[3] are denied the possibility of participation in explicit action for change. In part, then, I am suggesting the importance of learning to hear, and to be 'answerable' (Rosen, 2015b), to both the interventions and silences of young children's play in deliberations over the political and activism. Put simply, play may be many things, but it is deserving of political attention.

While I have suggested that political issues of inequality, oppression, and exploitation generally need to be addressed through collective activism, such social action is largely motivated by what matters or comes to matter to people. Rational logic and dialogue are not the only, or even primary, motivations (Sayer, 2011). The characteristics of play mean that it is a significant arena for gaining insights into issues which matter or come to matter for participants. Perhaps more importantly, it offers a space for collectively exploring and building a sense of what matters 'to us'. As an easily ruptured space which necessarily requires that someone or something 'responds in satisfying ways' (Henricks, 2006, p. 201) in order for it to continue, some element of play themes, partners, and/ or processes must matter to players in order for play to be maintained. In the monster saga, it mattered to Cecilia and Kaltrina that they were not excluded. The existential survival of the children, and later the fish, became of crucial concern to the collective group of players. Maintaining the interactive play space mattered: children offered contradictory suggestions for stopping the monster but did not 'block' other interjections to the extent of collapsing the play space.

Play – and its affective, interactive, and subjunctive characteristics – can provide a counter-point to cynicism engendered in a world where actions seem futile or are co-opted before even being realised. There is *always* an alternative in play. As a slightly more liminal and less existentially fraught space, play allows for experimentation, creation, as well as imagining and enacting new ways of being and living. The monster saga prompted this group of children to find ways to come together in a common struggle against the monster. This enactment of a form of solidarity, albeit a contestable one, was different from many everyday interactions in Westside Nursery, where these children were often at odds with each other. Verbal and physical fights, and efforts at being *individually* recognised and praised, were not uncommon. Building common cause is a critical challenge in activist movements: important both because it works against the short-termism of 'new capitalism' which erodes the possibilities of sustained commitment to others (Sennett, 1998) and as a political strategy in the face of fragmentation and intensifying global inequities.

In discussing these points, I have provided examples from the monster play. However, I have explicitly left open the matter of who players can be, hinting that there is an 'us' which moves beyond young children. If adults approach play within openness, rather than attempting to contain that which seems risky or recuperate it for developmental purposes, imaginative play has the potential to allow for those constituted as adults and children to *engage together* with the possibilities of a more just future. Before expanding, it is perhaps instructive to be clear what I am *not* saying here. This is not a point about educational theory or pedagogical practice per se. I am not advocating play as, yet another, forum in which adults might constitute themselves as teachers in relation to children, and intervene to socialise children into 'proper' roles of citizenship and 'correct' types of political activity. Here, however, I am seeking to destabilise play as something that young children do and in which adults might occasionally intervene, precisely because play allows for political dilemmas and strategies to be explored in slightly more liminal spaces. As a player in the monster saga, the rapid breathing, whispered voices, and expansive physical movements of players produced feelings in me of both fear in the face of the monster's voracious appropriations and subjugating acts, as well as a sense of strength (and admitted unease) in bodies coming together to stop the monster's destruction.[4]

Finally, children's historically situated expertise as players can serve to destabilise adult–child power relations, an important counter balance to critiques of solidarity as conditional and paternalistic (Benson & Rosen, in press). This is not a naïve claim that play is immune to historically sedimented power relations. For example, adult–child play in this ethnography was often treated by educators as an opportunity to help students meet nationally determined learning goals. The historically specific constitution of the 'child as player' does, however, exemplify that the 'competent adult' and 'deficit child' is not a monolithic, a-historic, or static relation. Nevertheless, given the subordination of children broadly speaking, the proposal to engage in play intergenerationally is one which is well served by a consequentialist lens. Who speaks, influences, and acts in play; in what ways; and for whose benefit are central questions to be asked. I was compelled to wonder, for example, how important it was to maintain our common cause and how much my insistence on doing so might amplify adult dominance or muffle important debate about what is 'we' value.

Linking emotions and imagination to activism is not to discount the importance of rational deliberation, but to add to it. Political dilemmas that are opened up in ludic activity, as well as things identified as mattering to us, can continue to be explored both in future play and in other sites. Conversely, activism in turn can help shift the contours of play, including the exclusions, the hegemonic, and relations of domination which haunt such spaces.

Young children's play, then, is neither the same as, nor the antithesis to, activism. In offering a space where the world can be otherwise, play can perhaps simply be understood to share with activism the slogan: 'Another world is possible.' Imagining which worlds this might be, and how we might live and be in these worlds, is the subject of ongoing struggle, deep political-economic analysis, and creative explorations of the inter-generational 'matterings' of our lives.

## Notes

1. This 'critical moment' happened during an 18-month ethnographic study investigating socio-dramatic and fantastical play about themes of imaginary death and pretend physical violence. I spent one day a week at Westside Nursery as a semi-participant observer, joining as a co-player when invited and taking field notes either during or just immediately after observing a session. These 'scribbles' – with all the omissions and imprecisions this term implies (Jones, Holmes, MacRae, MacLure, 2010) – were turned into longer fieldnotes at the end of each day. I also conducted formal and informal ethnographic interviews with children and adults. Thematic coding was complemented by in-depth analysis of 'critical moments' such as the one in this article. Critical moments are not chosen because they are repeated events: even if a phenomenon is observed only once, it can still be interrogated in relation to the conditions of its production and the effects of its existence (Sayer, 2000). Analytically, the use of critical moments which either 'disturb or jar' or 'are so mundane that we may miss their presence' allows for analysis of 'entrenched assumptions' (Albon & Rosen, 2014, p. 6).
2. The term 'generational order' refers to 'a system of social ordering' which positions certain people as 'children' and others as 'adults' (Alanen, 2011, p. 161). Rather than reflecting a natural division, these categories are inherited and remade through human activity. Certain activities, behaviours, needs, and capacities become associated with each generational position, affecting possibilities for action.
3. I am using this age distinction somewhat rhetorically. Age is neither the only way to understand the processes whereby some humans are made into children. As a growing 'legal fetishism' (Vitterbo, 2012), age has, however, become a dominant way of defining childhood.
4. The use of such emotive terms perhaps sounds unbelievable, and I myself was surprised by the force of my responses. However, if it is accepted that fiction and images can produce emotional investments and interpellations in adults, I would argue that it is only 'adultism' which makes children's play seem so inconsequential that it cannot produce such sentiments. It goes without saying, however, that these embodied emotions are not transparently knowable and are more than likely bound up with adult anxieties of childhood.

## Acknowledgements

I wish to thank the SI editors, independent reviewers, and participants in the 'Activism on the edge of age' workshop (organised by the editors) for their insightful comments on earlier drafts.

## Disclosure statement

No potential conflict of interest was reported by the authors.

## ORCID

*Rachel Rosen* ⓘ http://orcid.org/0000-0001-9916-5910

## References

Ailwood, J. (2003). Governing early childhood education through play. *Contemporary Issues in Early Childhood, 4*(3), 286–299.

Alanen, L. (2011). Generational order. In J. Qvortrup, W. Corsaro, & M.-S. Honig (Eds.), *The Palgrave handbook of childhood studies* (pp. 159–174). Basingstoke: Palgrave MacMillan.

Albon, D., & Rosen, R. (2014). *Negotiating adult–child relationships in early childhood research*. London: Routledge.

Aries, P. (1962/1996). *Centuries of childhood*. London: Pimlico.

Benson, L., & Rosen, R. (in press). From silence to solidarity: Locating the absent 'child voice' in the struggle against benefit sanctions. *Children & Society*. Retrieved from http://discovery.ucl.ac.uk/id/eprint/1541263

Bobel, C. (2007). 'I'm not an activist, though I've done a lot of it': Doing activism, being activist and the 'perfect standard' in a contemporary movement. *Social Movement Studies, 6*(2), 147–159. doi:10.1080/14742830701497277

Bosco, F. J. (2010). Play, work or activism? Broadening the connections between political and children's geographies. *Children's Geographies, 8*(4), 381–390. doi:10.1080/14733285.2010.511003

Brown, W. (2002). At the edge. *Political Theory, 30*(4), 556–576.

Cook, D. T. (2014). Whose play? Children, play and consumption. In E. Brooker, M. Blaise, & S. Edwards (Eds.), *The Sage handbook of play and learning in early childhood* (pp. 283–293). London: Sage.

Dahlberg, G., & Moss, P. (2005). *Ethics and politics in early childhood education*. London: RoutledgeFalmer.

Dubinsky, K. (2012). Children, ideology, and iconography: How babies rule the world. *The Journal of the History of Childhood and Youth, 5*(1), 5–13. doi:10.1353/hcy.2012.0009

FindTheData. (2012). *Compare highest grossing movies*. Retrieved from http://highest-grossing-movies.findthedata.org/

Fisher, M. (2009). *Capitalist realism: Is there no alternative?* Winchester: Zero Books.

Fraser, N. (1990). Struggle over needs: Outline of a socialist-feminist critical theory of late-capitalist political culture. In L. Gordon (Ed.), *Women, the state, and welfare* (pp. 199–225). Madison: University of Wisconsin Press.

Henricks, T. S. (2006). *Play reconsidered: Sociological perspectives on human expression*. Urbana: University of Illinois Press.

Horton, J., & Kraftl, P. (2009). Small acts, kind words and 'not too much fuss': Implicit activisms. *Emotion, Space and Society, 2*(1), 14–23. doi:10.1016/j.emospa.2009.05.003

Hughes, P., & Mac Naughton, G. (2001). Fractured or manufactured: Gendered identities and culture in the early years. In S. Grieshaber & G. S. Cannella (Eds.), *Embracing identities in early childhood education: Diversities and possibilities* (pp. 114–130). London: Teacher's College Press.

Jones, L., Holmes, R., MacRae, C., & MacLure, M. (2010). Documenting classroom life: How can I write about what I am seeing? *Qualitative Research, 10*(4), 479–491.

Kallio, K. P., & Häkli, J. (2011). Are there politics in childhood? *Space and Polity, 15*(1), 21–34. doi:10.1080/13562576.2011.567897

Katz, C. (2004). *Growing up global: Economic restructuring and children's everyday lives*. Minneapolis: University of Minnesota Press.

Lester, S. (2011). *Moments of nonsense and signs of hope: The everyday 'political' nature of children's play*. IPA conference, Cardiff.

Martin, D., Hanson, S., & Fontaine, D. (2007). What counts as activism? The role of individuals in creating change. *Women's Studies Quarterly, 25*, 78–94.

McNally, D. (2011). *Monsters of the market: Zombies, vampires, and global capitalism*. Leiden: Brill.

Moss, P. (2007). Bringing politics into the nursery: Early childhood education as a democratic practice. *European Early Childhood Education Research Journal, 15*(1), 5–20. doi:10.1080/13502930601046620

Nakata, S. M. (2008). Elizabeth Eckford's appearance at Little Rock: The possibility of children's political agency. *Politics, 28*(1), 19–25.

Nolas, S.-M., Varvantakis, C., & Aruldoss, V. (2016). (Im)possible conversations? Activism, childhood and everyday life. *Journal of Social and Political Psychology, 4*(1), 252–265. doi:10.5964/jspp.v4i1.536

Oswell, D. (2009). Yet to come? Globality and the sound of an infant politics. *Radical Politics Today, 1* (1), 1–18.

Pellegrini, A., & Boyd, B. (1993). The role of play in early childhood development and education: Issues in definition and function. In B. Spodek (Ed.), *Handbook of research on the education of young children* (pp. 105–121). New York, NY: MacMillan.

Rose, N. (1999). *Powers of freedom: Reframing political thought.* Cambridge: Cambridge University Press.

Rosen, R. (2015a). Children's violently-themed play and adult imaginaries of childhood: A Bakhtinian analysis. *International Journal of Early Childhood, 47*(2), 235–250. doi:10.1007/s13158-015-0135-z

Rosen, R. (2015b). 'The scream': Meanings and excesses in early childhoods settings. *Childhood, 22*(1), 39–52. doi:10.1177/0907568213517269

Rosen, R. (2015c). The use of the death trope in peer culture play: Grounds for rethinking children and childhood? *International Journal of Play, 4*(2), 163–174.

Rosen, R. (2016). Early childhood subjectivities, inequities, and imaginative play. In N. Worth & C. Dwyer (Eds.), *Geographies of identities and subjectivities* (pp. 141–162). Singapore: Springer.

Ruddick, S. (2007). At the horizons of the subject: Neo-liberalism, neo-conservatism and the rights of the child part one: From 'knowing' fetus to 'confused' child. *Gender, Place & Culture, 14*(5), 513–527. doi:10.1080/09663690701562180

Sayer, A. (2000). *Realism and social science.* Thousand Oaks, CA: Sage.

Sayer, A. (2011). *Why things matter to people: Social science, values and ethical life.* Cambridge: Cambridge University Press.

Sennett, R. (1998). *The corrosion of character: The personal consequences of work in the new capitalism.* New York, NY: Norton.

Skanfors, L., Lofdahl, A., & Hagglund, S. (2009). Hidden spaces and places in the preschool: Withdrawal strategies in preschool children's peer cultures. *Journal of Early Childhood Research, 7*(1), 94–109. doi:10.1177/1476718x08098356

Skelton, T. (2010). Taking young people as political actors seriously: Opening the borders of political geography. *Area, 42*(2), 145–151. doi:10.1111/j.1475-4762.2009.00891.x

Sutton-Smith, B. (1997). *The ambiguity of play.* Cambridge, MA: Harvard University Press.

Vitterbo, H. (2012). The age of conflict: Rethinking childhood, law, and age through the Israeli–Palestinian case. In M. Freeman (Ed.), *Law and childhood studies* (pp. 133–155). Oxford: Oxford University Press.

Zeiher, H. (2003). Shaping daily life in urban environments. In P. Christensen & M. O'Brien (Eds.), *Children in the city: Home, neighbourhood and community* (pp. 66–81). London: RoutledgeFalmer.

ACADEMY
*SOCIAL SCIENCES

# Educational activism across the divide: empowering youths and their communities

Thalia Dragonas and Anni Vassiliou

**ABSTRACT**

This paper tells the story of the Creative Youth Workshops (CYWs), a social space for youths, members of the minority/Muslim and the majority/Christian society, in jointly constructing alternative possibilities of living positively together in the conflict-ridden social environment of Thrace, a North Eastern Greek province bordering Bulgaria and Turkey. The CYWs constitute a sub-project within the overall frame of a comprehensive intervention inside and outside the classroom, called 'Education of Muslim Minority Children'.

## Introduction

This paper tells the story of the Creative Youth Workshops (CYWs), a social space for youths, members of the minority/Muslim and the majority/Christian society, in jointly constructing alternative possibilities of living positively together in the conflict-ridden social environment of Thrace, a North Eastern Greek province bordering Bulgaria and Turkey.[1] The CYWs constitute a sub-project within the overall frame of a comprehensive intervention inside and outside the classroom, called 'Education of Muslim Minority Children'.[2]

The story of the CYWs is multi-vocal and multi-layered. While it is us who are telling, it is also the voice of those who engaged in this process. In our telling it, we do not adopt the side of the observer and we do not distinguish between the CYWs on the one side and us on the other.[3] In our long years in the field we have been navigating amidst a power game of identity politics prevalent in the Thracian society and have been constantly involved in a non-linear process of negotiation and mutual transformation. Thus in order to unravel our story, we will start by positioning CYWs inside the wider project and by grounding it within the specific contentious socio-historical and political context. The description of this multi-dimensional intervention is not prescription, as Gergen (2015) would caution in discussing the 'mirroring tradition' of research that favours the maintenance of the status quo. It is a narrative portraying the grounds of possibility, of practices in which social change is the primary goal. Hence our work is placed within a paradigm bridging action-research and activism.

We will guide the reader through our rationale informing the setting up of the CYWs, the resources the group drew upon in search of meanings and understandings, the encouragement of creativity, self-expression, imagination and dream-work, the nego-tiation of linguistic, cultural and ethnic identities, and the enhancement of collaborative skills in sharing and living together. We will finally highlight how the youths' engagement has had intergenerational consequences.

## The project on the 'Education of Muslim Minority Children' and its socio-historical and political context

The project on the 'Education of Muslim Minority Children' comprises the teaching and learning of Greek as a second language, the development of multiple educational materials, compensatory classes in various subjects, teacher training and extensive work with the community. It is a complex intervention, taking place amidst antagonistic political interests that have deep historical roots. Its content and the social, cultural, historical and political context within which it was developed and has been running since 1997, have been described extensively elsewhere (Dragonas, 2014a, 2014b; Dragonas & Frangoudaki, 2008, 2014).

Minority children are Greek citizens of Muslim religion, members of a territorial, histori-cal minority established by the International Treaty of Lausanne in 1923, sealing the exchange of populations between Greece and Turkey. Some are Slav speaking, few are Romani speaking while most of them are Turkish speaking and have a Turkish ethnic iden-tity. Locked within the wider Greek-Turkish conflict, these children bear the stigma of incarnating the lifelong archenemy of Greece.

Compared to the majority Christian population, the Muslim minority has suffered pro-found inequalities since it is far more economically deprived and far less educated than the majority. The biggest part lives in separate communities that are largely agrarian and poor. While there are trends towards modernisation, the minority is still greatly traditional, patri-archal and religious. Society in Thrace is divided into first- and second-class citizens: a dominant group freely exercising power and a subordinate one, socially, economically and educationally marginalised. As Bhabba (1983, pp. 24–25) says, talking of the colonial subject, the dominant is strategically placed within the discourse for the dominated subject.

The above socio-historical parameters permeate the educational system. Muslim chil-dren have suffered from poor education for a very long time. The result has been massive under-achievement. In 2000, 65% of minority children dropped out of the 9-year compulsory education while the national mean was 7%. In Thrace there exists a system of separate schooling that the overwhelming majority of minority children attend at the primary level, while, at the secondary level, common education is more fre-quent. While in the minority school children are segregated, in the state school which is largely mono-cultural in its orientation and reluctant to accommodate otherness, they are cut off from the maternal language and culture. Fine and Sirin's (2007) frame of hyphe-nated selves referring to youths living in conflict, striving to make meaning and negotiating the contradictory messages that swirl through them, is very pertinent in the case of Muslim minority children.

This intervention is situated at the intersection of activism and action-research in edu-cational policy and pedagogy. Activism and action-research are both polyvalent concepts drawing from different theoretical approaches and informed by various socio-cultural and political motivations. Activist education has drawn inspiration from Freire's (1970) work in terms of confronting and challenging the system of injustice, as well as from Dewey's (1899) pedagogy founded on the principle that learning takes place in social environments where there exist collaborative activities through which learners communicate, interact and consequently construct their own world of knowledge. Action-research on the other hand, as initially established by Lewin (1948), implies social engagement with problems and learning in the act of creating change. Enriched by Deleuzian ideas (Drummond & Themessl-Huber, 2007) action-research is conceived as open-ended in its creative forms of becoming. Thus the common denominator of activism and action-research is that of participatory practice and creative action in view of transformation and emancipation. Finally, in both concepts there is the inherent notion that the relation between problems and solutions dialectically enfolds and embraces a spiral process. Problems invite solutions as much as solutions solve and change aspects of problems (Drummond & Themessl-Huber, 2007, 440). A third meaningful concept to our work is that of empowerment – internal psychological and external political empowerment – enabling people to move from a state of powerlessness to a state of more control over their life, their fate, and their environment and to become more able participants in the political process and in local decision-making (Sadan, 2004).

In a nutshell, the project in question has aimed at the social inclusion of minority children, by confronting massive under-achievement and decreasing high drop-out levels from compulsory 9-year education. Thus, underlying this long-lasting educational intervention is the accommodation of demands emanating from a deeply contested diversity, the empowerment of educators, students and community in order to challenge the operation of coercive power structures, and the encouragement of an open-minded dialogue between the majority and the minority. This may be an educational project but is no less a political one.

## The CYWs

One of the most important developments in this project was the establishment of 10 Community Centres that have educational and socialising functions. They offer a wide range of activities, including creative play and artistic expression for preschool children, afternoon compensatory classes and summer courses for primary and secondary school students, the use of computers, Greek language classes for parents, Turkish language classes for Greek-speaking teachers, and vocational guidance for the youth. They maintain an on-going dialogue with parents, teachers and representatives of the community who are encouraged to join events, organised every few months, where children can show and share their work.

The Centres constitute *loci* where rigid boundaries are disrupted, both those set by the majority to exclude the minority as well as those raised by the minority to protect itself. They are staffed by equal numbers of minority and majority personnel and they constitute the sole spaces in Thrace where majority and minority members are actively engaged in a collaborative task, striving for a common goal. Moreover, they represent the only state institution where children, and most importantly their parents, can use their preferred language for communication. They are a microcosm, where different identities coexist and languages alternate, where knowledge is generated and identities are negotiated, and there is an active contribution to the discourse of identity politics in Thrace. The dynamics developed within the Centres, as well as between the Centres and the overall society, reaffirm that the act of claiming identities and claiming the spaces of identity are political acts.

The CYWs are situated within the Community Centres in the two big towns of Xanthi and Komotini. They are known to the local society as DEN by their Greek acronym coined by the youths themselves.[4] DEN, however, is not only an acronym. As a word, it means 'NOT', denoting a negation or an opposition, expressing a rebellious tendency. The CYWs are real, imagined and symbolic spaces that host activities for children, adolescents and young adults across the various divides of Thracian society – minority/majority, Christian Orthodox/Muslim, rural/urban (Vassiliou & Dragonas, 2015). Nolas (2013) makes a pertinent distinction between the instrumental focus of structured 'positive youth development' programmes and informal youth learning spaces informed by the language of relationships, identity and belonging. The latter, according to Nolas, draw from a more radical youth work practice. Following this distinction, CWYs belong to this second category centring on communities of place and identity practices.

The CYWs are venues that offer the potential for collaborative learning and the material reality of a workshop with lots of resources, tools, supplies and equipment. Youngsters are urged to explore their psychosocial environment, to look both inwards towards themselves and outwards towards their community and express themselves creatively through various artistic means – such as drawing, theatrical games, narration and written text, constructions, clay modelling, collage, photography, video and computer processing. They are encouraged to exercise collaborative skills and participate actively in every project's stage – namely, to envision, plan and implement a project, and finally to reflect upon their experience. In essence, the CWYs have strived for a shift from the self-contained 'I' to the related self, from the bounded and limiting 'us' to the dialogical 'we'.

In the 14 years since the CYWs were set up, a total number of 36 youth workers – across diverse divides of the Thracian society – have been engaged with developing the project. In total, diverse project cycles have engaged more than 3000 children, adolescents, youth and adult community members. Several young people have grown up parallel to the project's lifetime, and have become youth workers themselves during and after their university studies. This fact has put into practice one of the main tenets of the project – namely empowering community members to meaningfully engage in processes of social change concerning their own communities.

Conceptualising the evaluation of the CYW project as a process which connects social research and social action, our evaluation design focused on revealing the ways in which all those directly or indirectly involved experience and perceive the workshops – before, during and after diverse project cycles. Considering the CYWs as part of a wider social system, groups of interest included the youth workers and their coordinators, children, adolescents and youth who participated in the activities and the wider local communities in which they are embedded. Data were gathered using methodological tools such as interviews, focus groups, participant observation, open-ended questionnaires, journals and a study of material involving youths' creative expression. The evaluation process was designed as an integral part of the project's evolution as its results were continuously fed back to all involved. Thus new cycles of activities were built upon older ones, informed by multiple narratives engendered by the evaluation process and relevant fieldwork conducted within diverse communities. As part of this feedback loop, a website (www. museduc-mm.gr) was developed as an additional relational space for all involved – documenting and mapping the project's lifespan as it evolved.

### Entering the field

In setting up the CYWs, we relinquished our roles as authorities and a priori 'experts'. Instead, we adopted an interpretative attitude relying on the on-going analysis of experience as it was occurring in the specific context. In embracing such a framework, we did not employ trained youth workers brought in from the outside. A mixed group of a small number of young people in their 20s and 30s was formed, representing the diversity and richness required by the project – female and male, members of the minority and the majority, of various ages and life courses, differing in educational and training background.

We were well aware that language and history are both limits and conditions to understanding. We also knew that understanding is not an individual but a relational achievement (Gergen, 2009). Critically reflecting through dialogue on the complex and conflict-ridden social environment in Thrace was a prerequisite for negotiating a common reality and for mapping the context within which the CYWs would take root.

The entire Thracian society has been nurturing antagonistic traditions, expressed in parallel monologues. Both minority and majority social groups have been practicing mutual blame and have known how to operate in opposing realities. As Bakhtin says 'monologism denies the existence outside itself of another consciousness with equal rights and equal responsibilities, another I with equal rights' (1984, p. 292). Monologue is deaf to the other's response. The young people who were trained as youth workers and the youngsters who were to become members of the CYWs have been socialised in seeing the world in monologic and exclusionary terms. The big challenge lying ahead was how to create a culture of being together.

The first steps in the youth workers' training involved shaping the actual physical space the CYWs would occupy. This decision was intricately connected with what the youth workers – who were to actively participate in forming the initial youth groups which would, in turn, invite other young people to join in – would like to do in these workshops. Subsequent training concerned issues such as how to recognise the needs of the youngsters who would join the Workshop's activities; how to design a project that responds to these needs; how to implement and evaluate a project; how to make good use of the equipment and tools available; how to serve the role of the youth worker and, finally, how to be actively aware of the group process.

New verbs were practiced – such as to initiate, to propose, to connect, to dialogue and to negotiate. Each of these conversational modes opened up more mutually appreciative interchange. Youth workers were provided a space to connect and talk with each other, to reach out and to engage in shared mutual inquiry. This practice involved jointly examining, thinking, questioning and reflecting. Moreover, this new mutually shared construction presupposed imaginary moments in the dialogue in which participants were to join in visions of a reality not yet realised (Andrews, 2014; Gergen, 2009). It is in these imaginary moments that the orientation shifted towards cooperation and participants moved toward a common purpose. In doing so, they redefined each other as 'we'. A quickening of imagination led to new possibilities. Dreaming and fantasy were powerful resources in the dialogic search for meanings and understandings. Let us turn to the youth workers' own words, as they looked back at these first experiences of transformative dialogue:

> It was when we started sharing the same space, sharing our concerns, our dreams, our expectations. When we touched each other's soul. When we gradually started looking into each other's eyes, capturing the reflection of our gaze. A chain of gazes was formed, which got stronger and stronger as we stood in unity. This strength acquired shape. Who can tell me that there is no room for dreams? There is always room for dreams, they snuggle wherever they can, provided you allow them space. Dreams know where they come from and where to go, when they are to live and when they are to die, they know because they are free. (male, 40, majority member)

### Bringing out one's creative self

Society in Thrace demands that individuals, groups and communities change. There is evidence that creators change more easily.[5] Creativity and self-expression are personal skills, enabled or inhibited within a specific social context. The use of art for both individual and community expression and visioning is highlighted times and again in such liberating projects (Watkins & Shulman, 2008).

Activities within the CYWs produced the conditions that promoted greater creativity on all levels possible – be it on the intrapsychic, interpersonal, intergroup or intercultural one. The youngsters spent long hours discussing what 'being creative' meant and what a 'workshop' was, in essence. They utilised stimuli for creative expression, explored various different expressive tools and materials and practiced skills of communication and cooperation building on difference. As they reflected upon questions such as, 'how can the CYWs become a relational space that will have room for all?', 'where can our differences enrich what is jointly created, rather than separate us?', 'what skills need to be practiced in order to achieve this end?', 'how can we handle mistakes?' and 'how can we learn to process experience and draw knowledge that can be applied as we walk this relational path?', the notion of friendship took on new meanings:

> All the clay objects that we crafted had multiple meaning. You might ask how can friendship be related to a pencil-holder!? Of course, it too has its own meaning. It shows us the variety of friendship, just like the pencils it holds, it symbolizes unity, it creates the foundations of friendship and ensures unity and cohesion. (male, 12, minority member)

From a relational point of view, it is creating in a group, in deliberately relating and operating together that 'we construct worlds of good and evil, joy and sorrow, happiness and despair … and it is through relationships that personal well being is achieved' (Gergen, 2009, p. 107). In the words of another young member:

> The CYWs transported me to different worlds. It was a space where I expressed the artistic world I had inside myself. It is as if the world begun there. I learned to share my feelings there. It was a space I shared friendship … even if one quarreled, our room smelled of respect. (male, 13, minority member)

The initial image of the CYWs was that of an uninhabited rock which, in turn, became an island on which each inhabitant could practice (in the youth's own words) 'respect', 'cooperation', 'trust', 'involvement', 'cohesion', 'equality', 'love', 'freedom of opinion', 'dream', 'craze', 'faith'. New and exciting possibilities were born out of the shared group process. The youth workers jointly reflected upon the question 'how we may conceive of "group" and "synergy" so that they become useful tools for a youth workshop which is creative, multicultural, and interactive?'

> Individuals dream but teamwork gives wings to the dream. As individuals we have potential but a group has the power to transform … we need to mix our different shades. One's help mobilizes the other, and jointly we mobilize society. We cooperated towards a common goal. (male and female, 24–40, majority and minority members)

### From separate language worlds to new ways of meaning-making

Thrace is multicultural and multilingual. There is a complex, hierarchical interplay of national, ethnic, religious, linguistic and cultural identities among the minority groups constituting the Muslim minority and between these groups and the majority. The greatest part of the minority is Turkish speaking; at school Turkish and Greek are the languages of instruction. However, Turkish is not the mother tongue of all members of the minority. Some speak the Pomak language (a Slavic dialect close to Bulgarian) and some others Romani. The power status of these languages is not equal – Turkish having the highest status. Language use is tied to ethnic identity and is marked by political conflict. Furthermore, the members of the majority speak only Greek and do not know any of the minority languages. If the members of the minority want to communicate with members of the majority they have to do so in Greek.

Each year, the CYWs organise summer camps[6] with mixed minority and majority group youth at the banks of the river Nestos.[7] At one such summer camp, the youth workers devised a playful situation to address the issue of language use. The youth workers were not aware of language theories. They did not know Wittgenstein's (1953) analogy between language and game. Nor did they know Bourdieu's (1991) theory about language. Yet they have come to know that language signifies status. In a charade-like game, children were met every morning at a fresh water spring by a fairy who spoke an alien, fairy language and was accompanied by an 'interpreter'. In order to communicate with the fairy in her language, majority and minority children had to invent new codes of communication and translation between different languages. The purpose of the activity was to address issues of language use and linguistic hegemony in a playful way. Greek, Turkish, the Pomak or Romani languages were not an issue here. If children wanted to communicate in the fairy language, they had to go beyond traditional linguistic barriers, confront prejudice and invent new codes of communication. Children could also become fairies themselves, if they wished, and thus address the challenge of adopting new roles.

The game youth workers devised challenged traditional ways of meaning-making, and by using new forms of language/action children had new possibilities for extending their grasp of what goes on within relationships.

In this and other activities organised at the camp, children communicated in whichever language they preferred. Yet, we observed that all the children mainly used Greek – the language of the majority. It was clear that minority children, who were the numerical majority at the camp, accommodated to the needs of the Greek-speaking children who did not know the Turkish or Pomak languages. There was an obvious reversal of linguistic hegemony, and it was the minority children who were there to integrate the majority ones into the camp and create a shared reality.

### Coupling narrative with imagination

Narrative practice has been shown to be relevant in working with communities and groups experiencing divide and emotional distress (White, 2003). Such use of narrative practice is based on the premise that all communities have a stock of knowledge and living skills that provide contextually and culturally relevant proposals for action in addressing communal concerns.

Narratives were used extensively in the various groups – whether those of youth workers or those of youths within the CYWs. Individual stories soon gave way to collective stories narrated by the entire group. A wide range of themes emerged from these stories: 'the rainbow connecting two planets, so their inhabitants could cross and exchange goods and ideas', 'the multicolored tree in a field that had only known the colors of green, red and yellow', 'the cold planet deserted by its inhabitants who searched for warmth and love', 'the lord who died of loneliness', 'the magical almond tree that could make wishes come true, that helped the poor and healed the sick, and that could tell between truth and lies', and many more. The story metaphors were woven around concepts of love, colour, difference, misfortune, sharing, redemption, connectedness, hope. Stories were constructed drawing from traditions and practices, explicitly or implicitly within larger stories that alluded to the youths' interpersonal, social and political contexts. Youths grappled with questions such as: 'is there a "me" in "we?", can there be a "we" in "me" as well?', 'are they mirror images of the same process?'. It is this bond between narrative and imagination that Andrews (2014, p. 5) talks about that creates 'a bridge traversing the pathway between what is known, and what can be known, between the present and possible futures' (Figure 1).

A low round table (*sofra* – a common word in Turkish and Greek) became a symbol for a group of pre-adolescents, as they learned to cherish sharing stories as much as sharing food. Rigid self-narratives based on low self-esteem gave way to synthesising complex narratives based on self-confidence and recognition of ability. In the youth groups, stereotypes were continuously breaking apart in the process of sharing narratives of diversity. The skill of empathy acquired flesh and bone. Conflict between differently defined identities and conflict in relationships became entrance points for multiple narratives. By mutually shaping the storytelling, the re-telling, and the new telling, youth experienced the richness of different voices and sometimes the simultaneous contradictory feelings and opinions.

Journal entries of both youths and youth workers alike allude to this transformative process:

> Even if the community center closes permanently, memories from good – and even bad – moments will be in our minds and hearts. How could we forget them? It's like we could forget our own name. This space will remember too, that we once considered it like home, that it was beautiful, full of life. (female, 13, minority member)

> Over time we saw so much – a tree growing from a seed, which in turn grew into a tree. We learned how to nourish and protect growth. We learned how to take care of the process, how to see from another point of view. We got hurt, we cried, we felt anxiety and pressure, dedication, joy, satisfaction, a sense of reward. We cooperated for our own benefit and the

**Figure 1.** The magic almond tree that could make wishes come true.

> benefit of our goals. We've learned how to carefully build a network of friendship and we can pass this knowledge on. (male, 26, minority member)

Such practice resonates to what Nolas (2013) describes, when discussing youth spaces, as opportunities of identity development and the crafting of biographical narratives, both in terms of being and becoming, as old identities are shed and new ones are adopted.

### From parallel lives to co-existence

Minority members in their 90 years history have in the main employed non-violent protest methods in response to the restrictive and discriminatory measures they have been subjected to, while the government and the local majority population have been especially careful to avoid the use of physical violence. However, the Greek state has been ambivalent towards the Muslim minority that has been simultaneously subject to appropriation/assimilation and exclusion. Difference has functioned as a mechanism to create, in Elias (1994) words, a differentiation between the 'haves' and 'must-not-haves,' that has resulted in a sharp division between majority/first-class and minority/second-class citizens. The people of Thrace, especially those who are members of the majority Christian community, often claim that 'here in Thrace we live peacefully together'. Yet, in reality, what they describe are parallel lives in separate worlds that operate in parallel universes. The greatest percentage of the Muslim minority population lives separately in ethnically and linguistically homogeneous settlements. Thus, our entire intervention was geared towards strengthening practices of co-existence by fostering the understanding of the other, creating the conditions of interactive and collaborative relationships, challenging coercive relations of power and negotiating identities.

A project engaging pre-adolescents is an indicative example of the reluctance and fear, characteristic of both minority and majority, to transform parallel lives to co-existence. A group of youngsters, members of both the minority and majority, decided to envisage and actually build – with carton paper and various other materials – a village where both Christians and Muslims would live together. A dyad of both Christian and Muslim youth workers acted as facilitators. The youngsters engaged in long conversations, and came up with various suggestions that were soon discarded – there could be no river because a river divides; there could be no mosque because, if so, there should also be a church; there could be no school because they had to decide between a minority school where separate education is provided and a state mixed school; there could be no soccer field because the team supporters fight among themselves. Unable to confront conflict, the youngsters felt incapable of finding solutions. It took them several weeks of long conversations and shared deliberation before they could visualise the village of their dreams that finally had both a river with a bridge, a mosque and a church, a school and a soccer field. In this new space, group members were invited to live together in such a way that everyone would be included. During the course of the task, group ties were further developed. Issues of difference, cooperation and the significance of each individual and the group as a whole were elaborated. Conflict among group members led to exploration of 'who am I in the group'. Thus, the project served a double purpose: imagining co-existence in the common village as well as negotiating co-existence in the group process, here and now.[8]

The CYW's projects aimed at empowering youth workers and youths alike to bring imagination of co-existence into reality. During a summer camp, a mixed minority and majority group of university students expressed reflections around the themes of acknowledging diversity and striving for community.

> I'd read somewhere that diversity doesn't mean black and white. Necessary for giving color, meaning and purpose to our life, our existence, it connects us to our fellow human, enabling us to co-exist, co-decide, and in the end co-reveal life. I hadn't exactly understood what that meant. After the camp experience, the meaning of diversity was now clear. (female, 21, minority member)

One of the created artworks portrays two halves of a circle – a dark one described by the words 'discontent', 'inequality', 'inadequate education', 'exploitation', 'difficulties', 'pessimism', 'resignation' and 'entrapment' and a bright one, described by the words 'diversity', 'happiness', 'emancipation', 'dreams', 'effort', 'struggle', 'optimism', 'bright future', 'a better and dignified life'. Above the circle they wrote: 'we are changing the world around us and we are creating a new one by touching our inner souls!'.[9] This sentence is at the heart of our internal/psychological and external/political empowerment project, described in the beginning of this paper.

### Intergenerational consequences

Youths developed ways of speaking about and symbolising elements of their environment that slowly seeped out into the wider culture and began to affect community discourses. Parents were increasingly invited to attend and share the youths' projects.

Fieldwork before and after project cycles has been an integral part of the workshop's methodology, encouraging the opening of a dialogical space where family members engage in feedback and active participation in youth projects. As more actors were gradually brought into an on-going dialogue in ever widening circles, parents and the wider communities of families became partners in defining the various project cycles of the CYW. Joint parents–children and parents' workshops were held upon parents' initiative. As they reflected on their children's fervour to be members of the CYWs they said:

> Here at the CYW, our children succeeded in living within a micro-society, in being able to care for and deepen their relationship and communication skills with others – in a different way than they are used to in the outer world. Here they succeeded in paying attention to details that may provide us the stimulus for change. We, as parents, needed this very much; we thank you for the opportunity; we are glad that something like this [workshop] happened; we now understand why our children wanted to come. (male and female, 32–44, minority and majority members)

Parents' involvement in the CYWs and other activities in the realm of the wider project, had a ripple effect on their literacy. Mothers in a remote village were the first to timidly express the wish to learn Greek in order to help their children with schoolwork. The realisation of this goal, however, was not as easy as it seemed. Their husbands were reluctant to allow them to attend classes. After long negotiations, women had their way. A few years later, hundreds of women stood proudly in front of their own people, receiving their degrees at an end of year ceremony – all making a V sign. Women came to classes regularly, made impressive progress, developed their own traveling book on Thrace, and participated in excursions outside of the Thracian bounds. It was soon clear that the motive of helping their children was coupled by another, perhaps stronger, motive – that of claiming public space. Classes served as a springboard to important changes in their lives. After a year and a half of classes, one woman got a job for the first time of her life. 'I am part of life now,' she said 'I am not sitting in my corner anymore. It is as if a miracle came true.' 'We're living our dream,' said another. Classes gave women a voice, and as one of our mature students pertinently acknowledged: 'Language is freedom' (Zografaki, 2016).

## Conclusions

In the 20 years that have elapsed, the 'Project on the Education of Muslim Minority Children' has come a long way. There are many quantitative indices that point to the change, such as, for example, the lowering of the drop-out rate from compulsory education from 65% to 20% – still much higher than the national mean. There are many qualitative changes, such as those described above, that point to a process of empowerment and a shift from monologic to dialogic practices of meaning-making.

The processes of change, however, have often been met with resistance from both sides of the divide. When the project began in 1997, it triggered mixed emotions: suspicion from the local Greek authorities; anger, hostility and ambivalence at best on the part of the nationalists in the majority population; hesitation and timid hope in the minority; caution among its leaders. Establishing a relationship of trust was a long, arduous process. Steps forward gave way to steps backward. At times tensions were worked through with relative success. Despite the inevitable difficulties in the containment of differences, the creativity with which solutions were devised was impressive. However, regressive pulls were also noted toward more closed and oppressive modes of relating and away from more open ones. Diamond and Allcorn (2006) aptly discuss this movement forward and backward. There can be no pure states of experience and transformation.

As regards the CYWs – a smaller structure within the overall project – the challenge was how to transform traditions that have nourished splitting, coercive relations of power and suppression of voices. Our attempt was to give rise to a relational hub where all members would have a sense of connection, belonging, participation and ownership. Thus, collaborative processes were encouraged; relationships were strengthened; relational leading was adopted; dialogic practices were nurtured; dreaming and imaginary moments were encouraged; narratives were exchanged; creativity was enhanced; mutual inquiry and joint action were reinforced; critical thinking was enhanced and agency was strengthened. We witnessed the creative transformation of youths – as individuals and as a group – and that of their communities. The healing potential of small group and community-based dialogical approaches (Watkins & Shulman, 2008) was corroborated.

Freire's conception of activist education, Dewey's premise on active engagement in one's learning, and Martin-Baro's (Aron & Corne, 1996) psychology of liberation all call for transformation rather than conformity to status quo cultural arrangements that contribute to divisive practices. Spaces of participation were created, bringing people together across ages and cultures that shared dialogues on issues that mattered and realities that challenged them. Youth workers, youth, young adults and their families found themselves engaged in a process of multi-being and becoming. Processes were developed within the overall project and the CYWs in particular, that helped youths and their parents evolve a sense of a meaningful voice and discover their own capacities for transformative social action.

Borrowing from Deleuze's (1994) philosophical view that action-research has both an actual and virtual dimension feeding into each, and translating his concept of the virtual into our notion of imagination, we confirmed his proposition of opening up to new ways of thinking, feeling and acting that are emancipatory, transformative and life affirming. Deleuze talks about a cyclical process that is both fluid and grounded in creative action rather than a series of well-defined linear steps. An action-research project is imbued with a dimension of creativity that is open to new connections. We have talked about a process captured in the symbol of an upward spiral representing an always becoming, never-ending process of potentialities (Vassiliou & Dragonas, 2015).

A final note, drawing once more Deleuzian principles, concerns the relation between problems and solutions (Drummond & Themessl-Huber, 2007). Solutions, no matter how successful, change the nature of the problem in that they toss some aspects of the problem into obscurity and bring others into clarity. A new phase of our project is about to begin and two more years lie ahead. The youth workers aim for a larger recruit of majority youths, thus deepening the intercultural dimension. Minority youths are now much more confident than they were 20 years ago. Yet we are fully aware that new challenges await us, calling for a deepening of our reflection on where we are standing and placing our advocacies as regards youth work.

## Notes

1. Committed to a collaborative principle, authorship of this paper is fully shared. It is the product of a long-lasting exercise of interlacing our thoughts and words.
2. It was initiated by the Greek Ministry of Education, funded, in the main, by the European Social Fund; and has spanned four phases: Greek Ministry of Education, Life Long Learning and Religious Affairs, Operational Program in Education and Initial Vocational Training I (1997–2000), II (2002–2004), III (2005–2008), IV (2010–2016) V (2016–2018). It is directed by professors Anna Frangoudaki and Thalia Dragonas, www.museduc.gr.
3. Our diverse roles in this project have been complementary. Anni was the one who conceived of the idea of the CWYs, drawing from her long experience in socio-cultural youth work. She then went on to coordinate and facilitate the endeavour in its entirety. Thalia, being one of the two leaders of the wider intervention, has assumed a supervising role and has worked closely with Anni in developing the CWYs project.
4. The initials of DEN stand for three words «Δημιουργικό» (Creative), «Εργαστήριο» (Workshop), and «Νέων» (Youth)–hence «Δ.Ε.Ν.» translates into Creative Youth Workshop.
5. See https://youtu.be/9nkZmo4lEIM.
6. CYW summer camp videos 'Following the flow': (2003) http://tinyurl.com/CYWsummer2003 – (2011) http://tinyurl.com/CYWsummer2011 – (2013) http://tinyurl.com/CYWsummer2013.
7. The camp at the banks of the river Nestos encapsulates the essence of the CYW project. Co-existence is facilitated as youths spend time together. Relational flow coincides with the flow of the river. Being a geophysical frontier of Thrace, Nestos has served as a metaphor for negotiating boundaries. For more see Vassiliou and Ligdopoulou (2005), http://tinyurl.com/CYWfemact2005.
8. For this and other projects see CYW 2002–2004 presentation: http://tinyurl.com/CYW2002-2004.
9. The artwork referred to may be seen on the CYW website: http://tinyurl.com/CYWchanging.

## Disclosure statement

No potential conflict of interest was reported by the authors.

## Funding

This work was funded by the European Social Fund and Greek Ministry of Education and Religious Affairs, Operational Program in Education and Initial Vocational Training I (1997–2000), II (2002–2004), III (2005–2008) and IV (2010–2013).

# References

Andrews, M. (2014). *Narrative imagination and everyday life*. New York, NY: Oxford University Press.

Aron, A., & Corne, S. (1996). *Writings for a liberation psychology: Ignacio Martin-Baro*. Cambridge, MA: Harvard University Press.

Bakhtin, M. M. (1984). *Problems of Dostoevsky's poetics*. (Caryl Emerson, Ed. and Trans.). Minneapolis: University of Minnesota Press.

Bhabba, H. J. (1983). The other question – the stereotype and colonial discourse. *Screen, 24*(6), 18–36.

Bourdieu, P. (1991). *Language and symbolic power*. Cambridge: Polity Press.

Deleuze, G. (1994). *Difference and repetition*. (P. Patton, Trans.). London: The Athlone Press.

Dewey, J. (1899). *The school and society: Being three lectures*. Chicago, IL: University of Chicago Press.

Diamond, M., & Allcorn, S. (2006). Surfacing perversions of democracy in the workplace: A contemporary psychoanalytic project. *Psychoanalysis, Culture and Society, 11*(1), 54–73.

Dragonas, T., & Frangoudaki, A. (Eds.). (2008). *Addition not subtraction, multiplication not division: The reform of the education of the minority in Thrace* (in Greek). Athens: Metaihmio.

Dragonas, T., & Frangoudaki, A. (2014). 'Like a bridge over troubled water': Reforming the education of Muslim minority children in Greece. In V. Lytra (Ed.), *When Greeks and Turks meet* (pp. 289–311). London: Ashgate.

Dragonas, T. (2014a). The vicissitudes of identity in a divided society: The case of the Muslim minority in Western Thrace. In K. Featherstone (Ed.), *Europe in modern Greek history* (pp. 135–152). London: C. Hurst & Co.

Dragonas, T. (2014b). A minority education reform in Western Thrace, Greece: Psychosocial and political perspectives. In T. Magioglou (Ed.) *Culture and political psychology: A societal perspective* (pp. 351–368). Series: Advances in Cultural Psychology: Constructing Human Development. Paris: Information Age.

Drummond, J., & Themessl-Huber, M. (2007). The cyclical process of action research: The contribution of Gilles Deleuze. *Action Research, 5*(4), 430–448.

Elias, N. (1994). *The civilizing process*. Oxford: Blackwell.

Fine, M., & Sirin, S. (2007). Theorizing hyphenated selves: Researching youth development in and across contentious political contexts. *Social and Personality Psychology Compass, 1*(1), 16–38.

Freire, P. (1970). *Pedagogy of the oppressed*. London: Continuum.

Gergen, K. (2009). *An invitation to social construction*. London: Sage.

Gergen, K. (2015). From mirroring to world-making: Research as future forming. *Journal for the Theory of Social Behaviour, 45*(3), 287–310.

Lewin, K. (1948). *Resolving social conflicts: Selected papers on group dynamics*. New York, NY: Harper & Row.

Nolas, S.M. (2013). Exploring youth people's and youth workers' experiences of spaces for 'youth development': Creating cultures of participation. *Journal of Youth Studies*. doi:10.1080/13676261.2013.793789

Sadan, E. (2004). Empowerment and community planning. *E-book*. Retrieved from http://www.mpow.org/elisheva_sadan_empowerment.pdf

Vassiliou, A., & Dragonas, T. (2015). Sowing seeds of synergy: Creative youth workshops in a multicultural context. In T. Dragonas, K. J. Gergen, S. McNamee, & E. Tseliou (Eds.), *Education as social* construction: *Contributions to theory, research and practice* (pp. 192–212). Chagrin Falls, OH: WorldShare E-Books.

Vassiliou, A., & Ligdopoulou, T. (2005). It takes two: Glimpses of the Creative Youth Workshop of Thrace. *Annual Review of Critical Psychology, Special Issue Feminisms and Activisms, 4*, 154–165. Retrieved from https://discourseunit.com/annual-review/arcp-4-feminism-and-activisms-2005/

Watkins, M., & Shulman, H. (2008). *Towards psychologies of liberation*. New York, NY: Palgrave Macmillan.

White, M. (2003). Narrative practice and community assignments. *International Journal of Narrative Therapy and Community Work, 2*, 17–55.

Wittgenstein, L. (1953). *Philosophical investigations*. Oxford: Blackwell.

Zografaki, M. (2016, May). *'Language is freedom': Minority women's literacy and empowerment at the support centres of the project of Muslim Children's Education in Thrace (in Greek)*. Paper presented at the conference: An alternative education for the minority children in Thrace, Athens.

# Housing choices in later life as unclaimed forms of housing activism

Andrea Jones

**ABSTRACT**

This paper explores how housing choices over a lifetime produce under-recognised and unclaimed forms of housing activism. It is based on qualitative interviews with two individuals in their sixties, living in intergenerational communities in the South of England. I argue that their stories of their housing choices and their future housing plans resist dominant housing discourses, particularly as they relate to ageing, and they illuminate a number of under-recognised elements of housing activism. Using Clapham's housing pathway concept, I describe their narratives of decision-making about where and how to live over their life time to show their agency and their resistance to norms of housing consumption in later life, which are key elements of housing activism. Whilst interviewees recognised the political nature of their housing choices, neither claimed the term 'housing activist' nor used the term in their narratives and I argue that this may be because their forms of housing activism were interwoven with domestic and caring needs, emotional experiences, intermittent commitment and ageing identities. Their housing pathways and life stories support emerging theories of activism that broaden definitions from public to private spaces and challenge stereotypes of older people's involvement in housing activism.

## Introduction

In this paper, I describe the housing pathways of two people in their sixties who live in intentional communities in the South of England, to explore what housing activism is. These individuals did not claim to be 'housing activists', but I argue that their housing choices resist dominant housing discourses, particularly in later life, and their complex life stories help to illustrate a number of under-recognised elements of housing activism.

Intentional communities are consciously and collectively built around the sharing of resources and living space, often sharing common cultural values (Bunker, Coates, & How, 2007; Christian, 2003; Coates, 2013). Bunker defines them as:

> Shared house, communal household, cohousing group, ecovillage, ashram, alternative community, commune, housing co-op ... with the locations and premises occupied being equally varied, as are the motivations and ideologies of the people who live in them ...

(with an) underlying commonality that links the groups together. A common thread that is the quest to create community.

For Sargisson intentional communities are:

> ... bodies of people who have chosen to live – and usually work in some way – together. They have a common aim or commitment. This commitment might be to such things as a political ideology, a spiritual path or to Co-operative living itself ... Intentional communities are sometimes referred to as 'utopias'. (Sargisson, 2000, p. 29)

Her work has shown how intentional communities are complex entities and subject to changing conceptualisations and definitions over time (Sargisson, 2007, 2012).

In this paper, I focus on two individual's stories, selected because these individuals talked the most explicitly of all my interviewees about the politics of housing and therefore provided fruitful narratives in which to explore the boundaries of what is considered housing activism and how ageing shapes our understandings of it. In the interviews, it was clear that political principles and values were important to the interviewees and were also implicit in their choices to live in intentional communities. I use the word *choice* without caveat here because these individuals were unequivocally *active* in choosing to live in these communities. The choices they made were not, and are not, part of norms of housing consumption in the UK: the vast majority of over 65's currently live in owner occupied or social housing (94%) and either in a couple (54%) or on their own (31%) (ONS, 2013). This provides a flavour of the orthodoxy of housing in the UK. Through the successful marketisation and commodification of housing over the last century and in the last 30–40 years in particular, norms of housing tenure (ownership, private and social rental) in the UK have a strong grip on housing choices (Flint & Rowlands, 2003; Gurney, 1999; Heath, 2008; McKee & Muir, 2013; Saunders, 1989; Savage, Barlow, & Dickens, 1992). People who are not in couples or stereotypical families are marginalised in private housing markets, including older people (Forrest & Leather, , 2002; Peace & Holland, 2001; Peace, Holland, & Kellaher, 2011).

It is in this normative context that I explore what housing activism means in the context of life stories. I share these two individual's stories of decision-making about where and how and with whom to live over their life time, drawing on a number of different theorists to shape my focus. I have drawn on Giddens notions of 'life planning' and lifestyle choices which he describes as having become more significant as traditional social ties have loosened (in a post-industrial world and conditions of post-modernity) forcing individuals to 'negotiate lifestyle choices amongst the diversity of options' (Giddens, 1991, p. 5), without forgetting that there remain 'differential access to forms of self-actualisation and empowerment' (p. 6). I have also drawn on Clapham's useful application of life planning to housing consumption, in the form of 'housing pathways' which provide:

> a way of ordering the housing field in a way that foregrounds the meanings held by households and the interactions that shape housing practices as well as emphasising the dynamic nature of housing experience and is interrelatedness with other aspects of household life ... the housing pathway of the household is the continually changing set of relationships and interactions that it experiences over time in its consumption of housing. (Clapham, 2005, p. 27)

Housing pathways resemble what Plummer calls 'topical life stories' (Plummer, 2001, pp. 42–43) focussed as they are on a particular aspect of an individual's life. Clapham similarly helps to locate housing choices as 'part of the search for identity and self-fulfilment' (Clapham, 2005, p. 30), but without reducing awareness of the structural inequalities that are fundamental to the housing sector. Using each individual's housing pathway, I describe the factors that these individuals considered to be significant in their housing choices, or lack of choices. Like Andrews, I see such stories as subjective truths co-created by the interviewee and interviewer (Andrews, 2014) and I do not make claims of objectivity. I illustrate out how these individuals became involved in their intentional communities drawing out forms of housing activism that emerged from their agential choices made in the context of domestic and caring needs, emotional experiences, intermittent commitment and ageing identities.

## Methodology

The stories I present here are taken from interviews conducted in 2014–2015 as part of my PhD research. I visited nine intergenerational communities identified through the Diggers and Dreamers website[1] and conducted 23 semi-structured interviews with individuals aged from 51 to 84 years, asking 'what makes it possible to live in intentional communities into older age?' (Jones, 2017). Interviews took place in participants living quarters and lasted between 1 and 2 hours. All interviews were audio recorded and transcribed verbatim. The doctoral thesis and the initial analysis undertaken were informed by a contemporary reading of Bourdieu (1998). In this paper, I extend the initial analysis to focus on the intersections between life course, narrative and activism drawing on the work Andrews (1991, 1999), Jolly (2011) and Brickell (2012a).

## Two stories of agency in housing choices

I start with Interviewee 4, and the stories she told me about her life and how she'd come to be living in her intergenerational, urban housing cooperative over the past 30 years. Her home consisted of a homely self-contained two-bedroom unit within the housing cooperative building that now mostly consisted of units shared by single people. Her housing pathway shows how she had moved in and out of different forms of housing when she left her childhood familial home which, though conventional in structure, she described as 'a very sort of radicalised environment' in that her parents were Marxists and atheists and strongly encouraged her involvement in politics (see Figure 1, housing pathway for Interviewee 4). She described how at aged 15–16 attending political meetings in squats in her local city had been her first experience of this way of living.

She left home to live in student accommodation, then spent time living in private rental properties, squats and communes in London and Ireland during her twenties. In the 1980s, in her early thirties, she found herself with a child, a dog and a piano and the onset of a long-term chronic condition. Living on the South coast of England, she found it difficult to find an affordable place to live in. So, with her partner, she got involved in setting up an urban housing cooperative locally. She describes her needs as practical:

> Because with those three restraints a Co-op was the only place that was going to be able to allow me to have a secure place on a long term basis.

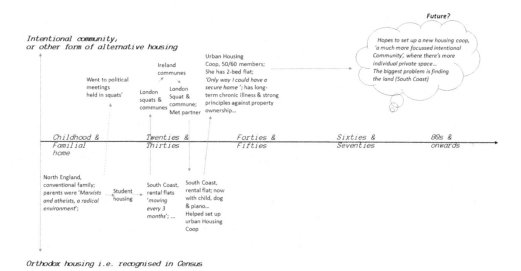

**Figure 1.** Housing pathway of Interviewee 4, community 3.

But interwoven within her accounts of the practical necessity of finding, a long-term secure home was also her critique of private property in principle – 'property *is* theft' – and in practice, based on her experience of the private rented sector:

> the story is you think you're going to be able to stay there, and then they don't like you, or you fall out with the people that you're sharing with, or the owner decides to sell, or they put the rent up too much. And that happens to everybody in (town in which community 3 is located) in the rented sector. Or the accommodation is awful, with bed bugs and damp and people upstairs who are banging on the ceiling, all these things. And that's the common experience of everybody using the rented sector generally in [town in which her community is located], especially for students. Even now actually.

These negative accounts of the housing choices offered by the private market in housing were contrasted with her articulations of the positive experience of working with other single parents from the local Gingerbread group and other founder co-operative members, to create their own housing opportunities. Over a period of four years they organised together, as a group of volunteers, to build a new block of flats for around 25 households, that she moved into with her children. They managed to secure one of the last state housing grants available in the late 1980s, an experience she described as a 'massive learning curve' for her. She also described the efforts of other individuals who did not end up living there – 'there was a lot of altruism'. They worked with architects to design the building around the needs of young families, mostly single parents, to achieve a lifestyle that she described as 'amazing':

> it was brilliant for the kids because they had a lot of other grown-ups, they were growing up around other adults, who they got used to interacting with them and the grown-ups, the non-parents, were in a … living in an environment where they could hang out with kids. So it was win-win really. And there was a very supportive sort of um, not co-parenting exactly but you know, communal kind of (pause) … as parents we all felt our job was a lot easier because there were other people stepping in and you know stewarding our kids and taking them out on day trips collectively.

Her children had now left home. Asked about her future plans she talked about how she hoped to set up a new Housing Co-op with a group of people that were mostly in their forties or older, which she described as 'a more focused intentional community' than her current Housing Co-op. She hoped that there would be more individual private space in this new community than most members had in the current situation.

I asked her if she was not just a little bit daunted by the thought of doing it all again. She recognised the considerable obstacles to achieving this in the current socio-economic and political environment, including the difficulty of finding land in an area of now extremely high property prices. She was also aware of the lack of the kinds of state grants that they had secured in the 1980s, but she was also optimistic:

> there's new money, there's ways in which we can get new money. [Speaking softly] That doesn't rely on the State and doesn't rely on Grants … there was a commission that was, um, set up by the Confederation of Co-operative Housing and other groups, um, into finance for mutual owned development and all that. So there's all that there, you know …

In her reflections on why she was considering moving on, while she was not explicitly critical of her existing Co-op, it was evident in her accounts and her rationales that she had become tired of some of the interpersonal dynamics, had become frustrated by elements of the design within the community (poor soundproofing in particular) and was desiring of a more coherent sense of community expressed through sharing and working together than her current community was achieving. She also desired to have more individual privacy.

She also alluded to some pressure she felt to relinquish her slightly larger living unit since her children had left home because, now, as a single person, it was hard to justify her having more self-contained space than the other single people in the Co-op. She did not suggest that her age nor the fact that she had lived in that unit the most of her adult life, bringing up her children there, gave her any sense of entitlement to remain in her home. It was unclear whether the pressure she felt came entirely from her own consideration, or partly from others within the Co-op.

What I want to draw out from this account and her story is how hard it is to disentangle her practical housing needs and her quest for stability and security for her family, with her political commitment to co-operative and egalitarian principles and practices. I also want to foreground her sense of agency in the face of a number of constraints that she had to deal with in life. She freely admitted that she had never had the choice to own a house (no financial capital nor sufficiently stable earning capacity, given her illness) irrespective of her principled opposition to individual homeownership. But she was sufficiently empowered to join with others in driving through a logistically and politically challenging project (even in the 1980s) in order to achieve a home and away of life that suited both her needs and beliefs. These were illustrations of her agency and how this agency was interwoven with her practical needs and caring responsibilities as a parent.

My second Interviewee (2), was living in a tent/bender within an 'eco-village' which was a squat of woodland adjacent to a large, derelict development site, that had been going for 2 to 3 years at the time that I interviewed him and he had been living there all that time. There were around 30–40 people living on the site in various self-build forms of accommodation; they had built a shared lounge and kitchen and play area; their water was from a spring and they manage their waste using compost toilets.

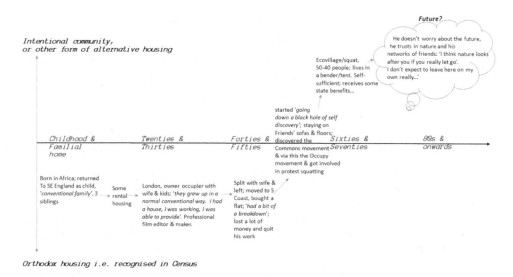

**Figure 2.** Housing pathway of Interviewee 2, community 2.

His housing pathway shows a conventional familial start to life and a conventional family and housing pathway through into his forties, including a professional career that included employment within conventional commercial sectors (see Figure 2 – housing pathway for Interviewee 2). He described splitting up with his wife, leaving his family and having a mental breakdown as a critical turning point in his life, during his early forties. He used the term 'going down a black hole of self-discovery' to encapsulate what had clearly been a difficult time of losing his connection to his work, his family (temporarily), many of his friends, getting into debt and losing any sense of having a permanent home. During this process, he described 'discovering' the Commons Movement (a contemporary movement drawing on historic rights of un-propertied people's entitlement to 'common' land) and, through this, made connections to the Occupy movement and protest squatting in London, which he then become involved in.

His stories and narratives included many expressions of political opinions and beliefs (such as anti-contemporary foreign policy in Iraq) and many philosophical reflections about loss of social connections in contemporary society that recall Bauman's theorising of the search for security and sense in conditions of liquid modernity (Baumann, 2001). His reflections were combined with identity seeking:

> I think we're looking for something, as a peoples. And I think, in the West, we've kind of lost touch with, with ourselves a bit … I'm not into family so much, I believe in tribes and that actually we're looking for our tribes, and that we will find them if we look for them.

In relation to how he thought about home he considered that wherever he was now, *was* home, and he talked about himself as more as a traveller:

> I see myself as a traveller now … So basically I'm seeing civilisation as a Roman road and I'm just passing through it, and I'm kind of looking around what's going on around me, hanging around for a bit, and then I'll be off again. So yes, I consider it (this place) home … because I just feel more rooted in myself, which is not about necessarily a building that goes with it; it's

very much about Earth, knowing your place, er, and your relationship to Mother Earth, if you like, and how you, how you feed into the great story, if you like.

He talked also about how most family, friends and colleagues considered that he had 'gone mad' and were always trying to persuade him to return to a mainstream way of life and his career, but how most had not even come to see his current way of life, what he felt to be his home. He described his chosen way of life not only as a rejection of contemporary and commercial values but something more positive – as a way of life that he felt was more beautiful than anything else he had experienced before:

> They're (his friends and colleagues) faced with someone who's rejecting the world that they're living in and who's er, standing up and saying, 'Look, this isn't really what I'm interested in anymore, I'm moving on ... ' It's showing me another different aspect to life which I, I, I'd ignored for, for most of my life (pause) you're actually touching nature here. I've got robins here; I've got three generations of robins that I know (pause). I missed this most of my life. I wouldn't miss it for, for anything now.

In his accounts, he interweaves his narratives of political discontent – outright rejection of conventional ways of life – and poetic expressions of attachment to the land that he was camped on. He expressed a strong sense of personal fulfilment in living so close to nature, something that he had never experienced before. He also talked of the emotional roll-ercoaster he had been on through his break with his family, his loss of social connections and his interpersonal conflicts during this time. Once again, he never used the term acti-vism, nor described himself as a housing activist, though I see evidence of agential acti-vism in his housing choices, this time interwoven with his emotional journey through life and a personal quest for self-fulfilment.

In relation to my question about his future plans, he responded that he no longer worried about the future and that he trusted in nature and in his network of friends. He expected that if and when this eco-village/squat came to an end he would move on with the community of friends he had made on the site. He seemed undaunted by the hardships associated with this way of life as he moved into his sixties and described how he felt freed by living this way.

## Discussion and analysis

### Agency and activism

The Oxford English dictionary defines activism as 'the use of vigorous campaigning to bring about political or social change'. Living in a squat that challenges established laws about land ownership and rights of land use can easily be seen as part of wider campaigns for political and social change. Both interviewee's stories of how they became members of their intentional communities also reveal a range of other processes and dynamics that, I argue, are equally valid as active forms of political and social change.

These individuals were also quests for self-fulfilment through finding a better life-style than that which they felt conventional society offered them. These stories support shifting definitions of activism to include what have been called 'lifestyle movements' (Edwards, 2014). As McNay (1999) and others (Bourdieu, 1998) remind us, it is important of recognise individual's lifestyle choices and life chances as being constrained by their upbringing, their class, their primary social experiences, whilst not foreclosing on the potential for individual and collective agency. I use the term unclaimed to refer to the power and agency that is evident in the stories of these individuals that is insufficiently recognised in the politics of housing. This is as part of what Massey describes as a quest to develop a politics of consumption that aims to build awareness of the global ramifications of local daily lives' (Massey, 2004, p. 101) instead of perceiving the impacts of globalisation to operate in one direction, from the global to the local.

I argue that these individual's housing pathways constitute an expression of agency, manifested in contrast to their familial legacy, that is a key element of housing activism. But there were many other elements of their complex life stories that were woven into their housing activism that are under-recognised in narratives of activism.

## Activism, domesticity and caring

Analyses of social movements continue to talk of successful strategies and 'famous activists' (Goodwin & Jasper, 2014) and banner-waving on the streets is a common image of activism. Certain forms of housing activism, such as campaigns to defend social housing in London, are being rightfully made more visible through academic engagement with community groups and journalistic exposure (Minton, 2012; Watt & Minton, 2016) and new alliances are being made all the time as the housing crisis in London deepens (Humphry, 2016).

However, such visible forms of organised activism contrast with quieter acts of resistance. In Interview 4's housing pathway, domestic parenting responsibilities were interwoven with her politics and it was impossible to disentangle these from her agential housing choices. Such domestic responsibilities have been neglected as spheres in which political and housing activism takes place (Brickell, 2012a). Brickell has argued for recognition of activism in the private domain of the home rather than just in the public domain (Brickell, 2012b, 2014). Interviewee 4's housing activism emanates from local, everyday housing choices, that, nevertheless, challenge deep-seated and taken-for-granted assumptions about how it is possible to live in contemporary Britain. Her story is about making her and her children's lives more liveable (Skeggs & Loveday, 2012) in a way that rarely achieves widespread media attention – a recent exception being the fight of the Focus E15 mothers to remain housed locally in London (Watt, 2016). Away from the obvious and well-covered battle zones of housing activism it is common for women's involvement in *determining* the course of their housing to be 'unexpected' (Feldman & Stall, 2004, p. 7) and I suggest that this lack of recognition the domestic duties that underline Interviewee 4's account of her housing choices contributes to the unclaimed status of such forms of activism.

## The emotional landscape of housing choices

It was also impossible to disentangle the emotional histories that were also within my interviewee's stories of their housing choices. Their resistance to housing orthodoxy was formed through deeply personal and emotional experiences of separation, illness, parenthood amongst many other dimensions of living. My analysis here draws on the growing interest in understanding the place of emotions within the social sciences (Davidson, Bondi, &

Smith, 2005; Holmes, 2010; Martin, 2007). Feminists have made the case for including affective dimensions in research (Thomson, Moe, Thorne, & Nielsen, 2012) and emotional capacities as legitimate forms of capital (Reay, 2004) thereby enhancing the range and breadth of social science researchers' approaches and understandings.

This interest has lead researchers to focus on a 'sense of emotional involvement with people and places, rather than emotional detachment from them' that is particularly relevant here (Davidson et al., 2005, p. 2). We cannot understand these housing journeys without recognising the significance of emotional experiences in how their stories turned out.

As Brickell points out, this increasing awareness of the emotional landscape of activism has emerged from feminist perspectives. In her work on forced eviction in Cambodia, Brickell draws out the 'emotive topography' of activism in both public and private spaces. With reference to a number of disciplines, including housing studies, she argues:

> Although "the home is invested with meanings, emotions, experiences and relationships that lie at the heart of human life" (Blunt and Varley, 2004, p. 3), this literature has tended to neglect the emotionally saturated nature of domestic loss and resistance. Existing work privileges technical and theoretical language to describe the scale of dispossession, the contentiousness of property rights, compensation arrangements, the adverse employment impacts of resettlement, the ideological and practical constitution of social movements, and governmental policy. (Brickell, 2014, p. 1260)

What Interviewee 4 in particular revealed, was the emotional roller coaster that was a significant part of this emerging resistance to conventional housing choices. Interviewee 4's housing pathway also illustrates how housing activism can be intermittent and fleeting.

### Intermittent activism

Interviewee 2 talked about how he had moved in and out of conventional forms of home and work life for most of his life. His current home in a squat was the most radically transgressive of the communities I encountered and one which had a clear and specific purpose to challenge wider society and government. Glynn makes this distinction between different forms of squatting and their significance for housing activism:

> Squatting can be seen as the ultimate example of individual self-help, but there have been times when co-ordinated groups of squatters have been able to effect wider change beyond their own homes … Many squats have little or no impact on other households and can take pressure off immediate demand, while organised mass squats can provide an important source of pressure in campaigns to force government action and legislative change. (Glynn, 2009, p. 266)

Interviewee 2's involvement in living in a semi-public[2] squat and taking up legal challenges to the rights associated with the land they were squatting on, represents a clear and widely recognised form of housing activism. But it was also evident from his housing pathway that his activism was intermittent over his lifetime. How are we to make sense of this temporal dimension in understanding and weighing up forms of housing activism?

Interviewee 4's story more closely fits with the 'lifetimes of commitment' that Andrews has described in her research with people who she describes as having 'dedicated their lives to progressive social change' (Andrews, 1991, p. 1). In the 15 stories Andrews tells in her book, she highlights how:

political commitment has become the cornerstone of their lives. It is not only an expression of the way in which they see and understand the world around them, but also has strong implications for the way in which they perceive themselves and the purpose of their lives. (Andrews, 1991, p. 141)

Interviewee 4 described her ongoing involvement in campaigning for equitable access to housing and saw housing co-operatives as part of this political struggle in the UK. There was continuity in her beliefs and her housing pathway. But my research illustrates how activism is interwoven with complex motivations, needs and emotions over an individual's lifetime and how activism is often intermittent, as oral historian Margaretta Jolly has also found. Jolly's work focuses on what life stories reveal about political dissenters and activists; she argues that life stories help to understand that patterns of dissent and consent, of being insiders or outsiders, are complex. She makes the case for combining life course studies and social movements studies to help recognise the complexity of a lifetime of decisions and better grasp the nuances of how individuals move in and out of being activist (Jolly, 2011).

Her argument seems highly relevant in relation to the stories of Interviewee 2, who had been a conventional homeowner in the past, yet was strongly critical of the ideology of home ownership and propertied relations in the UK. Many of the interviewees in my research had been married, but were also critical of the convention of marriage. Some interviewees talked about how they had 'played the (housing) system' in order to secure themselves a stable home, but also recognised the inequitable nature of that system and campaigned for change in it. Jolly's work helps us to see these contradictory principles and practices as part and parcel of an understanding of activism. As reflexive social science has taught us, individuals are both constituted by, and constituting of, society (Giddens, 1991). What these individual's housing pathways illustrate is precisely these tensions and this complexity of a lifetime of decisions and how this needs to be recognised in our understandings of housing activism.

Andrews acknowledges some of this in her encounters with lifetime activists. She recognises that commitment is no simple word nor a simple matter (Andrews, 1991, Chapter 7). Furthermore, some individuals in her research talked about the sense of purpose and satisfaction that their activism gave them, recognising their endeavours as part of self-fulfilment. Her work foregrounds the more traditional forms of political activism, in the more public arenas of workplaces, political debate, poverty, inequality and human rights. But her work is relevant here because of her life stories approach and her focus on activism in later life.

## Ageing activists

Dominant discourses of housing and ageing are still disproportionately preoccupied with residential care, even though this less than 4% of the population of people aged over 65 lived in residential care in 2011 (ONS, 2013). Contemporary discourses are also dominated by critiques of residential care and policies and practices are orientated towards 'staying put' and *receiving* support (Demos, 2014; Department for Communities and Local Government et al., 2008; Department of Health, 2005). Campaigns that challenge housing orthodoxies can reinforce conventional ageist stereotypes: images of young housing activists abound, whilst older members of housing campaigns are too often used as representations of vulnerability and powerlessness (Duxbury & McCabe, 2015).

Andrews has done much to recognise older political activists and to tell their stories in order to defy ageist stereotypes (Andrews, 1991, 1999) and Brenton has drawn attention to new initiatives and forms of agency in later life housing choices that are emerging in the UK (Brenton, 1998, 2013). The housing pathways of both interviewees presented here suggest continued and strengthened agency, irrespective of getting older. Their thoughts about their future living arrangements seem to be resisting any notion that their capacity for agency later life is in any way blunted. Their future plans resist the dominant narratives of 'staying put'. Their agential housing choices show, as Andrews has argued, that ageing ought not to be equated with disengagement and conservatism as it often has been in the past (Andrews, 1991, 2007; Gilleard & Higgs, 2000).

Recent critical and cultural gerontology is contesting well-established concepts about ageing and what it means, including rejecting traditional dominant narratives of ageing as primarily in terms of physical decline (Twigg & Martin, 2015b). New anti-ageing discourses and identities are emerging. Marshall has described contemporary anti-ageing identities as being as much about choice as anything else:

> those qualities identified as defining the late modern subject – reflexivity, agency, flexibility, mobility, responsibility, individuality – have now been extended to older adults, transforming the contexts and resources for later life identities. (Marshall, 2015, p. 211)

My interviewees current housing choices and their future housing plans resonate with this theory of modern later life subjectivity. There was no talk of conventional housing choices associated with people in their sixties, such as 'staying put' or sheltered housing. There was acknowledgement by both that ageing altered their perspective on life and Interviewee 2 talked about how he felt different to the younger activists in his squat, but this difference did not negate their alternative housing ambitions. Once again, I see their activist status as under-recognised because of an underlying ageism in contemporary UK society that permeates narratives of housing activism, as well as orthodoxies of housing choices in later life.

These interviewee's stories are contributing to slowly changing perceptions of ageing identities in Western societies. Woodspring (2015) refers to 'boomer generation' narratives of agency and empowerment and that illustrate something of the 'differences in the shape and significance of old age for the post-war cohort' compared with previous generations. There are movements afoot in housing specifically, indicating new forms of housing choices are being made by older people themselves (Baker, 2014; Bynorth, 2015; Glass, 2009; Morrison, 2011; Motevasel, 2006; Toker, 2010) and these individuals seem to be part of a re-writing of not only their expected housing pathways, but also their scripts for older age.

## Conclusions

These individuals did not claim to be 'housing activists', but I argue that their housing choices resist dominant housing discourses, particularly in later life, and their complex life stories help to illustrate a number of under-recognised elements of housing activism.

Using Clapham's housing pathway concept, I described these two individual's stories of decision-making about where and how and with whom to live over their life time to show how they were unequivocally *active* in choosing to live in these communities, resisting norms of housing consumption in the UK. I have illustrated how their forms of housing activism were interwoven with domestic and caring needs, emotional experiences, intermittent commitment and ageing identities and I argue these dimensions of housing activism are under-recognised and may contribute to why my interviewees did not claim the term 'activist' in their narratives and stories.

Brickell reminds us that we are beginning to reclaim the home as 'a material and ideological entity of geopolitical significance' and that it is important to open our minds to what is recognised as 'home' and not take-for-granted what is 'homely' (Brickell, 2012a, p. 585). The unusual housing choices made by these individuals illustrate what has been possible, despite the ideology of home ownership (Glynn, 2009). Their stories and future plans also resist dominant expectations of housing choices in later life, though it is important to acknowledge these interviewees are in what gerontologists refer to as the third age (Twigg & Martin, 2015a) and are not yet in 'the fourth age', where managing declining physical independence is likely to become an issue (Peace & Holland, 2001; Price, Bisdee, Daly, Livsey, & Higgs, 2014). Perhaps the challenges of fourth age later life will, after all, dent their housing activism. As Woodspring concludes about the boomer generation, time will tell. There is a fascinating longitudinal research project in that.

## Notes

1. Diggers and Dreamers is a non-for-profit organisation in the UK that produces publications and supports a website providing a directory of intentional communities.
2. The squat was semi-public because even though they were occupying privately owned land, the boundary was not fully secured and it was regularly accessed by members of the public, walking their dogs for example.

## Acknowledgements

I am indebted to the Economic and Social Research Council and the University of Sussex for funding my PhD.

## Disclosure statement

No potential conflict of interest was reported by the authors.

## Funding

This paper is based on doctoral research funded by the Economic and Social Research Council.

## References

Andrews, M. (1991). *Lifetimes of committment. Aging, politics, psychology.* Cambridge: Cambridge University Press.

Andrews, M. (1999). The seductiveness of agelessness. *Ageing and Society, 19*, 301–318.

Andrews, M. (2007). *Shaping history: Narratives of political change.* Cambridge: Cambridge University Press.

Andrews, M. (2014). *What is narrative interviewing?* Retrieved from http://www.ncrm.ac.uk/resources/video/RMF2012/whatis.php?id=b6235e4

Baker, B. (2014). *With a little help from my friends creating community as we grow older.* Nashville, TN: Vanderbilt.

Baumann, Z. (2001). *Community. Seeking safety in an insecure world.* Cambridge: Polity.

Blunt, A., & Varley, A. (2004). Introduction: geographies of home. *Cultural Geographies, 11*, 3–6.

Bourdieu, P. (1998). *Practical reason: On the theory of action.* Stanford, CA: Stanford University Press.

Brenton, M. (1998). *'We're in charge' CoHousing communities of older people in the Netherlands: Lessons for britain?* Bristol: Policy Press.

Brenton, M. (2013). *Senior cohousing communities – an alternative approach for the UK?* York: Joseph Rowntree Foundation.

Brickell, K. (2012a). Geopolitics of home. *Geography Compass, 6*, 575–588.

Brickell, K. (2012b). 'Mapping' and 'doing' critical geographies of home. *Progress in Human Geography, 36*, 225–244.

Brickell, K. (2014). "The whole world is watching": Intimate geopolitics of forced eviction and women's activism in Cambodia. *Annals of the Association of American Geographers, 104*, 1256–1272.

Bunker, S., Coates, C., & How, J. (2007). *Diggers and dreamers. The guide to communal living 2006/7.* London: Edge of Time Limited.

Bynorth, J. (2015). Pioneering Scottish housing project for over-55s comes closer. *Herald Scotland.* Edinburgh. Retrieved from http://www.heraldscotland.com/news/home-news/pioneering-scottish-housing-project-for-over-55s-comes-closer.116861103

Christian, D. (2003). *Creating a life together: Practical tools to grow ecovillages and intentional communities.* Gabriola Island: New Society.

Clapham, D. (2005). *The meaning of housing: A pathways approach.* Bristol: Policy Press.

Coates, C. (2013). *Communes Britannica.* London: Edge of Time.

Davidson, J., Bondi, L., & Smith, M. (2005). *Emotional geographies.* Aldershot: Ashgate.

Demos. (2014). *"A vision for care fit for the twenty-first century … " The commission on residential care.* London: Demos.

Department for Communities and Local Government, Department of Health and Department for Work and Pensions. (2008). *Lifetime homes, lifetime neighbourhoods. A national strategy for housing in an ageing society.* (Government DfCaL, Health Do & Pensions DfWa, Eds.). London: HMSO.

Department of Health. (2005). *Independence, well-being and choice. Our vision for the future of social care in England.* (Health Do, Ed.). London: HMSO.

Duxbury, N., & McCabe, J. (2015). *The Rise of the Housing Activist.* Retrieved from http://www.oceanmediagroup.co.uk/features/housingprotests/

Edwards, G. (2014). *Social movements and protest.* Cambridge: Cambridge.

Feldman, R. M., & Stall, S. (2004). *The dignity of resistance: Women residents' activism in Chicago public housing.* Cambridge: Cambridge University Press.

Flint, J., & Rowlands, R. (2003). Commodification, normalisation and intervention: Cultural, social and symbolic capital in housing consumption and governance. *Journal of Housing and the Built Environment, 18*, 213–232.

Forrest, R., & Leather, P. (2002). *Our homes, our lives: Choice in later life living arrangements.* London: Centre for Policy on Ageing.

Giddens, A. (1991). *Modernity and self-identity: Self and society in the late modern age.* Stanford, CA: Stanford University Press.

Gilleard, C., & Higgs, P. (2000). *Cultures of ageing: Self, citizen and the body.* Harlow: Prentice Hall.

Glass, A. P. (2009). Aging in a community of mutual support: The emergence of an elder intentional cohousing community in the United States. *Journal of Housing for the Elderly, 23*, 283–303.

Glynn, S. (2009). *Where the other half lives: Lower income housing in a neoliberal world*. London: Pluto Press.

Goodwin, J., & Jasper, J. M. (2014). *The social movements reader: Cases and concepts*. Chichester: Wiley-Blackwell.

Gurney, C. (1999). 'We've got friend who live in council houses': Power and resistance in home ownership. In J. Hearn & S. Roseneil (Eds.), *Consuming cultures: Power and resistance* (pp. 42–68). London: MacMillan Press.

Heath, S. (2008). *Housing choices and issues for young people in the UK*. York: Joseph Rowntree Foundation.

Holmes, M. (2010). The emotionalization of reflexivity. *Sociology, 44*, 139–154.

Humphry, D. (2016). The London's housing crisis and its activisms conference, associated with CITY's special feature (issue 20.2). *City, 20*, 495–506.

Jolly, M. (2011). Consenting voices? Activist life stories and complex dissent. *Life Writing, 8*, 363–374.

Jones, A. (2017). *Alternative capital, friendship and emotional work: What makes it possible to live in intentional communities into older age* (p. 266). Brighton: Social Care & Social Work, University of Sussex.

Marshall, B. (2015). Anti-ageing and identities. *Routledge handbook of cultural gerontology*. New York, NY: Routledge, 210–216.

Martin, W. (2007). Embodying 'active' ageing: Bodies, emotions and risk in later life. *Sociology*. Warwick.

Massey, D. (2004). The responsibilities of place. *Local Economy, 19*, 97–101.

McKee, K., & Muir, J. (2013). An introduction to the special issue – housing in hard times: Marginality, inequality and class. *Housing, Theory and Society, 30*, 1–9.

McNay, L. (1999). Gender, habitus and the field: Pierre Bourdieu and the limits of reflexivity. *Theory, Culture & Society, 16*, 95–117.

Minton, A. (2012). *Ground control. Fear and happiness in the twenty-first century city*. London: Penguin.

Morrison, S. (2011). Come together: Could communal living be the solution to our housing crisis? Sarah Morrison visits five of the country's 'alternative' co-habitational projects to find out. *Independent*. London.

Motevasel, I. N. (2006). Senior housing in Sweden - A question of class differences and collective aging: An interview study in rental apartments and housing cooperatives. *Journal of Housing for the Elderly, 20*, 77–93.

ONS. (2013). *What does the 2011 census tell us About older people? Full infographic*. Retrieved from http://www.ons.gov.uk/ons/rel/census/2011-census-analysis/what-does-the-2011-census-tell-us-about-older-people-/what-does-the-2011-census-tell-us-about-older-people--full-infographic. html

Peace, S., & Holland, C. (2001). *Inclusive housing in an ageing society: Innovative approaches*. Bristol: Policy Press.

Peace, S., Holland, C., & Kellaher, L. (2011). 'Option recognition' in later life: Variations in ageing in place. *Ageing and Society, 31*, 734–757.

Plummer, K. (2001). *Documents of life 2. An invitation to a critical humanism*. London: Sage.

Price, D., Bisdee, D., & Daly, T., Livsey, L., & Higgs, P. (2014). Financial planning for social care in later life: The 'shadow' of fourth age dependency. *Ageing and Society, 34*, 388–410.

Reay, D. (2004). Gendering Bourdieu's concepts of capitals? Emotional capital, women and social class. *The Sociological Review, 52*, 57–74.

Sargisson, L. (2000). *Utopian bodies and the politics of transgression*. London: Routledge.

Sargisson, L. (2007). Strange places: Estrangement, utopianism, and intentional communities. *Utopian Studies, 18*, 393–424.

Sargisson, L. (2012). Second-Wave cohousing: A modern utopia? *Utopian Studies, 23*, 28–56.

Saunders, P. (1989). *The meaning of 'home' in contemporary English culture. Housing Studies, 4*, 177–192.

Savage, M., Barlow, J., & Dickens, P., et al. (1992). *Property, bureaucracy and culture. Middle-class formation in contemporary Britain*. London: Routledge.

Skeggs, B., & Loveday, V. (2012). Struggles for value: Value practices, injustice, judgment, affect and the idea of class. *British Journal of Sociology*, *63*, 472–490.

Thomson, R., Moe, A., & Thorne, B., & Nielsen, H. B. (2012). Situated affect in traveling data. *Qualitative Inquiry*, *18*, 310–322.

Toker, Z. (2010). New housing for new households: Comparing cohousing and new urbanist developments with women in mind. *Journal of Architectural and Planning Research*, *27*, 325–339.

Twigg, J., & Martin, W. (2015a). The field of cultural gerontology: An introduction. In J. Twigg & W. Martin (Eds.), *Routledge handbook of cultural gerontology* (pp. 1–15). New York: Routledge.

Twigg, J., & Martin, W. (2015b). *Routledge handbook of cultural gerontology*. New York: Routledge.

Watt, P. (2016). A nomadic war machine in the metropolis: En/countering London's 21st-century housing crisis with focus E15. *City*, *20*, 297–320.

Watt, P., & Minton, A. (2016). London's housing crisis and its activisms: Introduction. *City*, *20*, 204–221.

Woodspring, N. (2015). *Baby boomers: time and the ageing body*. Bristol: Policy Press.

# Enduring ideals: revisiting *Lifetimes of Commitment* twenty-five years later

Molly Andrews

**ABSTRACT**
This article examines political commitment to work for progressive social change as a lifelong activity. Challenging assumptions that idealism is something which is associated with youth, and, appropriately, later to be 'grown out of', the article presents an alternative model for examining social activism as a lifelong engagement. Revisiting research published 25 years ago (*Lifetimes of commitment: Aging, politics, psychology*, Cambridge University Press, 1991), the author re-examines key aspects of the study, including its most central contribution concerning activism as a feature across the life course. The discussion addresses recent debates on old age and political inclination as they are manifested in the global mourning of the death of Nelson Mandela, and the Brexit vote.

> The knowledge of life … which we grown-ups have to pass on to the younger generation will not be expressed thus: 'Reality will soon give way before your ideals,' but 'Grow into your ideals, so that life may never rob you of them.' (Schweitzer, 1925, p. 102)

Thus, I opened the concluding chapter of my book on British political activists who had worked for progressive social change for 50 years or longer. I had come to this interest firstly as someone who had attended many demonstrations from a very young age, gatherings which were crowded with young and old alike. And yet despite what I could see with my own eyes and the knowledge that I could surmise from my own experience, there was nonetheless another message which existed somehow outside of the demonstrations, a received wisdom summed up by a phrase often attributed to Churchill, though appearing in slight variations and in an impressive range of public figures including the French monarchist Guizot, the politician Clemenceau and the writer George Bernard Shaw amongst others: 'if you are not a liberal (or "republican" or "socialist") at twenty, you have no heart; if you are still a liberal (or other variant) at forty, you have no brain'. The message was clear: liberal or left-leaning politics was for youth, and while appropriate for that phase of life, it was nonetheless something to be grown out of. Indeed, only those who had crossed to the other side of the bridge, as it were, could look back on their earlier, naïve selves and see reality for what it was.

There have been many versions of this construction of the political life cycle, which associates youth with a time of idealism. And yet, I wondered, where did this leave me, with my political sensitivities, and where were those older activists who I always saw at protests? It was as if they (and indeed my imagined future self) had been completely whitewashed out of the picture, out of our idea of what it means to 'grow up'. And so it was that I dedicated myself to a study of 'lifetimes of commitment' to both document and better understand this phenomenon, of those people who as they increased in years, found in life a deepening of their commitment to work for progressive social change. This study was published as my first monograph, *Lifetimes of commitment: Aging, politics and psychology* (Cambridge University Press, 1991). The purpose of the present article is to revisit some of the key arguments I made at that time, and to reflect on the observations I made a quarter of a century ago.

I conducted my study on lifetime socialist activism in the mid-1980s, in the height of Thatcher's Britain, interviewing 15 women and men who had been politically active on the left for 50 years or longer, most of whom had become engaged in the interwar years. At the time of our interviews, I was in my twenties, and they ranged in age from 75 to 90. Most of the people who participated in my study were interviewed a number of times, and I became and stayed good friends with them. Over the years which followed my investigation, we entered and indeed left each other's lives in ways that were deeply affecting, and on more than one occasion I found myself delivering a eulogy, sharing with gathered mourners some of the stories which I had heard in the course of our many conversations together.

Twenty-five years later, what do I make of that study? How do the findings stand the test of time, and do the observations I offered then about the ways in which political engagement develops across the life cycle still pertain today?

Sadly, our world now is just as permeated with ideas about age bringing with it a bend towards conservativism as it was when I began my research in the 1980s. There are, of course, examples of numerous world leaders well into their eighties and nineties who are revered around the globe for their visions of progressive social change and inclusiveness. Amongst these, none is more well known than Nelson Mandela, who died at 95 years of age. Not only did South Africa designate 10 days of mourning for Mandela, but his passing was marked around the world, with heads of state attending the funeral service in – it was here that Obama and Castro first shook hands after 50 years of chilly relations between their two countries – and millions of others watched the service as it was live streamed from the stadium. Accolades were issued from every corner of the globe; here was a man who was virtually universally revered, for having an image of a more just society and for retaining his commitment to realising that vision, despite the personal cost to him for doing so. Few would be willing to openly state that they did not admire Mandela, and one could be mistaken for thinking that the characteristics which he embodied– perseverance, determination, a deep moral and political sense of purpose, conjoining belief and action, enduring and indeed deepening across a long life – were generally recognised and admired by the world at large, not only in his case, but indeed, in those unsung heroes who people our everyday lives. However, there is not much evidence of this. Rather, Mandela (and Mahatma Gandhi, Bertrand Russell, W.E.B. Du Bois, Eleanor Roosevelt, Gloria Steinem, Paul Robeson, Thurgood Marshall, I.F. Stone, Margaret Sanger and countless others who made it into their 8th, 9th and even 10th decades of life, with their commitment to working for social justice still burning bright) is still portrayed as an exception to the general paradigm that as we age, we become more inward, more insular, with a diminished concern about the fate of others less fortunate than ourselves. And this master narrative is so pervasive that it is almost impossible to recognise it, much less to challenge it and thereby more difficult for us to see around us our own ordinary heroes and heroines who lead extraordinary lives.

The first and most important comment, then, that I would offer about my research into lifelong political commitment and activism is that it was and remains a neglected area of research. Moreover, there is a widespread tenacity to hold onto the idea that as age increases, so does the lure of an insular politics – even amongst those whose earlier lives had been dedicated to redressing social injustices. While on a personal level that might be rewarding – confirming in me a sense that my work in this area retains some significance – more broadly it is disappointing, as I feel that we strip ourselves, and those who come after us, of inspiring examples of how we all might live out our lives even into old age, if we are given that opportunity. In depriving ourselves of these inspiring examples, we deplete the resources from which we might draw on for our own 'blueprints for living' (Andrews, 2009).

There are numerous factors which help to produce this arid landscape, and important implications which follow from it. Amongst these, perhaps the most salient is the intergenerational divide (which here features as both factor and implication). The acute decimation of the life course into discontinuous 'stages' is alarming, enhancing as it does a sense of cohort at the expense of a wider vision of life's horizon. While there is no denying that certain physical attributes attach themselves more to one age than another (Shakespeare's portrayal of the seven ages of man resonating 400 years later), this need not be at the cost of severance from all that has come before and all that will follow, not only generationally but even in our own lives. The distancing of ourselves from ourselves is commonplace – to our detriment, we cannot identify ourselves in those who are significantly younger or older than ourselves, and we are the weaker for it. Our over-reliance on a vision of the life cycle compartmentalised into stages means that we cannot participate in intergenerational exchanges, which are after all the ligaments of connection between the world we have been born into and that which we will one day leave behind. If we are to live purposeful lives, whose contributions will extend beyond our own lives, then we must recommit ourselves to such intergenerational conversations, which will help us to gain a broader perspective not only of our own lives, but of the social movements we care about – and from this follows naturally that activism in its most profound sense must be regarded as potentially reaching across the whole of the life cycle. Our actions build not only on our previous actions, but also on the shoulders of others, and in turn will help to create the conditions of our own future lives, as well as ultimately the world our progeny will inherit.

Revisiting my research on lifetime political activism, then, I still find my central focus one which merits attention. However, there are other aspects of the research which leave me with some questions.

## Lingering Questions

### *What is activism?*

This has always been a difficult nut to crack, and in selecting those who would participate in my study, I selected a more restricted definition of what constituted 'activism.' Those whose contributions, for instance, were primarily writing were not included. Thus, though I was at Jesus College, Cambridge, when Raymond Williams was there, and even discussed my study with him, I felt that his 'activism' was much more of an academic nature, and therefore related to but not of the same phenomena which formed the basis of my study. In this, I might add here that I was definitely influenced by some of those I had already interviewed: while they tolerated intellectuals, and sometimes even said their work was important to the cause, they nonetheless refrained from identifying scholarly work as being, in and of itself, a form of activism. However, this work differed in kind to my subsequent longitudinal study in East Germany, where I was able to re-meet activists 20 years later in their lives and find in them a similar political worldview, but in most cases transformed modes of 'activism'. I am aware of the growing body of work in which researchers identify the actions of very young children as being those of activism. (The Connectors Study, and particularly, its development of the concept of 'circuits of social action' is very engaging on this issue.) In Christos Varvantakis's very thoughtful blog on the meaning of 'activism', written from Athens in 2014, a place and time where activist/solidarity/grassroots initiatives were in abundance, he observes the

> … unimaginable diversity among social activism and solidarity initiatives – in their scopes, in their purpose, in their prospect, in their organization and in their political perspectives. Facing this diversity I have been led to think that the complexity of the phenomenon is thus probably best also approached in its particular expressions rather than merely as a macro-sociological whole. (Varvantakis, 2014)

But must activism include not only agency, but also a sense of political consciousness, and is this possible in those too young to have developed their cognitive capacity to think in the abstract? Not only as a scholar of activism, but also as a mother, I am very clear that many individuals form their ideas about the political world beginning at a very young age, and this is manifest in the playground, in negotiations with friends and sometimes even in participation in organised political activity. As important and fertile as this engagement is, it is nonetheless distinct from the depth of intellectual analysis that is a feature of political consciousness. Additionally, are all forms of group membership a manifestation of political commitment? Must belonging to a religious group, a sports organisation, a resident's association, or joining the governing body of a school also be considered activism, as indicated by the World Values Survey (http://www.worldvaluessurvey.org/wvs.jsp)? (see Nolas, 2014 for a discussion of this). I would argue not, but I think there are important conversations to be had on these issues. Some might regard this debate as one of semantics, but for me it is more than just that; I think if we dedicate ourselves to the study of sustained activism, then clarifying and perhaps even justifying our meaning of the terms we use is important. De Lemus and Stroebe (2015) define activism broadly as 'efforts to promote social change and improve the status of a marginalised group as a whole.' This might include a range of different behaviours, which exist along a continuum from weaker to stronger versions of activism. In my own research, I have emphasised stronger versions of activism, both in terms of their content (e.g. more than donating money, or signing a petition) and their duration; in retrospect, I would decide the same again, but would make my argument for doing so more explicit, and here's why.

In spring 2017, Pepsicola issued an ad which featured activism as a life style, fun and trendy but ultimately not very meaningful. In the ad, model Kendell Jenner is seen at a photoshoot, when a group of protesters appear. The crowd is diverse, and they carry signs with words like 'love' and 'conversation' painted on them. An attractive young man signals to Jenner that she should join – and so, whipping off her blond wig, she becomes not only one of the masses, but their leader. Staring down a line of riot police, she offers one a cold Pepsi. The crowd cheers, he smiles and the social tension dissipates. Almost immediately, the ad attracted strong criticism across social media. Bernice King, youngest daughter of Dr. Martin Luther King, tweeted a photo of her father being shoved by the police, and wrote 'if only Daddy would have known about the power of #Pepsi'. Other tweets evoke a bitter humour: cops with truncheons beating a black man, 'Kendell please, offer him a Pepsi', or another with police whose bottle of tear gas they are spraying at the protesters has been replaced by a large can of Pepsi. Though Pepsi pulled the ad very quickly, its initial airing sparked *The Independent* to ask 'Is this the worst ad of all time?' and veteran commercial director Joseph Kahn to write a series of tweets, including WHO THE FUCK THOUGHT OF THIS? THE AD WORLD JUST ENDED ITSELF and finally 'I've been studying commercials for 30 years. Kendall's Pepsi ad is legitimately the worst one I've ever seen' (Schultz & Diaz, 2017). Amongst the most offensive aspects of the ad was the portrayal of Jenner as utterly lacking in political consciousness – epitomised in the accusation that Pepsi had demonstrated itself to be profoundly 'tone deaf'. My interest in political activism stems from the conviction that such behaviour is about something, and emerges in response to perceived injustice. It is meaningful, conscious collective action, not a generic life style choice.

### A model of lifetime activism

In my doctoral dissertation, I included a model of what I termed 'the habit of responding.' For reasons mostly to do with style, I decided not to include this in the monograph which followed from my dissertation. And yet looking at it now, I can see that while perhaps a bit simplistic (as models often tend to me) it nonetheless encapsulates a sense of the basic movement through the life course that I was trying to convey. While previously much of the work on political activism had been oriented towards either initial political engagement, and/or one time involvement with a social movement, my attempt in this model was to represent how this develops not in a linear fashion, but rather as spiral. In the words of Eileen Daffern, one of my respondents, describing her own political development:

> You don't come back, it isn't the wheel has come full circle. You come in a spiral. This is the Marxist theory of progress ... Life doesn't go back to where it became, it comes up a bit further, and that's where you see progress. (Andrews, 1991, p. 176)

The basic premise of the model is that identification as an activist happens over time, through an accumulation of political engagements, and that the more one not only allows themselves to see injustice, but, in conjunction with others, to seek to combat it, the more one is likely to do so again. Over time, this dynamic reproduces itself repeatedly, until ultimately it becomes embedded into a 'habit of responding' (cf. Pedwell, 2017 for a recent analysis of the relationship between habit, revolution, routine and social change), an integral part of who one perceives themselves to be. With the women and men I interviewed, this persisted throughout their very long lives, and indeed was a primary defining feature of them.

## Activism and scholarship

I received a tremendous gift in pursuing the research which I did, effectively setting myself up for conversations with very inspiring people with whom I spent many, many hours over a number of years. Clearly those I included in my study were people with whom I had (for the most part) a political infinity. But what is the relationship between activism and research on activism? I do believe that there is merit in understanding how activism and political engagement more generally operates, and I also think that spending time speaking in-depth with people whose lives are marked by their high levels of continued involvement is a good way to obtain insight into this phenomenon. People have asked me if I consider myself an activist, and I am hesitant to claim this label, feeling that my own level of participation is not sufficient to justify this self-description. Related to this question is who is the intended audience for such works of scholarship? While I always aimed to write in way which was as accessible as possible, I was committed to the importance of intellectual rigour. This meant that while *Lifetimes of commitment* might be of interest to other people studying activism – and was even chosen by my publisher as one of the books they had selected for digitisation, thereby meaning that I continue to receive royalties on this title to this day, 25 years after its publication – it was never going to reach a wider audience of political activists.

## Methodologies

I have always been most inclined to working with word-based methodologies. However, in more recent years, I have had the privilege of working with colleagues who are more innovative, including a range of visual and material approaches. While I felt very satisfied with the quality of the conversations I did have, nonetheless I wonder what might have happened if I had more actively pursued other pathways for learning about their experiences. While I only regarded interview transcripts (and on occasion, written communication) as 'data', nonetheless I did spend ample time with participants and much of what I learned in these informal settings permeated my understanding of their lives. Two examples come to mind: (1) On the first day I met Eileen, when she was 'interviewing me for the job of interviewer' she had spent a significant amount of time going through old photographs so that I could get a sense of Yorkshire Dales where she was a child in the early twentieth century. We spent the afternoon looking at these photos together, as she 'introduced me' to her family members, and the dramatic natural environment which had profound influence on the woman she would become. But I did not regard these photos as 'research materials' in their own right, though they certainly helped to give me an impression of her life. (2) The second example was with Jack Dash, renowned organiser of dockers trade union. When he heard that I had a friend visiting from Germany who had come to London to study what was billed as the successful gentrification of the London Docks, he volunteered to walk around with us, exploring the sites of what used to be one of the most active seaports in the world. As we meandered, he explained to us how many homes and jobs had been lost, leaving us with an acute sense of a way of life that was no longer. I recorded Jack, and even took photos, but for me this was not research data. Now, nearly three decades later, I would not only include those 'extra bits' but would more actively solicit and document them.

## Whom to include?

The process of deciding whom to include in my study was rather convoluted, but in the end boiled down to pursuing a few snowball pathways. Were I to do this study again, I would more actively seek to create a pool with more diversity, particularly in terms of 'race' and geographic location. All of the 15 participants lived in England and had done so for many years – interesting then that I called them 'British socialists' rather than English, but this resonated with their own self-definition, and indeed one participant was Scottish. (The selection of participants was based mostly on logistical considerations – including travel and accommodation.) But when I once read a (mostly positive) review which referred to it as a study of 'little England' I could see that this was not without basis. The same can be true of my decision to have an all white sample. My reasoning at the time was that due to the ripples of migration in the UK, there were not that many non-white political activists in the UK in the interwar years (the period of political socialisation of the cohort I studied). In retrospect, I think I could have altered the design somewhat to include those who were residents of and had been politically active in the UK, and were roughly of the same age as the cohort I selected, but who might have come to the UK only as young people. I believe such an addition would have allowed me, for instance, to include some of the nearly 500 Caribbean people who came to Britain aboard the HMT Empire Windrush in 1948, bringing the first of what would become known as the 'Windrush generation,' whose arrival heralded a new face of Britain. While the design might have been rendered messier, the benefits of these voices would have outweighed the cost of the compromise.

## From the real to the imagined

Finally, most of my analysis of the interview data relied upon a close reading of what was told to be about events which had happened in the lives of my participants. I now wish that I had departed slightly from that conventional orientation, and had instead invited them to speak more about the worlds which they had imagined, the visions which had propelled them in their lifetimes' work. Creating more forums to explore the narrative imagination with them may well have produced results that uncovered more layers of meaning and understanding between us. Nonetheless, I am also very aware of how much time was demanded for the study as it was carried out, and perhaps it is more realistic to accept that sometimes decisions regarding research design and data analysis are by necessity heavily influenced by factors of convenience.

# Old age and its disregard for tomorrow's world: Brexit and beyond

Historian Peter Laslett, who has written extensively about intergenerational relations, argues:

> It could be claimed ... that many more duties of older people go forward in time than is the case in those who are young. This follows from the fact that they owe less to their own individual futures – now comparatively short – and more to the future of others – all others ... In this the elderly of any society can be said to be the trustees of the future. (Laslett, 1989, p. 196)

Similarly, I have already tried to demonstrate that for some, old age can be a time of life when people continue to fight for social justice, despite the fact that they might not live to see the fruits of their labour. But does it matter if this construction of old age is not one which is generally adhered by the world in which we live?

I think it does.

An examination of reactions of the British public to the outcome of the Brexit vote on social media is a very revealing case in point. The UK referendum on leaving the European Union, on 23 June 2016 produced results showing that age was a strong indicator of how citizens voted; indeed, while 25% of young voters (18–24-year olds) voted to leave, that percentage grew with increased years, culminating in the figure of 61% of those voters aged 65 and older (Bruter & Harrison, 2016).

This demographic breakdown produced a torrential outpouring of ageist abuse from those who considered themselves to be 'not old.' Giles Coren's rant was particularly noteworthy (Coren, himself 46, belonged to an age cohort 44% of whom had voted to leave). With his article leading with the heading 'Wrinklies have well and truly stitched us up' (*The Times* June 25, 2016), Coren writes:

> ... make no mistake, it is the old people who did this to us ... The less time a person had left on earth to live and face up to their decision ... the more likely they were to vote to leave the European Union. The wrinkly bastards stitched us young 'uns up good and proper ... From their zimmer frames, their electric recliner beds and their walk-in baths, they reached out with their wizened old writing hands to make their wobbly crosses and screwed their children and their children's children for a thousand generations. ... Old people are always wrong. About everything ... [they] give less and less of a damn what happens to the rest of us as time goes on.

It is of course surprising that Coren identifies himself as a young one; all things being equal, one thing that will happen 'as time goes on' is he will join the ranks of those he vilifies. But the point he makes here is that old people (those 65 and older) voted that way because they do not give a damn and cannot see beyond their own (now very limited) futures.

This anger at the old was all over social media. By lunchtime on the day following the election, David Vujanic's tweet (itself sent less than two hours after the result was announced), 'I'm never giving up my seat on the train for an old person again', had been retweeted 15,000 times. Another tweet 'you voted to leave the EU but you gonna die soon so it's not your problem' was retweeted 11,156 times and received 10,620 likes. And still comments elsewhere, exploding with rage: 'these fuckers should not have been allowed to vote for a long time. There's a reason why people grow old and die. If old people still had power, we would still be living in the stone age'.

There is good reason why young people might feel robbed of a future by those who will be affected for a shorter time by the outcome of the Brexit vote. Yet that does not really explain why this resulted in such vociferous vitriol towards the old. (Had the reverse been the situation, it is difficult to imagine that youth, as a group, would have been castigated in such a threatening way.) One of the reasons why the reaction was so prevalent and powerful was because it resonated with an already-existing master narrative that this is what 'old people are like.' Comments which appeared on social media and elsewhere, had they been written about women, or people of colour, or disabilities, or transgender, etc. would have been challenged. But this was not the case. Thus, my argument here is not a statistical one about voting behaviours, but rather concerns the ways in which the outcome of this vote functioned as a platform for the rehearsal of an ageist stereotypes, which often go wholly unchecked by researchers and the public alike.

And yet it remains true that in the Brexit vote, age was indeed an indicator of how an individual voted. This is also true of the British national elections in 2015. Of people aged 65 and older, 78% voted, and of those votes, 47% voted Conservative and 17% voted UKip (Mori, 2015). So how can this phenomenon be explained? My answer here is twofold: first, it is important to consider more fully who comprises the British population of those aged 65 and older? The British population aged over 65 is less ethnically and racially mixed than any younger age group, and 39% of whites who voted, voted Conservative, while only 23% of black and minority ethnics did. The statistics show that owning one's home was nearly as strong an indicator as that of age in the same election, with 46% of homeowners voting Conservative. These figures, when taken together, demonstrate that age as a single factor of analysis is an unstable indicator of the political propensities of any individual person, no matter how old. For a more comprehensive investigation of how older, or indeed any age, people vote, one would need to employ an intersectional analysis (Crenshaw, 1989) in which race, gender, ethnicity and other relevant variables were considered alongside or instead of age. This echoes back to the argument I made in the opening paragraphs of this article, that rigid segmentation of the life course by chronological age is a limited unit of analysis. It is, then, important to look beyond mere age when trying to assess how and why people vote as they do.

Moreover, to what extent are we prepared to make an assessment of political outlook based exclusively on voting behaviour? In 2014, the Pew Research Centre released the findings from a study with more than 10,000 Americans, using expressed values and attitudes to explore political typologies across the life cycle (Pew, June 2014). Far from older people being more conservative, Pew found the landscape to be much more complex, and a key determinant to political attitudes was the era in which one grew up, what Pew terms 'generational imprinting' (see also Grasso, Farrall, Gray, Hay, & Jennings, 2017). Of people 65 and older who were included in the study, 55% belonged to the typologies 'Solid Liberals', 'Faith and Family Left' or 'Next Generation Left', compared with 45% of those aged 18–29. Seventeen per cent of those in this younger category were classified as 'Bystanders' while that was true of only 3% of those aged 65 and older. Indeed, those who were born before 1949 (i.e. who were 65 or older in 2014) were the least likely of all groups to be classified as bystanders, which is not surprising when one considers that they were born in the shadows of the Second World War. The Pew study indicates that the impact of early political socialisation plays its part through the life course – bringing us back to our original discussion.

However, the debate about if and how political outlook correlates with old age is for me a bit of a red herring. My argument has never been that older people as a group are more or less conservative than other age groups; it is, rather, that such inclinations, in either direction, are not necessarily linked to age. Moreover, not only as a political psychologist, but as a human being, I think it is significant that people can and often do stay true to the moral principles which they adopt in early life; growing up does not mean growing out of our ideals, though it may include learning different ways of realising one's goals as political climates change and the body matures into old age. My interest has always been on how political engagement is expressed across the life course as a whole, not on any particular segment. Clearly, though, if one wishes to look at enduring political commitment woven into the fabric of a whole life, then one is directed toward those who have lived longest; thus, it was that my original study focussed on later life and activism.

## Closing thoughts

I would like to conclude this article by relating a personal memory. It was December 2000. The previous month, on 8 November 2000, voters around the United States had cast their ballots in the election for president. My heart sank as Al Gore conceded his defeat, only to recant his concession, saying that in the state of Florida, with its 25 electoral votes, the race was too close to call, with approximately 300 votes dividing the two main contenders. Ultimately, more than a month later, the Supreme Court ruled 5–4 that the clock had run out on the recount, and that the previously certified, though contested, total of votes in Florida should hold. Thus, it was that on 12 December 2000, George W. Bush was declared the winner of the election.

On that day, I had previously arranged that I would go see my dear friend, Eileen Daffern, for lunch in Brighton. Eileen had been one of the 15 people who had participated in my study on lifetime commitment years earlier, and we stayed in regular contact. Arriving at Eileen's house on the sea front, I felt completely deflated. Like many, my sense was that the election had been 'stolen' – decided by the Supreme Court (with a helping hand from Jeb Bush, brother of the candidate and at that time Governor of the state of Florida), rather than by the electorate. Knowing Eileen as I did, I should not have been surprised to be greeted by her, then in her early nineties, full of energy as she answered the door. 'Come' she said, taking me by the arm, 'I've prepared a little something for us.' And then she led me first into the kitchen, where she took a quiche out of the oven, and then into the front sitting room where a bottle of wine was chilling. She knew I needed her, and her very long-term perspective on the movement of history. By the end of our lunch together, she had very nearly convinced me that indeed, this dark moment was but a blip in the forward direction of history. Throughout that afternoon, she repeatedly made the case that we must not be thrown by momentary setbacks, but rather must always have our eyes set on making a future that was fairer, more just and egalitarian. Even if it is two steps forward and one step back, history always moves in that direction, she reassured me. I knew she had lived through much worse than this, and her resilience was inspiring for me; her commitment and experience helped me to imagine a future beyond Bush's presidency.

I was more than 40 years younger than Eileen, and she could offer me a perspective that few others could. We met and talked much during the dark days and years that followed, but I could not help but think of her when, at Obama's inauguration in 2008, I witnessed the helicopter taking Bush away from the White House, serenaded by many in the crowd who sang 'Na na hey hey, good bye'. The helicopter hovered, and then departed, leaving the crowd of over one million who had gathered to celebrate the end of a bleak era, and a new beginning.

## Disclosure statement

No potential conflict of interest was reported by the author.

## References

Andrews, M. (1991/2008). *Lifetimes of commitment: Aging, activism, politics*. Cambridge: Cambridge University Press.

Andrews, M. (2009). The narrative complexity of successful ageing. *International Journal of Sociology and Social Policy*. Special issue on Theorising Aging Studies, *29*(1-2), 73–83.

Bruter, M., & Harrison, S. (2016). *Did young people bother to vote in the EU referendum?* Retrieved November 18, 2016, from www.ecrep.org

Coren, G. (2016). Wrinklies have well and truly stitched us up. *The Times*. Retrieved November 18, 2016, from http://www.thetimes.co.uk/article/wrinklies-have-well-and-truly-stitched-us-up-qfz509cz8

Crenshaw, K. (1989). Demarginalizing the intersection of race and sex: A black feminist critique of antidiscrimination doctrine, feminist theory and antiracist politics. *University of Chicago Legal Forum*, *140*, 139–167.

De Lemus, S., & Stroebe, K. (2015, September). Achieving social change: A matter of all for one? *Journal of Social Issues*, *71*(3), 441–452.

Grasso, M. T., Farrall, S., Gray, E., Hay, C., & Jennings, W. (2017, January 26). Thatcher's children, Blair's babies, political socialization and trickle-down value change: An age, period and cohort analysis. *British Journal of Political Science*. doi:10.1017/S0007123416000375

Laslett, P. (1989). *A fresh map of life: The emergence of the third age*. London: Weidenfeld & Nicholson.

Mori, I. (2015, August). *How Britain voted in 2015: The 2015 election – who voted for whom?* Retrieved November 18, 2016, from https://www.ipsos-mori.com/researchpublications/researcharchive/3575/How-Britain-voted-in-2015.aspx

Nolas, S.-M. (2014, December). *What do we mean by 'circuits of social action'? A first stab of many, no doubt …* . Retrieved November 18, 2016, from https://connectorsstudy.wordpress.com/2014/12/16/what-do-we-mean-by-circuits-of-social-action-a-first-stab-of-many-no-doubt/

Pedwell, C. (2017). Transforming habit: Revolution, routine and social change. *Cultural Studies*, *31*(1), 93–120.

Pew Research Centre. (2014, June). *Beyond red vs. blue: The political typology*. Retrieved November 18, 2016, from http://www.people-press.org/2014/06/26/the-political-typology-beyond-red-vs-blue/

Schultz, E. J., & Diaz, A.-C. (2017, April 5). Pepsi is pulling its widely mocked Kendall Jenner Ad. *Advertising Age*. Retrieved April 13, 2017, from http://adage.com/article/cmo-strategy/pepsi-pulling-widely-mocked-kendall-jenner-ad/308575/

Schweitzer, A. (1925). *Memories of childhood and youth*. New York, NY: Macmillan.

Varvantakis, C. (2014, December). *Research encounters with activism and solidarity movements in Athens*. Retrieved November 18, 2016, from https://connectorsstudy.wordpress.com/2014/12/08/research-encounters-with-activism-and-solidarity-in-athens/

# Index

Note: 'n' indicates chapter notes; **bold** indicates tables; *italics* indicate figures.